I0762851

PHASES

PHASES

A MEMOIR

BRANDY

WITH GERRICK KENNEDY

HANOVER
SQUARE
PRESS

ISBN-13: 978-1-335-01327-9
ISBN-13: 978-1-335-00128-3 (Signed Edition)

Phases

Hanover Square Press
22 Adelaide St. West, 41st Floor
Toronto, Ontario M5H 4E3, Canada
HanoverSqPress.com

HarperCollins Publishers
Macken House, 39/40 Mayor Street Upper,
Dublin 1, D01 C9W8, Ireland
www.HarperCollins.com

Printed in U.S.A.

To Sy'Rai

Continue to be a light

CONTENTS

PHASES

PREFACE

ONCE, I STUMBLED upon a tale—a delicate thread of North African folklore—about a nameless, lonely little girl. She was beautiful and soft-spoken. Fragile yet resilient. She wandered Earth, searching for the pieces of herself that felt lost to the winds.

As her loneliness grew, her body filled with sorrow. The little girl swelled and swelled, her tiny body expanding like a balloon. Her grief grew so thick that she could no longer find her voice. So, she drifted along Earth, weightless yet heavy with despair.

Now, the Moon believed the warmth of her glow could bring comfort to this lost girl, but the girl's sorrow overshadowed the brightness radiating from the Moon's nightly beams. The Moon tried again, and again, to no avail. And so, the Moon whispered to the stars, and the stars twinkled and shone with all their radiant might. Even still, the little girl did not pay attention. She continued to believe she was alone in her anguish.

One night, the Moon decided she would not rise at all. Instead, she traveled down to Earth in search of the girl. She found her in a barren desert. The Moon scooped the girl up and flew her into the night sky. Bathed in the glow of the Moon's embrace, the girl felt a sigh escape her throat. The Moon gently rocked the girl in her arms. She had never felt such comfort. Such peace. Such warmth.

"You cannot stay up here forever," the Moon told the girl. "You belong on Earth, and I must stay in the sky for all the other people . . . but I will help you."

The little girl sat up. She did not understand what she was being told. She just stared back, blankly.

"Let your sadness *flow*," the Moon repeated. "It is okay to let out your sorrow."

Suddenly, an unfamiliar sensation overcame the girl. A stream of wetness poured from the corners of her eyes. She was unsure what was happening. The girl had never felt the tickle of a tear rolling down her cheek, the saltiness of a tear on her tongue.

As the girl wept under the glow of the Moon, she found her release. From that day on, the Moon reminded the girl that no matter how much sorrow filled her, she was never truly alone.

Ever since I was a little girl, I have been drawn to the moon and the folklore around her. The quiet of the night helps calm my racing thoughts, and the moon soothes me—down to my soul. I find so much beauty in her phases—an endless cycle of endings and beginnings. Rebirths. Cleanses. Second chances. As a child, I remember being told that my dreams were written in the stars, and the power of the moon could make them come true.

The earliest dream I can recall is me standing on a stage. The heat of a spotlight tingling my skin with excitement. There's a band behind me and a vast sea of faces looking up at me. Everyone is waiting for me to lift the microphone to my lips. Sometimes I'm in a flowing gown. Sometimes I'm in a simple T-shirt and jeans. But I was always onstage, performing. At one point in my life, that dream was all I was living for.

Sometimes my memories feel like a dream. Lived experiences enmesh with the fragments of my mind's creation. It has felt as if parts of myself are scattered across time, across selves, each holding different pieces of the same story, but the pieces never quite align. It only makes me question myself, and my mind, even more than I already have. That's why I believe memory can be a trap. It pulls at the edges of who we think we are, and who we might yet become.

My life has felt a bit like folklore, stitched together and passed along by others. One would think that after thirty years in the public eye, I'd have found a way to inoculate myself from the opinions of others. But longing to be liked has made that difficult. The hardest lesson of this book was learning how much that need for acceptance influenced my own happiness. It's time to give that girl a voice—and free her.

Still, even now, I'm afraid that I will disappoint people by sharing my story. I'm certain that details here will differ from how others might have told it. Because of that, some names and identifying details have been changed or omitted to respect their privacy. And some scenes and conversations recalled here are done from the spirit in which they were remembered and have been reordered and/or combined for narrative purposes.

The limits of my memory made me reconsider writing this book. I thought about just keeping all these stories locked inside. I'd gotten used to carrying them around, and they could vanish with my last breath and remain unknown. I'm afraid of what people might think. But my hope is that in surrendering my truths, that young girl who dreamed under the moon can feel understood. And, finally, find release.

PHASES

FEBRUARY 2024

MY HEARTBEAT THUNDERS in my ears, drowning out the cheers inside the Crypto.com Arena. Twenty feet away, beyond the thick LED video wall, eighteen thousand people are in the audience—and millions are watching live at home—unaware that my knees are trembling in my red leather boots. It's the 66th Annual Grammy Awards here in Los Angeles, and I'm waiting for my cue to perform with Burna Boy and 21 Savage.

"Five minutes, Ms. Norwood," whispers a headset-wearing PA, clipboard clutched to her chest. She couldn't have been more than twenty-two—probably wasn't even born when I last sang at the Grammys.

I nod, throat too dry for words, and adjust the big waving curls cascading down to my waist.

Twenty-six years after releasing "Top of the World," I'm here to sing it at the Grammys. Burna and 21 are nominated for their collaboration, "Sittin' on Top of the World," which samples my original record. I am always flattered when artists pull from my work. It never gets old watching younger generations find inspiration from music you created in your youth. Burna Boy is making history as the first Afrobeats artist to perform at the Grammys. He could have stood under the sun alone, or with only 21. Asking me to perform with them was a beautiful invitation.

It was 1997 when I'd last performed at the Grammys. I showed up in a slick all-black look—high-waisted pencil pants, babydoll blouse, and a choker. I performed "Sittin' Up in My Room," a song that set the stage for the meteoric career highs I'd experience next. I was up for my third and fourth Grammy nominations that night. I lost to Toni Braxton and a virtual duet between Natalie Cole and Nat King Cole, but these are not the things that mattered. I was eighteen, on the Grammys stage. *Singing one of my songs.* It really felt as if I were standing atop of the universe that night, and I wanted nothing more than to keep soaring. Higher and higher. What I didn't think about was the price it would cost to get there.

Now my nervousness and exhilaration dance a frantic waltz. I can hear the familiar, intoxicating roar of the crowd, and I stop to take a quick peek at the bay of monitors displaying the telecast from all angles.

"I need you to get up outta your seats immediately," Burna commands while walking from the center of the arena up to the stage.

For years, I dreaded events like these. I didn't feel worthy of such lauded spaces, and so I stopped going. Embracing the idea of being celebrated is ongoing work for me, and as I watch the camera panning to get close-up shots of the audience, a tiny jolt of fear hits me. Will they still care?

A disembodied voice spills out of the assistant's earpiece: "Go, for Brandy." I'm discreetly led around the video wall, behind an army of dancers, and into place at center stage.

The lights dim.

I inhale deeply, tasting the electricity of anticipation. The dancers part, revealing me underneath the blinding white spotlight, my back toward the crowd. I spin around, letting the floor-length trench coat whip around me dramatically, before singing a note.

"I'm just trying to be me, doing what I gotta do, some people think that I'm sittin' on top of the world."

The roar from the audience hits me like a physical force, thousands of voices creating a wall of sound that swallows me whole—unexpected, comforting, overwhelming. Every clap and cheer seems to whisper, *We still love you. We've been waiting for you.*

My gaze sweeps across the sea of industry faces in the front rows and the glittering phones speckled throughout the crowd, all pointed toward me, and I relish in the joy that shoots through my body.

These lyrics that once were an interrogation of fame now have a new, reimagined life. I close my eyes for just a heartbeat, transported back to that hungry girl in the recording booth singing "Top of the World." I think about the phase of life she was in then—the certainty she had, the absolute belief the world would see the real her.

What she couldn't anticipate was the vertigo that comes with sitting so high on a pedestal.

The dizzying fall that follows when the world realizes she can no longer live up to the image she projected or continue to match the success from her youth.

The bruises left by betrayed trust.

The hollow echo of being spoken of in the past.

One of the biggest lessons I have learned is to embrace the phases of life—all of them. For so long, I had been on a quest to find a new way forward, not just for my career, but for myself. But I can't move forward until I stop running from the past.

And so here we are, going back to the beginning.

PINK CAMELLIAS

MY HEART SANK like a stone through murky water, dragging me deeper into the abyss of my own terror. I could feel the weight of my five-year-old body collapsing into itself, my shoulders curving inward as if trying to protect what was left of my pride. My chest was tight with a panic so palpable I swore everyone could see it rising from my skin like steam hissing out of the bottom of an iron.

I prayed for just one note to escape. One single, solitary sound. If I could coax the first, I knew the rest would follow, spilling like a summer stream over smooth river rock. But my voice was held captive by my mind, locked away somewhere I couldn't reach.

"Jesus loves me, this I know . . ."

I had sung this hymn countless times—in the shower, in the car, at church with my dad and the choir. The lyrics were tucked firmly under my tongue, the melody and key nestled in the safest corner of my memory. But I stood frozen, my eyes wide and glassy, staring out at a sea of round-faced ladies wearing pillbox hats and dresses the colors of SweeTarts, and burly men in pressed tweed blazers. Dozens of expectant people sitting shoulder to shoulder in the pews before me.

Watching.

Waiting.

The comfort I'd found discovering my voice back home with my dad had evaporated like morning dew under a merciless sun.

I wanted to be anywhere but here. Anywhere but standing before these people, these kind strangers whose faces had morphed into a foggy haze of leering eyeballs. This was church, after all—a place where a little girl too scared to sing would only ever be met with kindness. And yet my face burned hot with embarrassment, the heat crawling up my neck and settling in my cheeks like an unwelcome guest. I wasn't just embarrassed for myself, but for my family. For my grandfather. I wanted—needed—to make him proud.

I had been working on my voice, and I wanted to show him that I was sprouting into my own. My grandfather worked in construction and was instrumental in erecting the 24th Street Church of Christ, the place I loved most in all of McComb, Mississippi. It was my sanctuary whenever we went back to visit. However, on this morning, we were visiting another church in McComb. It's what you did. You visited other church houses and sang and fellowshipped with neighboring congregations. Now, my grandfather never missed an opportunity to boast about his daughter and grandbabies who lived out in California. I can't recall how I was nudged up to the pulpit for a solo, but there I was, nervous and motionless in front of a crowd of kind faces waiting—and expecting—to hear this special child from California who they had been hearing about from her grandfather.

"Take your time, baby girl," an elder's voice called gently from the back, her words floating toward me like a lifeline. "The Lord ain't in no hurry."

A chorus of "Amen" and "That's right" rippled throughout the congregation, a wave of encouragement that somehow only made the pressure more suffocating. This was my first awareness of what it meant to have expectations placed upon your shoulders—how even the kindest intentions could feel like concrete blocks when you weren't ready to carry them.

Without warning, hot tears spilled over my lashes, carving glistening pathways down my cheeks. I turned and ran, the sound of my footsteps on the wooden floor echoing like thunder in my ears.

When I was four, my parents moved us from McComb—a small, pine-circled town tucked away in the southwestern corner of Mississippi—to Carson, a suburb thirteen miles south of downtown Los Angeles. My dad had received an offer to become the minister of music at the Church of Christ in Inglewood—an opportunity that Willie and Sonja Norwood believed too divine to ignore. My brother, Ray J, and I were small enough that we could stretch our bodies across the entire back seat of our faded blue Subaru and still have plenty of space—a blessing that came in handy for a cross-country journey that seemed to stretch on for an eternity.

"How much longer, Dad?" I'd whine, my face pressed against the window glass, watching the landscape transform from the lush green of the South to the sunburned browns of the West.

"Just a few more miles, Bran-Bran," he'd answer, his eyes meeting mine in the rearview mirror, twinkling with a promise.

My father was the first to tell me my voice was an anomaly—something precious and rare. He heard it in me long before any awareness had blossomed in my own consciousness. I have this fuzzy memory of him kneeling before me, his hands gentle on my shoulders, his eyes boring into mine with an intensity that made me straighten my spine.

"You have a unique voice, Bran," he told me. "Let's train it. Let's get it to where God wants it to go."

My dad is a phenomenal vocalist, a man who sings not from

his throat but from the marrow of his bones. As a teacher, he possessed a patience that seemed otherworldly, a gentleness that made me believe I could touch the stars with nothing but the power of my voice. And make no mistake—he was a master of his craft, a virtuoso who cared deeply about helping vocalists realize the full breadth of their potential.

He taught me to follow scales with meticulous precision, encouraging me to take my voice up and down, and how to better understand the range of my own instrument. Under his guidance, I learned the delicate dance between power and restraint, between letting your voice soar and knowing when to rein it in. Since he was the minister of music at our church, he placed me in every choir he could. Gospel music became my first language. The choir welcomed all who came, but there was one doctrine that remained unshakable—you only sang a cappella. No pianos. No organs. No drums. Just voices working together to create something that transcended the sum of its parts.

Church was where I first unraveled the intricacies of my voice—how to blend and match across different ranges and harmonies. It was where I learned how to let my voice soar above the rest when it was my turn to shine, and how to tuck it neatly into the fabric of the collective when it wasn't. It was at the Church of Christ, surrounded by voices both young and weathered, that I began to understand that my gift wasn't just mine—it was meant to be shared.

Growing up, summering in the South was my favorite slice of the year. The way people romanticized Los Angeles, with its swaying palm trees and omnipresent sunshine, was precisely how Ray and I viewed McComb, with its weeping willows and front porch swings. We couldn't wait to go back each year, counting down the days until our parents would pack us into the car or put us on a plane bound for Mississippi. Our family had constructed a beautiful life on the West Coast—a life filled with opportunities—but reconnecting to the roots that awaited us in McComb felt like a homecoming.

I craved the languid breeze of Mississippi summers, the way the air hung heavy and sweet like ripe peaches waiting to be plucked. I was drawn to everything about this place—the melodic drawl of the people who shaped their words like they had all the time in the world to release them, the kindness and care that seemed to ooze out of everyone so effortlessly, the way folks moved like they were constantly swaying to music only they could hear. In McComb, everyone seemed . . . free. Free in a way that the tight-laced suburbs of Southern California could never quite replicate.

Life in McComb unfurled at its own pace, slow and deliberate. Time seemed to move like thick molasses dripping from a spoon, sweet and unhurried. The railroad tracks that had once given this town its purpose and pride now sliced through it like an old scar—a physical reminder of division that separated the white neighborhoods with their elegant magnolias and wraparound porches from the Black neighborhoods where clapboard churches stood defiant, their steeples reaching skyward as if in perpetual prayer or silent protest.

It was a stark contrast from life in Southern California. Our parents never shielded us from the harsh realities of our world—they didn't have that luxury—but they also never allowed us to believe that there were other ways to live. Returning to the South was their way of ensuring we stayed connected to the values and traditions they had grown up with, and that we understood there was more than one kind of community, more than one way to exist in our skin.

One of those cherished traditions was braiding—an ancestral art form passed down through generations of women in our family. Perched between the sturdy legs of my grandmother, an ancient ritual would begin. Oils, creams, and butters were massaged into my hair with loving fingers, worked gently from root to tip until each strand glistened the deepest shade of obsidian.

A glowing hot comb, heated on the blue flame of the kitchen stove, would be pulled ever so delicately through my kinky coils, straightening them with a precision that bordered on reverence. If I fidgeted—as children are wont to do—I risked a scalding kiss from the metal, leaving a dark, scaly spot on my ear or nape that would be a reminder of my impatience for days to come.

"Be still now, Bran," my grandmother would murmur, her voice a soothing balm.

A delicious sting would follow as the hair was separated into small parts, meticulous squares created by the pointed end of a rattail comb, before the strands were woven together, snugly, by taut fingers that had performed this dance countless times before. The ache was familiar, a sensation as old as time itself, a pain that connected me to every woman in my lineage who had sat just as I was sitting now. With each pull and tuck, a braid began to form—a testament to both pain and beauty, to endurance and grace.

There's a quiet magic in the gathering of Black girls getting their hair braided, a divine time that feels less like an appointment and more like an ancestral birthright. It's a tapestry woven across generations and geographies, uniting us. Braiding is an ancient conversation. A communion shared by Black girls everywhere.

Just the thought of those ripples in time unleashes a dam's worth of memories—sensory explosions that transport me back to my grandparents' house on Summit Street or to the first salon my mom took me to get braided after a perm left my hair singed and brittle. It was a small shop in Carson that always smelled of sage and baby powder. The sound of combs clicking against glass jars of Blue Magic or Sulfur 8. The room filling with vapors, steam rising from boiling pots like ghosts across the ceiling. The smell of shea butter and coconut oil melting between practiced fingers, of stretched Kanekalon hair being prepared for installation, of pungent chemicals and sticky elixirs being stirred together to create magic—scents that hung in the air like sacred incense, marking the space as hallowed ground.

Braiding was a language I first inherited from my grandmother, who inherited it from her mother, and so forth—a matrilineal tradition spoken without words but articulated through tender touches and tiny tugs. It was a language that whispered, *This is ours. This is sacred. This belongs to us alone.* Some of my earliest memories involve a ritual around hair being pulled into cornrows or separated into neat plaits for school or church. I remember the colorful barrettes and wooden beads and golden clips that adorned my finished styles, like little punctuation marks.

My grandmother would prop me up on a pillow between her legs and get to work, her fingers moving with a rhythm all their own. The whole time she told me stories—rich, vivid tales that unfolded like road maps to a past I was too young to have known. Stories about her own childhood or about my mom and her sister, my aunt Beverly. About the things her mother had passed down to her that she passed to my mother. I felt like those stories were held in my braids, like her fingers were weaving not just hair but history, a legacy I got to carry atop my head like the most precious crown.

Never would I have imagined that my hair would become such an essential part of my story—the iconography people remembered and celebrated, a visual signature as distinctive as my voice. Later on, when I began recording my music and stepping into the spotlight, I only wanted to be myself—which meant showing up with my braids intact, my heritage proudly displayed. What I didn't realize then was how much that would come to matter, how those braids would transcend mere style to become symbolic. That they would come to mean something not just to me, but to countless young girls who had never before seen someone who looked like them shine so brightly on their television screens.

Those trips to the South also offered me a glimpse of my parents before they were *my* parents—when they were just Willie Norwood and Sonja Bates, two young souls finding their way to each other across college campuses and concert venues. They met while attending different historically Black colleges in Mississippi, their paths crossing in a way that seemed both inevitable and miraculous.

My dad grew up in the Delta town of Greenwood, where cotton fields stretched toward the horizon like an endless sea of white when harvest time came. He earned his way into Jackson State University on a band scholarship, his French horn and trumpet playing as smooth and bright as polished brass. But it wasn't just in the marching band that my father found himself. He was also the charismatic front man of a popular local soul group called the Composers, a band that played shows all over Mississippi, their reputation growing with each performance.

At one of those shows—a packed, sweltering club in Jackson where bodies swayed and voices called back every line—was my mother. Her eyes found him immediately. She was drawn to the way he commanded the stage as if he'd been born on it.

"When he sings, it melts me down," she would tell me years later, her eyes growing soft with the memory. "It was like he was singing directly to me, even though we'd never met. Like he knew I was out there somewhere, waiting."

My mother was a liberal studies and psychology major at Southern University Baton Rouge, her mind as sharp as the creases in her perfectly pressed jeans. Like my dad, she was in her high school's marching band. She was a baton twirler, marching the field with the same military precision she used to get Ray and me up and ready for school. I loved watching my parents fall back into their young adult selves whenever they'd shuttle Ray and me to their respective campuses during our summer visits—how their postures would change, their voices taking on a different cadence, their eyes lighting up with memories before they became who they were.

They were so proud to have gone to HBCUs—so proud, in fact, that they pulled us into their good-natured marching band rivalries, forcing us to always choose sides. Naturally, I chose Mom (the way girls often do), while Ray picked Dad (following a similar unwritten rule). But secretly, what we really wanted wasn't to pick sides but to hear the songs, the chants, the call and response that electrified the air during halftime shows and campus gatherings. Ray and I knew them all and couldn't wait to shout along with our parents, to feel connected to a tradition that had begun long before us and would continue long after.

My maternal grandparents lived on a modest street lined with dogwoods and redbuds, their single-story house distinguished by the meticulous care with which my grandfather tended the yard. These weren't big homes by any means—not like the sprawling ranch houses with swimming pools that dotted the neighborhoods we saw on drives to Hollywood and Beverly Hills—but they were nice, solid, and everyone took such pride in maintaining their slice of the community.

Lawns were freshly manicured with vibrant azaleas that stood as tall as I was in those early years of our summer vacations. Each year, Ray and I tracked our growth against these living measuring sticks. The shrubs grew taller, but so did we, marking the passage of time in a way that felt tangible, visible.

Come spring, pink camellias would bloom like whispers of blush against the green, their petals so soft they looked like spun sugar dusting each house along the street. Their scent would drift through the air, light and delicate, carrying a hint of earth and honey. It was a fragrance that enveloped you, a tender, powdery sweetness that seemed to say, *Slow down. Stay awhile.* In those times, McComb felt like paradise—a world crafted just for Ray and me, a safe haven where time moved at a glacial pace.

Summers in McComb were an escape from life in Carson. Back home, I was being bullied incessantly, my too-skinny frame and quiet demeanor making me an easy target for girls whose words cut deeper than any knife could. Ray, meanwhile, found his own trouble to get into, his boundless energy and quick temper often landing him in the principal's office or confined to his bedroom as punishment.

The South offered us peace away from all of that. Being surrounded by so much family and genuine kindness offered a sense of protection that I felt nowhere else outside of my home or in church. In McComb, I wasn't the awkward girl with big eyes and gangly limbs—I was little Bran, Sonja's girl, Willie's daughter, Freddie and Mary Ethel's grandbaby. I belonged to people who belonged to this place, and that connection was like armor. If only I could bottle up that feeling and take it back home.

My grandfather—Paw Paw as we called him, the name rolling off our tongues like a sweet melody—had this peculiar tradition that Ray and I lived for each summer. He would hide pennies and quarters all over the backyard before we came down, planting them like seeds that would yield a harvest of childish delight rather than crops.

Some coins were buried in the ground, others neatly tucked behind shrubs or hidden beneath carefully arranged rocks or foliage. He gave us hints and tasks that steered us toward the bounty, creating elaborate treasure hunts that kept us occupied for hours.

"Look for the most wilted flower in Grandma's garden, then count three steps to the right," he'd instruct, his weathered face breaking into a mischievous grin.

Finding those coins was so satisfying, the metal warming in our palms as we clutched our bounty. But the real value lay not in the coins themselves but in the lesson Paw Paw was teaching us about gratitude, about finding joy in small treasures that others might overlook.

"Every penny you find is a blessing counted," he'd say, helping me drop my coins into a mason jar labeled with my name in his careful handwriting. "And every blessing counted is a prayer answered."

There was a gentleness to Paw Paw that seemed at odds with his powerful build. He had hands that could crush stone, but he chose to create with them instead. The yellowed newspaper clippings he kept tucked away in an old Bible revealed a McComb that was foreign to me—one where hatred once burned as hot as the summer sun. The more I read, the more I wondered how exactly Freddie Bates managed to hold on to that gentleness in a place that worked so hard to remind him that he was not equal, not worthy, and not deserving of a basic quality of life. I traced my fingers across the clippings, stories detailing unspeakable violence.

TIME magazine called McComb "the toughest anti–civil rights community in the toughest anti–civil rights area in the toughest anti–civil rights state in the Union."

Segregation was suffocating—total and complete. Every aspect of life in McComb was divided by an invisible line. Restaurants, schools, businesses, government, churches, drinking fountains, parks, pools, even the jail. Black residents were born in segregated hospitals and buried in segregated cemeteries. From first breath to last, the system ensured separation. And work followed the same patterns, with Black folks only having access to menial jobs.

The Supreme Court desegregation orders of 1954 and 1956 laid the groundwork for change, and Dr. Martin Luther King Jr.'s Montgomery bus boycott planted seeds. In 1961, the first wave of Freedom Riders hit the McComb bus station and everything broke loose. Black families boycotted the segregated schools.

The backlash was swift and brutal. Freedom Riders were beaten, their bodies broken and bloodied on the concrete. School protesters were expelled and thrown behind bars. Paw Paw was a member of the NAACP and was heavily involved in what became known as the McComb Movement—a series of voter registration drives and direct actions that sought to dismantle the segregation that strangled the South. When fifteen-year-old Brenda Travis was expelled from Burglund High School after being arrested for participating in a bus station sit-in, she and one hundred students walked out in protest, their young voices raised in defiance of an unjust system.

They marched to McComb city hall singing "We Shall Overcome," their voices wavering but resolute, only to be met with police batons and cruel words. Brenda was sent to a juvenile correctional facility an hour outside of the city without her mother or attorney being informed, a punishment meant to break not just her spirit but the will of an entire community.

My grandfather owned a gas station, bus and taxi transportation service—enterprises that were themselves acts of resistance in a time and place where Black business ownership was viewed with suspicion and often met with violence. Paw Paw used his fleet of buses to transport folks to visit Brenda in detention, ensuring she wasn't forgotten. Paw Paw also covered the transportation for her expelled classmates, who were forced to continue their high school education an hour away in Jackson.

The town folded in on itself after that, collapsing into the terrorist grip of the Americans for the Preservation of the White Race and the Ku Klux Klan. There were men who wore badges by day and white robes by night—a dual existence that kept the Black community in constant fear.

Paw Paw's involvement with the Freedom Riders made him—and by extension, his family—a target. On a muggy night in the summer of 1964, a stick of dynamite was tossed onto his doorstep, ripping boards from the ceiling, shattering windows, and blowing the front door clean off its hinges. My mother was thirteen years old then, a girl on the cusp of womanhood who learned that night what it meant to be hated for the color of your skin and the audacity to demand to be seen as equal. Prior to that, at the age of nine, she'd written to the president of the United States himself, asking for protection for her father. A letter came back, saying that it wasn't in his jurisdiction. In total, sixteen homes, churches, and businesses were lit ablaze.

Crosses as tall as trees were burned. Phone calls came in the dead of night; threats whispered through the line that made hearts stop. To register to vote, Black folks had to read a section of the Constitution and interpret it—a test designed to keep them from the ballot box. But they studied those words until they knew them by heart, gathered in church basements and back rooms to practice. Knowledge was their weapon, and the white establishment knew it.

The town's businesses withered as violence flourished—empty cash registers have a way of speaking louder than moral arguments ever could. McComb's reputation bled across state lines, and finally, a sense of revulsion settled in the pit of the town's collective conscience.

By that fall, six hundred and fifty civic and business leaders issued a plea for law and order. Restaurants began to desegregate. Whites and Blacks started talking to each other—not as friends, not yet, but as people who shared the same streets and the same sky and maybe, just maybe, could share the same future.

The schools, though—those bastions of separated worlds—they held out. Nominal desegregation came in 1967, under a voluntary "freedom of choice" plan that was more symbol than substance. It wasn't until 1971, under court order, that the full integration of schools was achieved.

By the time I was born in 1979, change had come, but like a cautious visitor, not yet ready to unpack its bags and stay. Social integration existed mainly on paper. Most folks kept to their own, not by law anymore but by choice—or at least what passed for choice when generations of separation had carved such deep channels in the landscape of human connection.

If any of that heaviness still hung in the air, I had no idea during those golden summers of my childhood. To Ray and me, McComb was our slice of heaven, a paradise where we could be carefree kids in a way that the streets of Carson never quite allowed.

Every single day, Ray and I would ride our bikes all over town, the wind in our hair, the sun on our backs, freedom in our hearts. It was our absolute favorite thing to do—just riding around, for hours and hours, exploring every nook and cranny of this place that held so much of our family's history. Not even the drowsy heat deterred us from spending the day together, creating our own little world on two wheels.

Our route always started on Summit Street, where our grandparents lived. We would pedal down to Bullock's, this little mom-and-pop shop we loved, its screen door slapping shut behind us as we entered the cool dimness to grab Goobers, Funyuns, and little plastic barrels of neon-colored juice.

"Y'all be careful now," Mrs. Bullock would call after us, her voice carrying the weight of a woman who had seen too many children grow up too fast in this town. "Don't go wandering where you ain't supposed to be."

With promises still fresh on our lips, Ray and I would mount our bikes once more, picking up speed as we sliced through the neighborhood streets like blades through butter. The faded glory of brick storefronts along Main Street told stories of better days, of a bustling downtown that had thrived before malls and highways diverted the lifeblood away from there.

Every time we passed the old, abandoned Palace Theater, I would slow my bike to a crawl, staring up at the rusty marquee with dreamy eyes. In my mind, I could see it lit up, bulbs chasing each other around the perimeter, my name spelled out in bold black letters: "An Intimate Evening with Brandy."

"Come on, slowpoke!" Ray would shout, circling back to get me. "You can daydream at home!"

We were given only one rule for our daily rides: we couldn't go over to the projects on the other side of the tracks, a complex of houses that had fallen into disrepair, its buildings crumbling under the weight of neglect and systemic abandonment. The whole family put the fear of God in Ray and me about venturing over there, their warnings taking on an almost mythic quality.

"Nothing good happens in those parts," my grandmother would say, her mouth set in a firm line that brooked no argument. "You stay where people know you belong to me."

A narrow cemetery surrounded by ancient oak trees separated the old development from the newer, yet somehow rougher, development—a strip of hallowed ground between two worlds we were forbidden to cross. Once dusk fell, Ray got a kick out of daring our cousins to ride through the cemetery, their refusals only emboldening him further.

"I ain't afraid of no ghosts," he'd declare, though I noticed he never volunteered to go first.

Now, the thing about being given only one rule to follow meant breaking said rule was all the more enticing—a forbidden fruit hanging low and ripe for the picking. A year had passed since my failed solo attempt at the neighboring church, and I'd since grown bolder in more ways than one. I was finding my voice in our home church choir, my confidence blooming like the camellias that dotted our grandparents' yard.

That afternoon, with the sun high overhead and boredom nipping at our heels, we made a decision that would end in the kind of story families tell for years afterward, embellishing a little more with each retelling. We snuck our way over to the very place we had been warned, repeatedly, never to go—only to get promptly chased out by a group of kids who made it very known just how unwelcome we were in their territory the second we came into view.

We hauled it up out of there quick, dodging the rocks being hurled toward us, our legs pumping furiously, hearts pounding in our chests like drums, the sound of jeers and threats fading behind us as we put distance between ourselves and our poor decision.

"Race you to the church!" Ray shouted, already pedaling furiously ahead of me, his bike kicking up dust from dry red clay soil.

"No fair!" I yelled back, pumping my legs harder, the wind whipping against my face. Our bikes skidded to a stop in front of the 24th Street Church of Christ, which our Paw Paw helped build with his own hands, brick by brick, a testament to what he always called "stubborn faith"—the kind that persists even when all evidence suggests surrender would be easier.

"I win." Ray grinned, dropping his bike on the patchy grass and racing inside, his energy undiminished by our narrow escape.

"You always win," I muttered, but there was no real bitterness in it. Ray was faster, stronger—these were just facts, like the color of the sky or the sweetness of the peach cobbler Grandma made for church.

The 24th Street Church of Christ was the only place that got as much of Ray's and my attention as our bike adventures. It was another home—a place where we felt safe, protected, embraced by something bigger than ourselves. The heavy wooden door creaked as we pushed it open, the sound echoing through the empty church like a greeting.

Early-evening light streamed through the stained-glass windows—simple designs of crosses and doves, painting the wooden pews with pools of gold, navy, and crimson. The air smelled of lemon polish, old hymnals, and something else—something that felt like history and belonging, like roots that went deeper than I could possibly understand.

"Hey, baby girl?" my dad's voice boomed from the back room, startling me. "I've been thinking, when we get back home, I'd like you to lead us with a solo. What do you think?"

My stomach dropped. The memory from earlier in the summer rushed back—standing frozen in front of everyone, my voice catching in my throat, the awful silence that followed. "I don't know, Dad. What if I freeze up again?"

"You won't," he said simply, placing a hand on my shoulder.

"But what if it doesn't sound right? What if—"

"Listen to me," my dad interrupted gently. "When we get back, we're going to keep working. You're ready for this."

I wanted to believe him, but the fear still sat heavy in my chest. The thought of all those eyes on me.

"I'll be right there with you. You know that," he continued. "And so will everyone who loves you."

I nodded slowly, still uncertain but trusting in the confidence I heard in his voice.

"Okay," I whispered. "I'll try."

"Trying is half the battle," my dad said, pulling me into a hug. "Remember, you have a gift from God, a gift that is meant to be shared. Never forget that."

OUTSIDER

IT SEEMED LIKE every kid in Carson hated Brandy Rayana Norwood.

The terror began each morning, when the weight of the day ahead settled in my chest like an anvil. Ambler Elementary sat nestled on a street lined with jacaranda trees, just close enough to our home to walk—close enough that my mom wouldn't drive me.

To get to Ambler, I had to pass Montez Hickmon's house.

At thirteen years old, Montez was lean and sinewy, with skin the color of walnut. He went to a different school on the other side of town, but he got kicked out. The reason for Montez's expulsion was unknown, but various stories floated among the kids in the neighborhood: He beat up a boy so badly the kid was hospitalized. He busted a teacher's nose. He brought a loaded gun to school. I didn't know the truth, but Montez spent his days at the corner house where the older boys who ran the streets gathered—and that was enough for me to know he was trouble.

Montez made the morning walk to school hell. At least two or three times a week, I could count on him popping out of the house to terrorize me as I hurried past, head down, backpack clutched to my chest like a shield.

"Hey, lil' skinny girl!" His voice would slice through the morning air. He had pure menace in his eyes and would walk within an inch of me. He had a particular obsession with my body, and he was relentless about tracking my development.

"Turn around, girl. Let me see if you wearin' a bra today," he'd sneer, yanking the back of my shirt so hard the collar would bite into my neck. "Still flat as a board! When you gonna grow some titties?"

He'd erupt in laughter that echoed in my ears long after I'd escaped. His voice bounced off the inside of my skull during math class, during lunch, during the walk home.

"Mom, I don't feel good. My stomach hurts," I'd whisper some mornings, my face buried in her neck, inhaling her familiar scent of cocoa butter.

She'd lean in close, take the palm of her hand, and gently press it against my forehead.

"Humph," she said. "Maybe I gotta try again."

She'd take her other hand, nice and slow, and rest it on my forehead longer, with assuring eyes that told me she was at least taking me seriously, even if we both knew what the results of her exam would show.

"Well, you're not feverish, baby," she'd say.

"Are you *sure*?"

"Bran," she'd say, her voice firm but tender, eyes searching mine for the truth. "You can't hide from the world, baby. Whatever's waiting for you out there, *you're* stronger."

But was I? Strong felt like a foreign concept, a quality reserved for girls in the books I read under my covers at night—girls with magic powers or swords, or at least a group of loyal friends. I had none of these things.

What I did have was a shortcut.

I discovered it while I was out riding bikes with Ray one weekend. There was this narrow gate covered in overgrown vines between a neighbor's house and an abandoned lot where street vendors sold incense, body oils, and fish plates on Sundays after church let out. It bypassed Montez's house entirely, spitting me out just a block from school.

The discovery felt like finding lost treasure. For weeks, I executed my covert operation with laser-focused intensity. I'd peek around the corner to ensure the coast was clear, tie my braids into a tight bun, sprint to the gate, slip through the narrow opening, leap over the broken fence on the other side, and emerge victorious onto safer ground.

I mastered the art of invisibility. For a blessed stretch of days, Montez's voice faded from my morning ritual. The tight knot in my stomach loosened. Maybe, just maybe, I'd beaten him at his own game.

Until the afternoon I didn't.

I remember everything about that day with sparkling clarity—the vivid yellow of my favorite sweater that I wore with everything, the baggie of candy I won in Mrs. Thompson's spelling bee that I clutched in my hand as I approached my secret passage, the excitement I had about sharing my bounty with Ray the second he came home. The gate creaked as I pushed it open, same as always. The vines caught at my sleeves, same as always. I landed on the other side with a small grunt, same as always.

And there he was. Standing on the other side of the fence. Arms crossed. The sight of Montez made me trip and fall backward onto my tailbone. I let out a sharp squeal.

"Thought you was slick, didn't you?"

Montez stood over me, his bulk blocking out the afternoon sun, casting me in his shadow.

"Please, Montez, leave me alone," I whispered, the words barely audible even to my own ears as I slowly got back up and dusted specks of gravel from my now dirt-stained sweater. "I just want to go home."

What happened next played out in slow motion, like watching someone else's nightmare. His fist, enormous from this angle, drew back. And then—*whoosh.* He crashed it into my mouth with the force of a brick falling from the sky. He said nothing. He just punched me with all his might and then stood there. *Waiting.* What did this boy think I was going to do? Hit him back? Fight him? I was eight and barely half his size.

I swear I saw stars. Actual stars, like in the cartoons, exploding behind my eyes. The taste of pennies filled my mouth. The ground rushed up to meet my knees. Pieces of candy scattered across cracked pavement.

When my vision cleared, Montez was still standing there, looking almost proud of what he'd done. In that second of stunned silence between us, instinct took over. I ran.

I ran until I reached my front door, fumbling with the key, falling inside, collapsing against the wall as sobs tore through my body.

"Bran! What in God's name—" My mom's voice cut through my hysteria as she rushed from the kitchen, still holding a dish towel. Her face went from confusion to fury in an instant as she took in my split lip, the blood on my favorite sweater. "Who did this to you? *Who did this?*"

But I couldn't speak his name. Couldn't relive it. So, I made up some story or other. On top of everything else, I didn't want my mother to worry.

By some divine intervention, Montez vanished shortly after. He'd gotten caught up with some of the older boys in the neighborhood who ran the stretch of Avalon Boulevard that *everyone* knew not to lurk on. Montez was sent down South to live with his father. I never saw him again after he attacked me. I like to hope that the low and slow of life in the South lightened whatever darkness lived inside him.

But Montez was just one part of my day. The torment continued at school.

At Ambler Elementary, I approached each interaction with

a desperate smile, a plea in my eyes: *Please like me. Please just see me.* But my yearning for connection became the very thing that marked me as a target.

The hallways of Ambler felt endless, stretched out like fun-house corridors where dangers lurked around every corner. I mapped safe routes between classes, identified bathrooms where bullies rarely ventured, and perfected the art of becoming invisible while sitting in plain sight.

Teachers moved through their days in the same fog of survival as their students. Mrs. Thompson was my favorite person at Ambler. She taught English language arts, and I loved how fun she made learning. She'd give pop quizzes and spelling bees and always had the best prizes. Troll dolls. Candy. Stickers. Pins. Yo-yos. The cutest colored pencils. I must have won *one* too many prizes, because Tyler Anderson went from paying me no mind to pulling my hair and whispering obscenities anytime he sat behind me. I'd pick another desk. And so would he.

When I finally gathered the courage to report him after class, Mrs. Thompson patted my hand with distracted sympathy.

"Oh, honey, don't you know? When a boy is mean to you, it usually means he likes you." Her smile was tired around the edges, her eyes already drifting to the stack of ungraded papers on her desk. "It's just his way of getting your attention."

The boys were predictable in their torment—direct, brutal, but straightforward. They struck and moved on, the pain intense but mercifully brief.

But the girls? The girls were artists of anguish, painting masterpieces of humiliation with delicate, deliberate strokes. Their warfare was methodical, designed to keep me perpetually off-balance, constantly vigilant.

Shanice Jones was the undisputed queen bee of Ambler Elementary. Her reign of terror was so legendary she could part the hallways with just her presence.

Shanice stood nearly five foot two in the third grade, her body developed far beyond her years, with curves that drew both envious and predatory eyes. Her confidence was bulletproof, her tongue a weapon honed to lethal sharpness. When she laughed—and she laughed often, usually at someone else's expense—the sound rolled through the hallways like thunder.

I'd feel her eyes on me before I'd see her, that prickle of awareness at the back of my neck, the subtle change in the air.

"Eww," she said one morning, her nose wrinkling as though she'd smelled something rotten. The crowd around us went quiet, sensing the beginning of a performance they'd been waiting for. "Anybody ever tell you that you look like E.T.?"

The words hit their mark. My eyes—my big, expressive eyes that my mom called "soulful" and "beautiful"—were my deepest insecurity. Shanice had found the tender spot and pressed down hard.

I froze as laughter rippled through the hallway, heat flooding my face. Any response, I knew, would only prolong my suffering. So, I stared at the floor, counting the specks in the linoleum tile (seventeen in the square directly beneath my left foot), and willed myself to become invisible.

But Shanice wasn't finished. She never was after just one strike. Later, in the cafeteria during lunch, her fingertips brushing my shoulders as she passed, leaning down to whisper just loud enough:

"E.T. phone home."

The next day, she cornered me by the water fountain, standing close enough that I could smell the powdery sweetness of the Love's Baby Soft she doused herself with every day.

"One of these days," she said, her voice soft, "I'm gonna beat your little ugly ass. Just you watch."

It was the anticipation that broke me—the constant vigil, watching for signs, reading meanings into casual gestures. Every day was a countdown to an explosion that never came. My shoulders lived permanently around my ears, my stomach a knot of anxiety, my sleep fractured by nightmares of Shanice finally making good on her promise.

"Hey, Pippi!" she'd yell from across the hallway. It only took Shanice calling me Pippi Longstocking a couple times before the name stuck with the other kids. *At least it's better than E.T.*, I told myself.

I started taking the long route to Mrs. Thompson's class, even if it meant being late, just to avoid the stretch of hallway where Shanice held court with the other mean girls. Counting the days until summer break like a prisoner marking time on a cell wall got me through the last stretch of classes.

Just three more months!

Just three more weeks!

Just three more days!

Just . . . three . . . more . . . hours!

When Shanice uttered those blessed words—"You lucky I'm not coming back here next year"—in my ear on the last day of school, I nearly collapsed with relief. All summer, I lived in a state of suspended joy, walking lighter, breathing deeper, tasting freedom like a physical thing on my tongue.

The air in McComb felt sweeter. The sky stretched wider. Colors seemed brighter. For three glorious months, I existed without the shadow of fear, rediscovering parts of myself that had gone quiet under Shanice's reign of terror.

Until the first day of fourth grade arrived.

I walked through Ambler's double doors with something approaching optimism, my new Lisa Frank unicorn trapper keeper proudly clutched to my chest, my hair freshly braided—barrettes click-clacking with every step.

There she was. Shanice Jones, leaning against the wall outside Mr. Jackson's classroom, her eyes finding mine across the crowded hallway like she'd been waiting all summer for *this* moment.

Cue the unraveling.

No. No, this isn't happening, I thought.

Every ounce of that golden summer joy drained from my body in an instant. My fingers clutched the straps of my backpack until my knuckles ached.

She had promised—*promised*—she wouldn't be back.

"Thought you got rid of me, didn't you?" she said, pushing off the wall and gliding toward me with predatory grace. The crowd parted for her automatically, no one wanting to be in her path. "You really thought I was gone?"

Shanice's family was supposed to move, but their plans changed last minute, so here she was, back at Ambler. Somehow, over the summer, she'd grown even bigger and more imposing.

This is it, I thought. *She's gonna beat my ass the first day of school.*

"I just wanna get to homeroom, Shanice," I said, summoning every ounce of strength I saw in my Paw Paw. I stood tall and firm, like one of the church walls he'd built. My voice came out shaky but resolute. This girl couldn't knock me over. *"Please leave me alone."*

Something shifted in her eyes then—surprise, maybe, that the mouse had finally squeaked. She sucked her teeth and made a sudden lunge toward me. I flinched, hard, despite my best efforts at bravery. Shanice's laugh echoed off the lockers as I darted past her into the classroom.

"Little punk!" she yelled after me. "You lucky I don't feel like whooping yo ass today."

Shanice ran with a crew of girls at Ambler. Katrina Wallace. Vanessa Washington. Crystal Pittard. It was unclear if these girls genuinely admired Shanice and liked being around her, or they simply recognized that standing in her shadow was safer than being in her path. Either way, these girls were straight-up lapdogs. Whoever Shanice couldn't stand, *they* couldn't stand. If she told one of them to do something—anything—they surely complied. So now that I had more sharks to swim from, I couldn't escape.

I had once found relative safety in certain corners of the school—a quiet spot in the library, a particular bathroom rarely frequented by the popular crowd. Now nowhere felt secure. If it wasn't Shanice, it was one of her flunkies. Even girls who once paid me no mind now joined the teasing.

The only place where I felt free, and seen, that wasn't my home was church. Standing with the choir, I felt accepted and embraced. The kids in the choir didn't tease me or ice me out. No boys pulled my hair because I got a solo, and no girls made fun of the gap in my front tooth or the flatness of my chest.

But summer? I lived for summer vacation. A chance to breathe without the shadow of torment falling across my day. And then fall brought the return of dread, settling in my stomach like a stone. Every night during summer break, I prayed the same desperate prayer:

"Please, God," I'd whisper into folded hands. "Please make Shanice leave Ambler. Make her dad get transferred. Give her mom a big fancy job in another state. Or put her into some special school for all the mean girls. Anything, Lord. I'll be good forever, I promise. Just make her go away."

My prayers seemed to bounce off the ceiling, falling back unheard. Until they weren't.

On the first day of fifth grade, I walked through Ambler's front doors with my body armored in anxiety, eyes darting left and right, scanning for Shanice's tall figure among the crowd. The hallway buzzed with excited chatter, kids comparing summer growth spurts and new sneakers, but I moved through it like a zombie. My entire being was focused on one task: spotting my bully before she caught me slipping.

But Shanice wasn't posted up by homeroom. She wasn't holding court outside the girls' bathroom. She wasn't waiting to ambush me at my locker. Minute after minute passed, and the familiar dread of seeing her began to give way to a new, equally unsettling feeling—hope mixed with suspicion.

I found a corner in Mr. Jackson's homeroom and kept my head down, just in case she was about to run up on me in front of everybody. Maybe this was her plan all along? Waiting until the first day of school of our final year at Ambler to truly humiliate me. But she never popped up.

At lunch, I sat with my turkey sandwich untouched, that strange lightness continuing to grow around the edges of my fear. Was this another one of her games? Was she waiting until I let my guard down? Was today finally the day she'd make good on years of threats?

Lisa Jefferson slid up a chair beside me and leaned in real close. I'd signed up to be in a local drill team because I liked to dance, and my mom thought it could be a way to make friends in the neighborhood. Lisa was never mean to me at school. She never spoke to me, either, until we saw each other at practice and realized we were the only girls from Ambler who had joined the team.

"Did you hear about Shanice?" she asked, her expression solemn.

"What about her?" I asked, working to keep my voice casual even as my heart thundered in my chest.

Lisa leaned closer, glancing around to ensure we wouldn't be overheard. "She's—" a heavy pause "—dead."

The cafeteria seemed to fade around me, sounds muffling as though I'd been submerged underwater.

"What?" I yelled.

"My mama works at the district office. I heard her on the phone this morning. They are gonna tell us at the end of the day." Lisa's words tumbled out in a rush now, her voice barely above a whisper.

I pushed aside my sandwich. I definitely had no appetite now.

"So, um, what happened?" I stuttered.

"Shanice was spending the summer down in Atlanta with her auntie. Day before yesterday, a gang of dudes broke into the house. And—"

I waited for the rest, something in me already knowing.

"They shot everybody," Lisa finished, her eyes wide with morbid excitement. "Shanice, too."

The cafeteria lights suddenly seemed too bright, the sounds of kids' chatter too sharp. I nodded mechanically, unable to form words. A strange buzzing filled my ears as one thought rose above all others:

I did this. My prayers did this.

All I could mutter was a low "Oh my God."

I spent the rest of the day in a haze. Sure enough, before the last bell, Mr. Johnson brought in a very kind older woman with graying hair and the softest baby blue eyes. She was a grief counselor sent by the district to share the very sad news that Shanice had been killed by some bad guys during vacation, and she ensured us that she'd be here for the beginning of the year to help us adjust to never seeing our classmate again.

"Does anyone want to share a memory of Shanice?" the nice lady asked to a class full of stone-faced fifth graders, many of whom had been tormented for years by the girl they were being asked to eulogize.

I eyed Vanessa. She was applying a fresh coat of lip gloss. Unbothered. Shanice's own "friend" didn't bother to raise her hand. Guess I had my answer about how her clique really felt, and that made me sad.

But I let my guilt go. It was an awful tragedy. And I knew that.

In a twist of fate, I wound up becoming friends with Shanice's sister, Cheryl, who transferred to Ambler that fall.

Cheryl and Shanice were only six months apart. They had different moms and looked almost nothing alike. Cheryl didn't have her sister's height or curves. She was short and bony. But unlike her sister, Cheryl was not about verbal tussling. She liked to actually fight.

Driven by a crushing guilt I couldn't name to anyone, I approached Cheryl during recess one day. She was sitting by herself on the bleachers, as she did almost every day for the first few weeks of school. My guilt aside, I also felt terrible for Cheryl. She was the new girl *and* the sister of the school's biggest bully who got murdered a few days before classes started. No one at Ambler was rushing to cozy up to Cheryl, and somewhere in my mind, I thought sucking up to the sister of the girl whose absence I had prayed for, whose death now weighed on my conscience like a stone, would help ease my guilt.

"Hey, I'm sorry for your loss," I said, my voice quiet and unsteady as Cheryl braided a thin plait into her hair without making eye contact. "Your sister didn't like me much, but . . . I'm really sorry about what happened to Shanice."

Cheryl pulled the finished plait around her loose hair to make a high ponytail. Pulled out her lip gloss and applied it. Only after she puckered her lips did she tilt her head up toward me. She looked at me for a long, assessing second, her eyes so much like her sister's that my stomach clenched in reflexive fear.

"You the girl that always beat everybody in Mrs. Thompson's class? You sit right up in the front," she finally said. "Can I ask you a question?"

"Sure," I said, nervously awaiting the accusation or the threat surely heading my way. Instead, Cheryl patted the empty space next to her.

She was inviting *me* to sit with *her*?

"Don't take this the wrong way. But why you be letting those girls dog you out? I see how Crystal and 'nem be pressing you in the hallway. You a punk or something?"

I didn't know what to say. So many people taunted me with that word, but no one ever said it to me in the context of a question that didn't appear to be an invitation for confrontation.

Cheryl must have read the disbelief on my face, because she let out a light giggle and patted my knee.

"I don't hang out with punks, so you gonna need to learn how to square up if you think we about to be cool," she said, smiling.

An unlikely sisterhood was born that day. Cheryl sat with me at lunch. I helped her with her homework. She walked me home from school and called me over the weekends. I never told her how I'd spent summers praying to never have to see her sister's mean ole face again. Why would I? I now had the one thing I craved: a loyal friend.

As the year went on, kids' imaginations ran fairly wild with the details of Shanice's case. All sorts of stories were passed around the school about Shanice's aunt. Once, we were in the cafeteria and Cheryl overheard a boy gossiping about it. Her face just went . . . blank. Like the lights had turned off. Cheryl calmly got up from our table, walked over to the boy, and popped him dead in the mouth with a closed fist so hard he fell backward off the bench.

"Keep my sister's name out 'cho mouth."

She might have been talking to the boy writhing around in pain at her feet, but *everyone* at Ambler got the message loud and clear. And now the sea parted for Cheryl whenever she took to the hallways. Shanice's old crew were especially jealous that she paid their cool girl clique dust!

Secretly, I *loved* it.

There was a day when I was really feeling myself. Cheryl brought me sparkly red Lip Smacker gloss, a gift for helping her raise her English grade. I raced to the bathroom to put it on in the mirror. Of course, Crystal and Vanessa were in there, hogging up the sink, scrunching their noses up at me.

"Girl, that cheap dollar-store gloss ain't gonna make you cute," Vanessa said, sucking her teeth.

"Yeah . . . Eeeeeeee! Teeeeeee!" Crystal yelled. They both burst out laughing—full-out cackling at the top of their lungs. Until Cheryl walked into the bathroom. Suddenly they were as quiet as church mice.

"What's funny?" she asked.

Silence.

The two loudest girls at Ambler, stone-cold silent.

"Y'all usually got so much mouth," Cheryl said, arms folded. "Why we quiet now?"

They both cowered. Looking to the ground, shrinking into themselves. Like I had so many times before.

"Thought so." Cheryl headed to the door, but before she left, she yelled out to me. "That gloss is *really* pretty on you, Brandy."

It was the last time any girl at Ambler so much as looked at me sideways.

I grew tired of feeling helpless—of needing protection, of being the victim. The drill team had become an outlet, a place where I felt capable and strong in my skin. There was a park at the edge of my street where we usually practiced, our synchronized movements drawing occasional audiences of neighborhood kids and parents.

One of those regular spectators was LaToya Williams—a tall, solid girl with a permanent sneer who lived a few blocks over. I could feel her eyes burning into me during every practice, tracking my movements with laser focus. Anytime I fumbled a turn or got tripped up in the routine, her derisive snort carried across the park, sharp as a needle.

LaToya was from a hostile family that was always in some mess in our neighborhood. The whole family liked to fight. There was no inciting incident between the two of us. Perhaps she didn't like the way I walked, or looked, or dressed. Whatever her reasons, she made me her target and picked at me for sport.

I tried ignoring LaToya, but that only made her try harder.

One afternoon, as I approached the park with my backpack full of homework I planned to finish before practice, LaToya made her move. She rushed me like a linebacker, ripping my backpack from my shoulders with such force I stumbled backward, nearly falling.

I should leave, a small voice whispered in my head. *Turn around. Go home.*

But I stood my ground, even as she closed in on my personal space, her finger jabbing my shoulder with each accusation she hurled.

"You think you cute, don't you?" Her face was inches from mine, her breath hot against my cheek, smelling of cinnamon Teddy Grahams and chocolate milk. "You think you all that because you can sing?"

Every word felt like a small explosion against my skin. She wanted a fight—needed it, almost. If I didn't engage, I was a punk. That was how it worked. Her finger stabbed my shoulder again, hard enough to leave a mark. Then again. And again. Each poke punctuated by words that crashed together as my heart hammered in my chest.

". . . stuck-up bitch . . ."

". . . think you better than everybody . . ."

". . . don't nobody care about your little singing . . ."

Her voice crescendoed until it seemed to fill the entire park. I couldn't make sense of half of what she was saying—only that it was loud, and mean, and relentless. But between the bursts of rage, I caught it—a flash of something like pleasure in her eyes. A quick upturn of her lips. She was *enjoying* this.

I glanced toward my drill team, standing in a huddle just a few feet away. They stood there, frozen in place.

Help me, I silently pleaded. *Somebody say something.*

LaToya shoved me, hard enough that I staggered back. Then another shove. And another. Each time I regained my balance, her hands were there again, pushing, pushing. Still, she didn't throw a punch. She didn't need to. This slow-motion humiliation was so much worse.

"What, you gonna cry?" she taunted, her face contorted in mock sympathy. "Little miss prissy choir girl gonna cry now?"

My throat burned with unshed tears. Fighting back would only make it worse. There was no winning move here, no right response—only endurance.

So, I stood there, a statue weathering a storm. LaToya's shoves became half-hearted. Her voice grew hoarse.

Finally, with one last venomous "You ain't shit," she stalked off, her performance complete.

The girls from the drill team approached cautiously, as if I were the dangerous one.

"You okay?" Staci asked, her voice small.

"Do you still feel like practicing?" Keisha asked, handing me my backpack while keeping her eyes toward the ground.

I stared at them, these girls I'd thought were my friends. And suddenly, something hard and hot unfurled in my chest—something I'd kept tamped down for so long I'd forgotten it was there.

"Do I look okay?" I repeated, my voice oddly calm. "Do I look like I feel like practicing?"

The embarrassment of being publicly humiliated burned away, replaced by something sharper: rage. Pure, boiling rage. The girls finished practice without me while I walked home alone, my mind churning not with shame, but with plans. This new feeling was . . . exhilarating. I thought about what Cheryl had asked me: "You a punk or something?" LaToya couldn't ruin what I had going in the choir. And so, she dogged me out in front of these girls because she thought I was a punk.

I knew in that instant I was absolutely going to get her back for it.

Most of the kids in my neighborhood were latchkey, parents working to keep food on the table and the lights on. I knew LaToya would be home alone during a specific window each afternoon—just like me, just like most of us.

First, I gathered every extension cord I could find around our house—from behind the TV, from the garage, from my parents' bedroom—and hid them under my bed. LaToya typically ran with a pack of equally intimidating girls, so I knew I'd need to wait for a day when her crew wasn't around. I'd watch from my bedroom window each afternoon, tracking her movements, learning her patterns.

Finally, the day came. The block was quiet, most kids still at after-school programs or friends' houses. From my lookout spot, I saw LaToya return home alone, the front door closing behind her. I retrieved my makeshift weapon—extension cords crudely braided together into a heavy, flexible whip—and marched across the street, my heart pounding so hard I could feel it in my fingertips.

Knock. Knock. Knock.

Like the fool she was, LaToya broke the one cardinal rule drilled into every latchkey kid: she answered the door. Our eyes met for a split second—hers widened in surprise, mine narrowed with purpose.

Before she could speak, I swung. The coiled cords whistled through the air and connected with a satisfying *WHACK* against her shoulder. She didn't even see it coming.

And then I did it again.

And again.

And again.

And again.

I whooped her ass right there on her own doorstep, the extension cord leaving angry red welts on her arms as she raised them to protect her face.

Standing over her, extension cord raised for another strike, I suddenly saw myself as if from a distance. I lowered the cord.

"Don't you ever," I said, my voice steady and unfamiliar in my own ears, "put your hands on me. You hear me?"

She nodded, a jerky motion somewhere between defiance and fear.

I marched off her doorstep, extension cord tucked under my arm, trembling with adrenaline.

No one in the neighborhood ever bothered me again.

SHOWCASE

TOWERS OF CASSETTE TAPES lined the walls of our family room. Even on my tippy toes, arms stretched until they ached, my fingertips couldn't graze the highest rows. I'd stand there, neck craned back, marveling at my father's musical metropolis.

My father's collection introduced me to sounds that changed how I wanted to use my voice. This was how I heard BeBe & CeCe Winans for the first time. And Whitney Houston and Mariah Carey. And the Clark Sisters. Rifling through my dad's collection was how I'd discover Boyz II Men and SWV. I was enraptured by all these incredible voices and would try to emulate what I heard.

My dad listened to an endless variety of artists and genres. Every type of recorded sound must have been in that room. I would stretch out on the floor and meticulously thumb through each stack. I read the liner notes and started a mental catalog of the writers and producers I enjoyed the most. My dad would fill in details about the recording process of a particular song. He'd tell me about different musicians and what to look for in their work. It helped my mind expand, particularly around how our voices can be used.

"Dad, how many tapes do you have?" I once asked.

He chuckled, that deep, warm sound that always made me feel safe. "Baby girl, I stopped counting somewhere in the hundreds. Music isn't meant to be counted—it's meant to be felt."

Sheet music wasn't simply scattered on the coffee table—it blanketed it in a patchwork quilt of my father's cramped annotations, coffee ring signatures, and dog-eared corners. His handwritten notes danced in the margins—"crescendo here," "try F sharp minor," "feel this part"—a road map to emotions I was just beginning to understand. Crates of vinyl records stood sentry between intimidating stereo equipment that blinked and hummed with mysterious importance. The turntable was a sacred object; I wasn't allowed to touch it until I understood just how to work it.

In the corner of our family room sat the piano—the vessel that carried my father and me through countless hours of discovery. Its ivory keys had yellowed slightly with age, each one holding the memory of every note we'd coaxed from its depths.

"Brandy, close your eyes," my dad would say, his voice gentle but insistent. "Don't just play the notes—feel them move through your fingertips. Music is about the spaces between the sounds as much as the sounds themselves."

He encouraged my curiosity to wander freely through the landscape of music, never redirecting my explorations, never suggesting some paths were worthier than others. I'd watch his hands, memorizing the way his long fingers stretched confidently across octaves, how they knew precisely where to land without his eyes guiding them.

Between learning how to harmonize with different tones at church and the records I listened to with my dad, I wanted to hear what my voice would sound like in harmony with itself. When I asked my father how I could record and duplicate my voice, he wasted no time walking me through how to use his four-track cassette recorder. He taught me the ins and outs of how to utilize the deck, and I began to unearth new textures, registers and ranges. My dad saw the elation pouring out of me as I played around producing harmonies. Eventually he surprised me with a four-track recorder of my own. That little machine is the reason I fell in love with my voice.

It also gave me the first taste of what my sound could be.

In church, my father wasn't just Willie Norwood, devoted family man. He was Minister Norwood—the revered minister of music whose gifts transformed the Church of Christ every Sunday without fail. His position commanded respect throughout the congregation, a sacred calling he'd answered long before I was born.

The Church of Christ takes the Bible verse "Sing and make melody in your hearts . . ." to mean we should only use our voices in church. No instruments. No outside music.

As minister of music, my father conducted with a surgical focus—a raised eyebrow to signal the sopranos, a slight tilt of his head to bring in the tenors, a barely perceptible lift of his finger to prompt the altos to swell. The slightest movement of his hand could transform a merely good performance into a transcendent one.

"Watch your father," my mom whispered to me as my dad led the adult choir during one service. "Notice how he doesn't need to speak to be understood. That's power, baby girl. That's mastery."

And I did just that. I watched him, studied him, absorbing his techniques, his mannerisms, his instinctive understanding of what each section needed in any given second. During Wednesday-night rehearsals, I'd perch on the edge of the front pew, homework sitting half-finished beside me, mesmerized as he worked with the different vocal sections.

"Altos, you're coming in too strong on the bridge," he'd say, his voice firm but never harsh. "Remember, you're the foundation, not the focal point here. Sopranos need room to soar on this passage."

He'd demonstrate exactly what he meant, his voice sliding effortlessly between registers to show each section precisely how their part should sound. This was my real music education—watching my father transform a group of singers into a unified force.

By age nine, I was no longer content to simply observe. I began asking questions during rehearsals—real, technical questions that sometimes surprised even the adult choir members.

"Dad, shouldn't the tenors hold back on that high G? It's competing with Sister Juanita's solo," I'd venture, my voice small but my conviction firm.

He'd pause, consider, then nod. "You're right, Bran. Tenors, let's take it down about 20 percent on that passage. Let Sister Juanita's testimony be heard."

The choir members would exchange glances—some befuddled, others impressed—but my father never once dismissed my input. Instead, he nurtured it, treating my observations with the same respect he'd give any adult musician.

When I turned ten, my father approached me after Sunday dinner.

"The youth choir needs direction," he said, taking a seat beside me on the living room sofa. "They've got good voices but need cohesion. And leadership."

I nodded, having noticed the same thing during our performances. The youth choir—ranging from ages eight to sixteen—had talent but lacked the polish and unity of my father's adult choir.

"I've been thinking," he continued, his voice casual, though I could tell this was anything but a casual conversation, "that you might be ready to take them on. As assistant director to start. See if you can help shape them into something special."

My heart nearly beat out of my chest. "Really? You think I could?"

"I know you could." His certainty washed over me like a blessing. "You've been learning from me since before you could talk. You hear things, Bran. You understand harmony and balance in ways some adults never grasp. It's time to put that gift to work."

That Wednesday, I stood before the youth choir for the first time—fifteen faces looking at me with expressions ranging from curiosity to barely disguised skepticism. At ten, I was younger than most of the members I was supposed to be directing.

"This is a joke, right?" one of the older kids, Nelson, muttered from the back row, just loud enough to be heard. "She's just a kid."

My father, standing at the piano to support me through this first session, raised an eyebrow. "So was David before he slew Goliath," he said simply. "Now, let's begin. Brandy has some ideas for our next performance."

And I did. I'd spent the previous two nights planning, selecting a contemporary gospel piece that would challenge us without being impossible, sketching out new harmonies that would showcase our strengths.

"We're going to try something a little different," I said, my voice wavering initially but gaining strength with each word. "Something that lets everyone shine."

For the next hour, I worked us harder than we'd ever been worked—drilling parts, rearranging vocal assignments to better suit each voice, demanding precision on passages they'd previously glossed over.

"Again," I'd say when we fumbled a transition. "From the top of the verse. And this time, feel it. Don't just sing it."

By the end of rehearsal, the skepticism had faded, replaced by a grudging respect and—more importantly—a new cohesiveness in our sound.

"That actually sounded . . . good," Nelson admitted as we gathered our things to leave.

My father, who had remained largely silent throughout the session, letting me find my own leadership style, squeezed my shoulder. "That wasn't good," he corrected. "That was excellent. They respect you now because you respected the music enough to demand their best."

Within a month, the youth choir had transformed. Our performances became highlights of the service rather than obligatory interludes. The congregation began to anticipate our contributions, murmuring with appreciation when we rose to take our place before the altar.

Then came the Sunday that changed everything.

Church was packed that morning—every pew filled, extra chairs lining the walls, latecomers standing in the back.

After we performed, and the adult choir rose to take our position, my father caught my eye and made a subtle gesture—a slight beckoning with his fingers. I froze, unsure if I had interpreted correctly. He repeated the motion, more definitively this time, and added a nod.

He was calling me to the front. To direct the adult choir *with* him. Publicly. During a packed Sunday service.

Sister Juanita gave me a gentle nudge. "Go on, child. It's your time."

With legs like jelly, I made my way to the front of the church, hyperaware of all the eyes following my movement. The youth choir looked as stunned as I felt, exchanging glances of surprise and confusion.

My father stepped slightly to the side, creating space for me beside him. He bent down, his lips close to my ear.

"You've earned this," he whispered. "Show them what you've built."

Time seemed to suspend as I stood there, the weight of uncertainty pressing on my chest. Then, somewhere in the back of my mind, I heard my father's constant refrain: *Music isn't about you. It's about the message. Be a vessel.*

I took a deep breath, lifted my hands the way I'd seen my father do countless times, and gave the cue to begin. The opening notes filled the church, and as the choir began to sing, something electric moved through the room.

They were perfect—every entrance clean, every harmony

balanced, every dynamic shift executed. But more than that, they were unified, their individual voices merging into a single instrument of praise.

As we moved into the second verse, I signaled for the youth choir to join, creating layers of harmony that seemed to physically lift the ceiling of the church. The congregation began to respond—first with gentle swaying, then with raised hands, then with spontaneous exclamations of "Yes, Lord!" and "Sing it!"

By the bridge, several people had moved into the aisles, overcome by the spirit. And through it all, I conducted with a confidence that seemed to come from somewhere beyond me—my small hands somehow controlling this wave of sound and emotion. Thunderous applause and praise rang out from the pews.

I turned slightly, seeking my father's approval, and found him wiping tears from his eyes. "That," he said simply, "is what music ministry looks like."

Later that afternoon, as we sat at the piano at home, still in our Sunday clothes, he placed his hands on my shoulders and looked directly into my eyes.

"What you did today wasn't about performance," he said. "It was about channeling something greater than yourself. Remember that feeling, Bran. That connection. That surrendering. That's what makes music transcendent. Never forget that."

I nodded, understanding even then that I had crossed some invisible threshold. I wasn't just Minister Norwood's daughter anymore. I wasn't just a girl with a pretty voice. I was a musician in my own right, capable not just of following but of leading.

"You were born for this," he added, his voice thick with emotion. "Don't ever doubt that, Bran. *Not for a single moment.*"

At ten years old, my sights were firmly set on a singular dream: getting a record deal.

This wasn't some vague childhood fantasy, the kind most kids cycle through weekly—astronaut one day, veterinarian the next. This was bone-deep certainty, a knowledge as fundamental as my own heartbeat. I wanted to make music. I wanted an album like one of the ones I ran my fingers across in our family room.

One Wednesday evening at choir practice, I overheard a cluster of the older kids huddled in a corner, their voices low but animated.

"They say there'll be people from labels there," Tanya whispered, her braces catching the light as she grinned.

"That's how Frankie got put on with Luther," Nelson added.

"I'm telling you, we just gotta get in front of the right people. And they ain't coming *here* to find us," Tyrone said.

They were talking about a talent showcase that had been advertised in the *Los Angeles Sentinel*, which was the essential publication for all things Black LA. I strained to catch every detail, my heart hammering so loudly I was certain my dad would call me out for creating a distracting percussion section all by myself.

I spent every quiet pause of that rehearsal fantasizing about what it would feel like to be on a stage—a real stage, with professional lights and shiny microphones. I imagined an audience that extended beyond the familiar faces of our congregation, people who might hold the keys to a future I could barely articulate but desperately craved.

On the drive home, with the courage of desire trumping the fear of rejection, I mustered up my voice.

"Dad, can I ask you something?" The words came out smaller than I'd intended.

He caught my eyes in the rearview mirror. "Yeah, baby, what is it?"

I twisted my fingers together in my lap. "Do you think I'm ready to sing outside of the choir?"

He was quiet for a second, navigating the left turn onto our street before responding. "Hmm," he said finally, that thoughtful sound I knew so well. "The question is: Do *you* think you're ready?"

"YES!" The word exploded from me with such force it surprised us both. "Dad, I heard there's going to be a talent showcase for kids. At the community center. I wanna do it. I need to do it."

"Okay."

"Okay?" I leaned forward, gripping the back of his seat. "Just like that?"

"Yes, Bran," he chuckled, pulling into our driveway. "If you think you're ready, you should do it."

"But . . ." I hesitated, suddenly needing more than permission. *"Do you think I'm ready?"*

He shifted the car into Park and turned to face me fully. I tried my hardest to read his expression, searching for any hint of doubt. Instead, I found his face broken open in a wide grin, pride shining from his eyes like sunlight.

"All the work you've put in?" He shook his head in amazement. "Leading the choir. Working on your voice every day like it's your job. Playing around with that four-track like you've been doing it your whole life. You're more than ready, Bran. Now, is that audience ready for you?"

I hopped out and raced straight to the kitchen counter. I knew I'd seen my mom reading the *Sentinel* the other day, and it was still sitting there, creased on a mostly finished crossword puzzle. I flipped through the pages, my fingers smearing the ink as I traced every line of the classifieds until I spotted the ad. I saw "calling all singers" and "all ages welcome" and that was all I needed to see. My dad hadn't even gotten to the front door before I yanked it open and showed him the ad.

"It's real! See!! It's real!" I shouted.

And just like that, my dad entered my name into the showcase. My mother, meanwhile, attacked the challenge of my appearance.

"If you're going to be a star," she declared, rifling through my closet with critical eyes, "you need to look like one."

We settled on a denim two-piece set she'd bought me for Easter but I hadn't worn yet—a vest and skirt combination that made me feel grown-up and important. She paired it with a powder-pink turtleneck that brought out the warmth in my complexion and put my hair up in a high ponytail using a tiny pink ribbon that matched perfectly.

"There," she said, stepping back to assess her work. "You look like someone they'll remember."

Whitney Houston's version of "Greatest Love of All" and Mariah Carey's "Vision of Love" were my go-to songs for any performance outside the gospel standards we sang at church. They were challenging enough to showcase my range but familiar enough that audiences connected immediately. That day, I chose Whitney, the song's message about believing in yourself feeling especially appropriate as my small hands trembled with nerves backstage.

"Remember," my father whispered just before I went on, "you're not just singing notes. You're telling Whitney's story through your voice. Make us believe it."

I walked onto that stage—my first real stage—feeling like I was floating three inches above the ground. The lights were brighter than I'd imagined, momentarily blinding me to the audience's faces. But when those opening piano notes poured out, I found my footing. The nerves dissolved, replaced by a strange, calm certainty. This was what I was born to do.

I sang my heart out that day, every run, every belt, every note carrying all my dreams and ambitions. When I hit the final note and the applause washed over me—louder, more enthusiastic than I'd dared hope—I felt something click into place in the universe.

There was no winner, but the rapturous applause from an audience outside of church was the ultimate prize. And there was the added bonus of knowing that executives from major labels and talent agencies were in the audience. The air buzzed with the hope that you could become one of the lucky ones to get a deal or be hired to go on tour to sing background for some superstar.

At ten, all I felt was hope and excitement. Talent showcases became my sanctuary, a temple outside of church where I worshipped at the altar of possibility. At one of these showcases, I met Danny J. Bakewell Sr. Danny is a pillar of South Los Angeles. A civil rights leader, property developer, and businessman, he would eventually become the publisher of the *Los Angeles Sentinel*. Danny was president of the Brotherhood Crusade. It was a grassroots nonprofit based in South LA that focused on addressing the unmet needs of underserved communities. The organization aimed to foster economic autonomy, health equity, and unity across South LA and did so through a range of programs and community events—many of which I would soon get booked for.

The Brotherhood Crusade was sponsoring a showcase I sang at. After getting a standing ovation from the audience—a feeling that would never get old—Danny approached my parents and invited me to sing at the organization's next event, the Black Family Reunion, a huge three-day celebration that would bring thousands of Black folks together in Los Angeles.

I had never performed for that many people before. I was too excited to even feel nerves, just adrenaline surging through my little body.

Standing on that enormous stage, looking out at a sea of beautiful Black faces spanning generations, I felt a different kind of responsibility. This wasn't just about my dream anymore; it was about representation, about showing other little Black girls what was possible.

Yet again, I chose "Greatest Love of All"—the lyrics about children being our future hitting differently in that context. The applause that erupted when I finished was deafening, a wave of love and recognition that lifted me higher than I'd ever felt.

Just as I was catching my breath backstage with my parents, I saw him walking toward me, his face alight with discovery.

"I heard you singing while I was in my dressing room, and I had to come out," the man said, extending his hand. "I'm—"

"RICKEY MINOR!" I screamed his name so loud the people out in the audience probably heard me. "You're Whitney's music director!"

He jumped back, clearly startled. "How do you even know that?" The genuine confusion on his face made sense—what ten-year-old would recognize a music director, let alone be starstruck by one?

"I am the b-i-g-g-e-s-t Whitney Houston fan in the WORLD," I gushed, words tumbling out faster than I could control them. "I want to be just like her! I've watched all of her performances, and I know all of the band." I proceeded to rattle off every single member of Whitney's touring band—the guitarist, the drummer, the backup singers—to Rickey's increasing amazement.

"Well, little lady," he said, shaking his head with a laugh, "your voice is remarkable. Truly special. Whitney would be impressed with what you did out there."

The world tilted on its axis. Rickey Minor—the man who worked with my idol every day, who helped shape the very sound I worshipped—thought I was good. More than that, he thought Whitney herself would approve. I nearly fainted right there on the spot.

"I have to meet her!" I blurted out. I'm pretty sure I actually grabbed the hem of his jacket, like I could physically anchor this opportunity before it floated away. "Would you please, *please* introduce me? I'll do anything. I'll sing for her. Or I'll just stand there and not say a word if that's what she wants."

I'm certain Rickey thought I was absolutely out of my

mind—this tiny, hyperventilating child making demands like she had any leverage whatsoever. But something in my desperation must have touched him, because his expression softened.

"Tell you what," he said, crouching down slightly to meet my eyes. "Next time there's a show in LA, I promise I'll get you tickets. That's the best I can do for now."

"Promise?" I pressed, needing to cement this verbal contract with all the seriousness of a Supreme Court oath.

"You have my word," he said solemnly, before exchanging information with my wide-eyed parents and heading off toward the stage.

Meeting someone who worked closely with my hero—someone who breathed the same air as Whitney Houston on a regular basis—was exhilarating enough on its own. But the fact that he had noticed me, had sought me out, had complimented my singing? And thought Whitney would like my voice? And promised me tickets to see her? It was almost too much for my young heart to process.

That chance meeting with Rickey put a battery in my back like nothing before. I went even harder after that, practicing with my dad until my voice grew hoarse, recording little demos on my four-track that I'd listen to critically, always asking myself: Would this impress Whitney?

The talent show circuit, too, was its own kind of bootcamp. "You can be standing up there and singing beautifully, but if you don't have any showmanship, it's not going to matter," Hollywood icon Don Johnson once told me. He was hosting a talent competition I'd entered, and I couldn't believe the guy from *Miami Vice* was giving me pointers! I placed third, but Mr. Johnson's advice imprinted itself in my brain—and it never left me. Nor did these words he offered before going back out onstage to greet the crowd: "People need to *feel* you as much as they *hear* you."

It was on that circuit that I first met Tyrese Gibson—a young performer with a confidence that radiated from him like heat from asphalt in August. Before one showcase, as we waited backstage among the nervous energy and last-minute warm-ups, he strolled over to where I sat softly running through scales.

"Those are cool," he said, pointing to my shoes—cherry-red leather Dr. Martens my mom had found on sale.

"Thanks," I replied, surprised by the compliment and immediately self-conscious.

When his turn came and he took the stage, I watched in awe as this kid who couldn't have been much older than me transformed under the lights. He sang with maturity and presence, his voice rich and controlled, his stage movements looking effortless rather than rehearsed. He sang that house down, leaving the audience on their feet.

All I could think while he was performing was *Wow . . . he sings* like that—*and he liked my shoes?* It seemed impossible that someone with that much talent and confidence would notice *anything* about me.

We continued to cross paths at other showcases, which blossomed into a genuine friendship. There was something comforting about seeing a familiar face in the wings, someone who understood exactly what was at stake every time we stepped onto a stage. That bond has remained intact through all the years and industry changes since, a testament to what we recognized in each other even then—that same hunger, that same certainty about our paths.

Rickey Minor made good on his promise. When Whitney was in town for her *I'm Your Baby Tonight* tour, he called my mom to tell her he'd leave tickets for us at will call. I was over the moon with excitement—literally bouncing off the furniture until my mother threatened to make me stay home if I didn't "get a grip on yourself, young lady."

For weeks, I told anybody who would listen—and plenty who tried not to—that I was invited to see Whitney Houston in concert. The checkout lady at Vons heard about it. The mailman heard about it. My teachers, my classmates, random people at church—nobody was safe from my ecstatic announcements.

Ray, always my biggest supporter, helped me decorate my favorite denim jacket with Whitney pins and ribbons we found at a record shop on Crenshaw. I wore that jacket everywhere. Might have even slept in it.

"Girl, you're going to wear it out before you even get to the concert," my mom warned, but I couldn't help it. I wasn't just some kid with a fantasy. I now had an actual connection to the world I desperately wanted to join.

In my mind, there was no doubt about it: I was meeting Whitney that night. The tickets were just the beginning—the first step toward what would surely be a meaningful encounter with my idol, maybe even a mentorship. I imagined Whitney hearing me sing, recognizing a kindred spirit, taking me under her wing. The scenarios grew more elaborate with each passing day.

But when we arrived at the Forum, we found our seats tucked *high* up in the rafters. Higher than the nosebleeds! From where we were sitting, the stage looked like a distant, glittering island in a sea of darkness.

I had come this far—I wasn't about to let something as trivial as assigned seating stand between me and destiny.

"If Rickey sees me," I whispered to myself, the plan solidifying with each word, "he'll bring me backstage. No question."

I started scheming with all the audacity only a twelve-year-old with stars in her eyes could muster.

When the opening act took the stage—I couldn't even tell you who it was, so single-minded was my focus—I shot up from my seat, heart pounding against my ribs. I located the nearest usher, a tall man in his fifties guarding the stairs that led down to the lower section.

I approached him with the straightest posture I could manage, channeling the confidence my father always told me was my secret weapon.

"Hi, my name is Brandy," I said, extending my hand for what I hoped was a mature, professional handshake. "I'm gonna be famous one day. If you let me down there—" I gestured toward the lower level "—I promise, I'll remember you when I make it."

I said those words with such conviction, such absolute certainty, that I think it disarmed him a bit. Maybe he felt sorry for this little girl in a handmade Whitney jacket. Or maybe he just wanted to see how the story would play out. Whatever the reason, he smiled—a small, conspiratorial quirk of the lips—and stepped aside.

I turned and waved frantically for my mom to follow, nearly delirious with success.

"Brandy! What are you doing?" she called out, the look on her face somewhere between embarrassment and disbelief.

"We gotta get to Rickey!" I yelled back. "He said he'd introduce me to Whitney!"

She shook her head, her eyes darting apologetically to the people turning to stare at us. "Bran, let's just sit and wait for her to come out. These aren't our seats."

"Come on, Mom!" I pleaded, bouncing on the balls of my feet with impatience. "This is our only chance!"

At the bottom of the section, another usher blocked our path, this one younger and less easily charmed. But I was on a roll now, emboldened by my first success.

"Hi, I'm Brandy, and this is my manager," I said with complete seriousness, motioning to my bewildered mother. "I'm gonna be famous one day. If you let us down, I promise, I'll pay your bills when I make it."

It worked! Again!

Step by step, usher by usher, we hustled our way closer to the stage. With each security checkpoint we passed, my confidence grew. I was unstoppable. I was destined for this. The universe was clearing a path specifically for me.

Eventually, we made it to the arena floor itself, where the real challenge began. The floor ushers were professionals, immune to the charms of an overeager child. So, I got creative.

"Rickey Minor is my uncle," I told one, my expression solemn. "I need to find him before the show."

"My mom works for Whitney's record label," I informed another. "We're supposed to meet Rickey before the performance."

I said whatever I had to—plausible or not—anything to keep inching forward toward that stage, toward the promise of meeting my idol.

Finally, I reached the side of the stage—and there he was, Rickey Minor himself, with a guy from the production crew. They were both stone-faced as they talked. Whatever this was, it seemed serious.

But this was my *only* chance to get his attention.

"Rickey!" I yelled, waving my arms like I was signaling a rescue helicopter. "Rickey!"

He was locked in conversation. So, I yelled his name again. Louder. Much louder.

"Riiiiickeeeeeey!"

He turned, scanning the crowd with slight confusion until his eyes landed on me—this tiny, frantic figure in a Whitney-decorated jacket jumping up and down at the edge of the barricade. I saw the recognition shimmer in his eyes, quickly followed by astonishment. He stared at me with this kind of wide-eyed, oh-my-God-she-really-did-it smile that was equal parts impressed and bewildered.

He waved back and motioned to a side door, then called for a security guard.

I took off running to grab my mother, who had maintained a slight distance, clearly torn between supporting my dream and wanting to apologize to every person we'd inconvenienced in our impromptu journey through the Forum.

"See? I told you!" I crowed, tugging her toward the door Rickey had indicated. "I told you we'd meet her!"

We stood where the guard told us to wait, my entire body vibrating with anticipation. The minutes dragged by like hours, each second a small eternity. My heart beat so wildly in my chest I was certain everyone could hear it over the music pulsing through the arena.

The music! It finally dawned on me that Whitney had gone onstage and started singing. And here I was, backstage, missing it.

. . . But I was backstage, waiting on Whitney! I looked up at my mom; she wore a strained smile on her face as she shifted on the balls of her feet.

"Maybe we should get back to our seats so we can catch the show," she said.

"Mom! We are backstage at Whitney Houston's show," I whispered. "I wanna wait for Rickey!"

And I waited as seconds folded into minutes as my mom kept watch.

When Rickey finally emerged from behind the door, he pulled me into the warmest hug, like a proud uncle genuinely happy to see his favorite niece.

"Hey, superstar," he said, his voice gentle. Then his expression shifted, and I knew before he spoke what was coming next. "I'm really sorry," he continued softly. "Whitney's too tired to see anyone tonight. She's heading straight to the hotel to rest. Next time, okay?"

His words hit me like glass shattering inside my chest. The dream that had carried me through security checkpoints and past professional ushers—the dream that had seemed *so* close I could almost touch it—crumbled into dust.

I collapsed into tears—not the pretty, dignified kind, but hot, heavy sobs that shook my entire body. The sky must have heard me and decided to join in my sorrow. As my mom and I made our way back out of the arena, clouds opened overhead and rain started to pour down, soaking us as we stood in the parking lot waiting for my dad.

The full weight of what had happened—or rather, what hadn't happened—settled on me. I hadn't met Whitney. I hadn't even seen her perform—too busy chasing a meet and greet. And now I was standing in the rain, mascara streaking down my face (my mom had let me wear a touch of makeup for the special occasion), my carefully decorated jacket dripping wet.

My mom crouched beside me.

"Bran," she said gently, brushing wet braids from my cheek with her free hand. "Cream always rises to the top. All you have to do is keep churning. Remember that."

She cupped my face, forcing me to look directly into her eyes, making sure I absorbed every word of what she said next.

"You're going to see Whitney, at the top. That is where you're going to meet her."

The rain fell harder, but something in her certainty calmed the storm inside me. My mom wasn't one for empty platitudes or false promises. If she said it, she believed it—and standing in a puddle of disappointment and rainwater, I chose to believe it, too.

I can't remember when Ray J caught the performance bug; that's how natural music felt in our household. My earliest memories of Ray are of him making music—beating on a drum to whatever was in his head, or sitting with my dad at the piano, absorbing his lessons. Ray would lie out with me in the family room for hours, digging through the record collection for inspiration. He jumped into the showcase circuit just like me. We were basically babies, just trying to be seen and heard all over Los Angeles, our young voices carrying dreams much bigger than our small frames could contain. We performed for whoever would listen, wherever they might be—community centers, school auditoriums, church basements—all in hopes that somebody, *anybody* with influence would take notice.

It was never about competition—until suddenly, it was. One of the local R&B radio stations announced a competition for local talent at Dockweiler Beach. A big to-do. Reps from labels and talent agencies were expected to be there, which meant *I* had to be there. By then, I had done enough of these showcases that I was feeling myself a bit. Between the Black Family Reunion performance and singing for Brotherhood Crusade, I had built a reputation around South LA. But so had all the other singers waiting backstage. The competition was stiff, the air electric with nervous energy and whispered rumors: "There's an A&R guy from Atlantic here." "I heard someone from MJJ Productions is in the audience." "My cousin's friend says there's a talent scout from LaFace Records watching."

There wasn't a tangible prize beyond local bragging rights and a silver trophy, but we all knew there would be people in the audience with the power to sign talent—to transform a dream into a reality. The stakes couldn't have been higher, at least for an eleven-year-old who fell asleep every night fantasizing about recording her first album and going on tour with Whitney Houston, because of course she was going to take me on tour to open for her.

The nicest thing I had in my closet was this poofy blush dress I'd worn as a bridesmaid for Sister Juanita's wedding. It was quintessential late-'80s formal wear—I'm talking high neckline with intricate lace overlay, and these balloon-style short sleeves that seemed permanently wrinkled no matter how much my mother steamed them. But in my mind, it was perfect—the kind of dress a future star would wear for her big break.

Backstage, I practiced my scales in a corner, rolling my shoulders the way my dad had taught me to release tension. "Relax your jaw," I reminded myself, massaging the muscles at the hinge. "Breathe from your diaphragm, not your chest."

When they called my name, I walked onto that stage with all the confidence in the world, convinced that this was my time, my breakthrough. The afternoon sun made my skin glow, like I was standing under a divine light. I sang Whitney's "Greatest Love of All" with everything I had, hitting every run, every note with the technical precision and emotional connection I'd practiced at the piano with my dad for hours.

I finished to enthusiastic applause, bowed the way my mother had taught me ("Don't rush it, Bran—let them appreciate you"), and made my way offstage, riding the high of a performance I knew in my soul was special.

That was when I saw them. Three boys in the flyest outfits I'd ever seen, huddled in a corner, waiting for their turn. Their swagger was as loud as their outfits—baggy denim that pooled around chunky work boots, top hats tilted at precise angles, and a mélange of oversized flannel shirts layered over garish cartoon prints that somehow looked perfectly coordinated rather than chaotic. They were pint-sized rebels who looked as if they'd been plucked from a distant galaxy and crash-landed in the middle of Dockweiler Beach.

When they strutted out onstage, they owned every square inch of that space with a confidence I'd never witnessed in performers our age. These boys couldn't have been more than ten years old, but the way they moved—shoulders back, chins up, eyes connecting with the audience—told me they had that inexplicable "it" factor seasoned performers spent lifetimes trying to cultivate.

"My name is Romeo, and I'm from the moon," the first boy announced with a sly smile, his voice carrying to the back row without effort.

"My name is Half-Pint, and I'm from Pluto." The smallest of the trio followed, bouncing on his toes.

"I'm Batman, and I'm from the stars," the third boy concluded, spreading his arms wide as if embracing the entire audience.

"And we're Immature."

The backing track kicked in—a thumping New Jack Swing beat that immediately had heads nodding—and those boys put on a show that made my heart sink to my patent leather shoes.

They were polished in a way I hadn't seen in performers our age—every move synchronized, every transition smooth, their stage chemistry electric. Their performance felt like a party.

Bell Biv DeVoe's "Do Me!" was dominating the airwaves then. New Jack Swing had exploded onto the scene, its fusion of R&B, rap, funk, disco, and synthesized percussion catapulting the sound to the top of Black music charts. BBD had found that sweet spot between mainstream pop accessibility and edgy hip-hop sensibility that appealed to both worlds.

I was too young then to grasp how provocative the lyrics to "Do Me!" actually were—the innuendo sailed straight over my innocent head. All I knew was the beat made my shoulders move automatically and the melodies were irresistible. Immature captured that same vibe but filtered it through a youthful energy. They combined the brash hardness of New Jack Swing and hip-hop with the sweet innocence of R&B balladry in a way that felt fresh and unexpected.

You could tell they were hungry to make it—that same hunger I felt burning in my own belly every time I stepped onstage. They won the crowd over that day not just with talent, but with the intangible chemistry between them, their showmanship, and, yes, their undeniable cuteness. Those top hats, those oversized clothes, those cheeky smiles—they were marketing gold, and even at my young age, I recognized it. The applause confirmed what I already knew—they were winning that damn trophy.

I felt defeated, standing there in my frilly bridesmaid dress. My careful a cappella rendition of a Whitney ballad seemed boring and old-fashioned compared to an adorable, confident boy band vibing to a catchy record. In my mind, the imaginary A&R executives were probably already backstage signing those boys to a multi-album deal while I stood forgotten in the wings.

I was about to retreat to lick my wounds in private when the man I'd seen accompanying Immature approached me and my parents.

"Your voice is exceptional," he said, extending his hand. "I'm Chris Stokes. I put Immature together and manage them."

My father stepped slightly forward, protective instinct kicking in. "Willie Norwood. This is my wife, Sonja, and our daughter, Brandy."

Chris nodded respectfully to my parents but kept his focus on me. "I was impressed by your performance. You have control and range that you just don't see."

"Thank you," I managed, my disappointment eclipsed by the unexpected praise.

He told us how he'd assembled Immature, bringing them together under his Teaspoon Productions banner. He was managing the boys and several other acts, working to develop a roster of young talent that could break into R&B.

"I would love to work with you and help develop you," he said, those magic words landing like raindrops in a desert. "Your voice is special—unique. With the right songs, the right production . . ."

My heart leaped so forcefully I felt lightheaded. This was my break—the divine interruption every young dreamer waits for, when someone with actual industry connections recognizes your potential. Chris had secured Immature a deal with Virgin Records and was writing and producing the group's debut album. He was in his early twenties, with a cool big-brother vibe—confident but not cocky, passionate about music and the business in a way that was infectious. The genuine belief Chris had in me was what got my parents on board.

"We're not looking for overnight success," my father told him during one of our early meetings. "We want someone who understands development, who sees what Brandy could be with the right guidance."

"That's exactly my approach," Chris assured him. "This is a marathon, not a sprint. I want to build something that lasts."

I was brought into the fold with Immature, joining their backing band as a vocalist. When Chris found out I had a younger brother who also sang, his eyes lit up with possibility. "Bring him in, too," he said. "Let's see what he can do."

Ray was ecstatic—his big sister had just pulled him onto a path he hadn't even known was available to him. We began hanging out with the group constantly. Chris's apartment became another home, its walls reverberating with melodies and the buzz of a group of kids who knew they were part of something special.

The reality, as I slowly discovered, was more complicated. I didn't want to appear ungrateful—I knew how fortunate I was to have a manager at all, let alone one who was actively working in the industry—but I was growing discouraged by how little time Chris actually devoted to developing me as a solo artist in that first year of working with him.

"Chris, what's your vision for me?" I finally asked one afternoon, cornering him while the boys were taking a break from rehearsal. "The solo stuff we discussed. When do we start working on that?"

He leaned against the wall, arms crossed, studying me with an expression I couldn't quite read. "I've been thinking about that," he said slowly. "And I've got an idea I think could be huge."

My heart quickened. This was it—the solo development plan I'd been waiting for.

"A girl group," he continued. "An answer to Immature. Same energy, same style, but with a girly twist. And I want you as the lead."

The words hit me like a bucket of ice water. A girl group? That wasn't the plan. That wasn't *my* dream.

"But . . ." I searched for the right words, not wanting to sound as upset as I was. "I thought we were focusing on my solo career."

"This is the faster route," Chris explained, his enthusiasm building as he outlined his vision. "The industry is all about groups right now. New Edition, Boyz II Men, TLC, En Vogue—groups are getting the deals, getting the airplay. We establish you in this group, build a fan base, then launch your solo career from that platform. It's strategic."

It made sense logically, but emotionally? Everything in me rebelled against the idea. I was a huge SWV fan, and I genuinely liked girl groups—the harmonies, the sisterhood, the combined stage presence. But something in my soul knew it wasn't for me. It was tough enough surviving the mean girls at school and in my neighborhood—I had no interest in potentially experiencing that dynamic with something I loved so much.

More than that, I had always seen myself as a solo artist. Whitney wasn't in a group. Mariah wasn't in a group. The voices I most admired stood alone, commanding attention through the sheer power of their individual gifts.

"Chris, I don't want to be in a group."

"Why not?" he sighed.

"Because I have what it takes to be a big star. On my own. You really should be working with me," I said, hands on hips, confidence on 100.

"Look, Darryl Williams at Atlantic already committed to seeing what I come up with. This is a huge opportunity that others would—"

"Okay, I'll do it!" I cut him off. "I'll do it!"

I'm sure he thought I was being an impatient, ungrateful brat, but I knew he was right. This was a once-in-a-lifetime opportunity. A meeting with a label? I hated the idea of being in a group, but I was sure Chris would find talented and, hopefully, nice girls. I was an inexperienced kid, and Chris was driven and ambitious. He was inspiring to be around, and I admired how much he genuinely wanted to win with us.

"Keep an open mind," my mother advised. "Sometimes God's plan looks different than what we imagined for ourselves."

A week later, I walked into Chris's apartment to find two other girls around my age already seated on his couch. Tanya was a tall, athletic-looking girl with skin the color of burnished copper and a smile that transformed her entire face. Beside Tanya sat her sister Jada, petite with delicate features and carefully styled box braids adorned with golden beads that clicked softly whenever she moved her head. I recognized them from some of the talent competitions. Tanya and Jada were fraternal twins. Incredible dancers, but I didn't recall them ever singing, so I wasn't sure how a group was going to work.

"Ladies," Chris announced, "meet your new sister, Brandy Norwood."

Whatever Chris named us has been long lost to memory. It was something sassy, like 3rd Degree. Or at least that's what I'm going to call us. Now, I may not be able to remember our stage name, but I do recall stretching my mouth wide to force a smile as I shook hands with my new "sisters," and trying my hardest to ignore the sinking feeling in my stomach.

"I've heard you sing," Tanya said, her smile genuine. "You're amazing. This is going to be so dope."

Jada offered a cooler reception, her eyes assessing me with barely disguised competition. "Chris says you've got range," she said. "We'll see."

That discomforting feeling danced on the back of my neck. *Sometimes God's plan looks different*, I thought, and mustered the best smile I could.

Chris had a specific vision for 3rd Degree. He styled us in the same oversized clothing, wanted us to adopt the same swagger and the same New Jack Swing sound.

"We're going for street but sweet," he explained during our first official rehearsal. "Tough enough to hang with the boys but still undeniably girly. Think TLC meets SWV with a dash of En Vogue's sophistication."

The outfits he procured for us were straight from the Immature playbook—baggy jeans, oversized flannel shirts tied at the waist, crop tops layered under masculine vests, chunky boots, and baseball caps worn sideways. It was the style then, but it still felt like a costume on me—like I was playing dress-up in someone else's identity.

"You don't look comfortable," Tanya observed quietly as we changed into our outfits one afternoon.

"Is it that obvious?" I sighed, adjusting the backward cap that kept slipping down over my eyes.

"Only to someone who's watching," she said with a small smile. "For what it's worth, I get it. This isn't exactly what I pictured, either. But it's a foot in the door, right?"

That simple acknowledgment of shared trepidation forged an immediate bond between us. Tanya, I learned, had dreams of Broadway—of belting show tunes rather than R&B hits. She saw 3rd Degree as a stepping stone, just as I did.

Jada, on the other hand, was all in. She embraced every aspect of the group identity, from the fashion to the attitude. She'd been in talent showcases and beauty pageants since she was five, pushed relentlessly by a mother determined to see her daughters achieve the stardom that had eluded her.

"This is our shot," she'd remind us during rehearsals, eyes blazing with intensity. "We have to want it more than anyone else."

Jada was talented, no question—with a clear, pure soprano that contrasted beautifully with my raspier tone and Tanya's rich alto—but her drive created tension as we prepped for the Atlantic Records audition.

"You're coming in too early on the second verse," she snapped at me during one particularly grueling rehearsal session. "Again."

"I'm following the beat," I defended.

"You're rushing," she insisted. "It throws off the whole harmony structure."

"Ladies," Chris intervened, his tone measured. "Let's take five and cool down."

As Jada stalked off to get water, Tanya squeezed my shoulder. "Don't let her get to you," she whispered. "She's just scared this won't work out."

Despite the intensity, we began to gel musically. Our voices blended well—surprisingly well, actually—creating harmonies that seemed to impress Chris. The choreography came together, our movements becoming more synchronized with each rehearsal. From the outside, 3rd Degree probably looked like a promising new act.

But inside, I felt increasingly disconnected from the music, from the image, from the very concept of being part of a group. I went through the motions, gave my all during rehearsals, but I was not feeling it.

"You seem distant lately," my father observed one night as we sat at the piano, working through vocal exercises after a long day of 3rd Degree rehearsal. "Is everything all right with the group?"

I hesitated, torn between honesty and what felt like obligation. "The girls are fine," I said finally. "Tanya's really nice. Jada's . . . intense, but talented."

"But?" he prompted, always able to hear the unspoken in my voice.

"But the clothes, the attitude, the whole vibe. I don't really like it."

He nodded, his expression thoughtful. "Have you talked to Chris about this?"

I shook my head. "He's so excited about the group. And he did get us a meeting with a label. I can't mess that up."

"Bran," my father said gently, "sometimes we have to walk through doors that aren't perfectly aligned with our vision to reach the ones that are. Just don't forget who you are in the process."

The Atlantic Records meeting loomed large in all our minds. Chris had talked it up relentlessly, assuring us that Darryl Williams had the power to change our lives with a single decision.

"This is it," Jada declared the night before the big day as we ran through our routine one final time in Chris's apartment. "This is our time to shine."

The Atlantic Records offices were everything I'd imagined a major label would be—sleek, modern walls adorned with platinum records and framed photographs of music legends. We were ushered into a conference room where Darryl Williams waited, along with two younger executives whose names I immediately forgot in my nervousness.

"All right, ladies," Darryl said after Chris had made the introductions. "Show me what you've got."

Our backing track started, and 3rd Degree launched into our carefully rehearsed performance—a medley of original material Chris had written, showcasing our harmonies, our attitudes, our potential commercial appeal. I sang with everything

I had, pushing aside my reservations about the style, the group concept, everything except the music itself.

When we finished, there was a second of silence as Darryl studied us, his expression giving nothing away. Then his eyes landed on me, and something in his gaze shifted.

"You," he said, pointing directly at me. "Brandy, right? Step forward."

I took a small step ahead of Tanya and Jada, my heart hammering in my chest.

"Sing something for me," Darryl instructed. "Just you. Something that shows me who you really are as a singer."

There was no hesitation. I launched into Whitney's "Greatest Love of All"—my showcase standard, the song that felt most like home in my voice.

I sang without the safety net of Tanya's and Jada's harmonies, without the distraction of choreography, without anything but my raw voice and the emotion I poured into every note.

When I finished, the room was silent. I could feel Jada's and Tanya's eyes on me, could sense Chris's tension from where he sat at the edge of the conference table.

Darryl leaned back in his chair, his expression thoughtful. Then, still looking directly at me—not at Chris, not at the group—he said something that would change everything: "Come back to me when you're fourteen."

The pronouncement hung in the air like suspended glass—beautiful but potentially shattering. I understood immediately what he was saying: he saw potential in me, but not in 3rd Degree. And he'd said it right in front of Tanya and Jada.

I darted a glance at my groupmates. Jada's face had gone completely blank, a mask that barely concealed the devastation beneath. Tanya's expression was more complex—disappointment mingled with what looked like resignation, as if she'd been expecting this outcome all along.

"Mr. Williams," Chris began, clearly trying to salvage the situation. "The group concept allows for—"

"The group concept doesn't interest me." Darryl cut him off, not unkindly but firmly. "What interests me is her voice." He nodded toward me. "It's unique. Distinctive. But she needs time to mature, to find what suits her. It's not that."

Pride and guilt collided inside me with such force I felt dizzy. This was exactly what I'd wanted—validation of my solo dreams, confirmation that I wasn't just another kid with a pretty voice. But the cost of that validation was written all over Jada's and Tanya's faces.

The ride back to Chris's apartment was painfully silent. Jada stared out the window, her profile rigid with hurt. Tanya fidgeted with the zipper of her jacket, her eyes occasionally darting to me with what seemed like sadness rather than resentment.

Chris tried to salvage the mood, his voice artificially upbeat as he dissected what had happened.

"This is a good thing," he insisted, knuckles white on the steering wheel. "Getting on Darryl's radar—that's huge. We can use this. We'll keep developing 3rd Degree while preparing for Brandy's solo meeting. Two paths forward instead of one."

Neither Jada nor Tanya responded. I couldn't bring myself to speak, either, torn between apologizing for something that wasn't really my fault and allowing myself to feel the excitement bubbling beneath my guilt.

Back at the apartment, Jada disappeared into the bathroom without a word. Chris stepped outside to make some calls, leaving Tanya and me alone in awkward silence.

"I'm sorry," I finally whispered, the words inadequate but necessary.

To my surprise, Tanya's face softened. "For what? Being good?" She shook her head. "And honestly? He was right."

"What?"

"You don't belong in a group," she said simply. "You're supposed to be solo. We all knew it. Even Jada knows it, though she'd rather die than admit it."

"But what about you? What about 3rd Degree?"

Tanya shrugged, but I could see the disappointment behind her casual gesture. "We'll be fine. Or we won't. But if I had your voice, I wouldn't want to share the spotlight, either."

"I didn't set out to—"

"I know." She squeezed my hand. "That's what makes you special. You aren't a backstabber or anything. You're just . . . talented. And now you've got your shot."

I hugged her then, grateful for her generosity in a time when bitterness would have been easier. When we pulled apart, I saw Jada standing in the doorway, her eyes red-rimmed but her expression composed.

"Congratulations," she said stiffly. It wasn't warm, but it wasn't hostile, either—just a formal acknowledgment of what had transpired.

"Thanks," I replied carefully. "But Chris is right—we can still make 3rd Degree work."

Jada's laugh was short and hollow. "Let's not pretend. What's the point of being in a group with someone who's gonna leave in a couple years? We'd just be your backup singers until you turn fourteen." She slung her backpack over her shoulder. "I need to go. My mom's waiting."

That was the last time Jada ever spoke directly to me. She stopped coming to rehearsals the following week, and Chris eventually replaced her with another girl who never quite fit in. 3rd Degree limped along for a few more months before quietly dissolving, exactly as Jada had predicted.

We spent the next year putting together a demo—with just me. No more group. Chris also cast me and Marques (aka Batman) in *We Are Family*, a pilot he wrote centered around a group of kids who lose their parents and move in together. The pilot didn't get picked up, but it gave me a taste of working on a television set.

In September 1992, Immature released their debut album, *On Our Worst Behavior*, which sounded like TLC and Bell Biv DeVoe's music dipped in sugar. They were still riding the New Jack Swing wave, which almost everyone was in those days because the sound was *that hot*. One of the better-known records off their debut is a syrupy romantic ballad, "Is It Love This Time." The song opens with a little skit of me calling into a radio station: *"Hello, I'm Brandy, and I would like to make a request out to Kevin by Immature, 'Is It Love This Time.'"* It's a cute puppy-love song that showcased the group's true magic. I wished more of that first album was like that. A lot of the songs Chris wrote were overly mature, trading on the tropes of adult relationships and experiences outside the boys' scope.

I was eleven, but Marques, Jerome (aka Romeo), and Don (aka Half-Pint) were all around nine when we first met. They had no business singing some of the lyrics being written for them. We were all barely hitting puberty. Why were these boys talking about "a honey dip is a girl with a big, old ghetto booty . . . and big potatoes"? They were at their best when they were doing sweet, romantic R&B and it could push the envelope without having to be crass.

What excited me the most about working with Immature was getting to do it with Ray. He would hype the crowd up and then join me off to the side as we sang and danced in the background. Getting to perform on big stages was a rush unlike anything I experienced singing in the choir, even if I spent the time imagining I wasn't in the shadows, and that the love and applause were for *me* and *my* gifts.

Working and performing with Immature was incredible—at first. Ray and I were over the moon when we got to perform at the famed Apollo Theater in Harlem. If there was a television in a Black household in the late '80s and early '90s, chances were the family was watching *It's Showtime at the Apollo.* We'd seen many an act get booed off that stage, shuffled off by Sandman Sims with his hook and trademark soft-shoe routine.

Being jeered and pushed offstage at the Apollo was the ultimate embarrassment for a performer! It didn't matter if you were fourteen or forty—if the crowd at the Apollo wasn't vibing with you, they made it known. Loudly. Without mercy. On the opposite end, if they loved you, they would erupt in applause so thunderous you'd swear your living room was shaking from the force of it.

This was our first trip away from our parents, and Ray and I were literally bouncing off the walls of our hotel room the night before the show. New York City—the concrete jungle where dreams are made—spread out twenty-two stories below our window, a glittering metropolis that seemed to vibrate with possibility.

"We're really here," Ray breathed, his face pressed against the glass, watching yellow taxis navigate the grid of streets below. "We're really in New York."

"Pinch me." I laughed, joining him at the window. "Seriously, pinch me."

He did, harder than necessary, prompting me to swat his arm.

"Ow! I didn't mean actually do it!"

"You said 'seriously.'" He grinned, dodging my retaliatory pinch.

We'd ordered room service—a luxury beyond imagination—and gorged ourselves on pizza and chocolate cake while flipping channels on the colossal TV. When we landed on MTV, we both fell silent, mesmerized by the music videos playing in succession—Janet Jackson, Michael Jackson, Whitney, Madonna, Prince. The soundtrack to our dreams, right there in our hotel room, with the Manhattan skyline twinkling behind us.

"That's gonna be us one day," Ray said softly, pointing to the screen where SWV was performing "Weak."

"I know," I replied, and I did know—with the certainty that only the very young or the very naive can possess. "Soon."

The next morning, we took a cab to the Apollo—another first. Ray pressed his face against the window, trying to absorb every detail of the city rushing past. I was quieter, mentally preparing for the performance, running through harmonies in my head, visualizing myself on that legendary stage.

"Look at how many people are out there!" Ray shouted after we snuck into the audience to catch the show taping ahead of ours.

It was surreal. Every seat in the house had a body in it. That didn't scare me—strangely, it energized me. It was the blinking red lights from the television cameras that sent butterflies swarming in my stomach—a reminder that the audience would be much bigger than the fifteen hundred people clapping (or potentially booing).

With everyone on their feet, dancing to the house band, we stood on the tips of our toes in the back of the Apollo and took it all in. Here we were in this huge, historic city about to perform on *television*. It was starting to sink in that things were in motion—that the dream wasn't just a dream anymore but something that was taking shape around us.

When the show's host, Steve Harvey, came out and introduced SWV as the next performers, I nearly lost my mind, clutching Ray's arm so hard he had to pry my fingers loose.

"Ow, Bran! Chill out!" he hissed, but he was grinning, too.

I was mesmerized when they strutted onto the stage in black leather vests, combat boots, and giant gold hoop earrings. They looked like superstars—confident, unapologetic, fully inhabiting their space. I couldn't keep my eyes off Coko especially. She wore these big sunglasses despite the dim lighting, and her nails were so long they seemed to wrap around her microphone *twice*! They launched into "I'm So Into You," and the crowd went wild from the first note.

They sounded exactly like the record I played obsessively when my dad had brought it home for me. He'd thought I'd like Coko's tone. I hadn't heard a soprano like her, with such a rich vocal texture. I was just starting to explore the lower register of my tone, and the way Coko harnessed the uniqueness of her voice inspired me to embrace the lower belts that came naturally to me. Onstage they commanded the audience, no elaborate choreography needed. When Coko hit her signature high notes, the theater erupted, and I felt something solidify inside me—a vision of my future so clear I could almost touch it.

Later that night, when it was our turn, the stage lights at the Apollo were so intense it felt like we were spinning in a rotisserie oven. Ray and I had to wear these oversized sweatsuits and giant beanies that matched Immature's aesthetic, which only felt hotter under the merciless lights. There was nothing but adrenaline and a desperate desire to not get booed to get us through that performance.

Ray and I were in the background, but it felt like we were so close to our dreams. What Immature had—the record deal, the music videos, the shows—was more within reach than ever. And it was happening for me and my brother. Together.

I loved this time. Chris was the cool big brother, and with the boys, I had inherited three little brothers.

I mistook familial for safe.

We were all hanging out at Chris's apartment. The boys were playing a video game and I was reading a book when I suddenly felt Half-Pint's uninvited, unwelcome hands making their way under my shirt. For a split second, I froze, my mind unable to process what was happening—this violation from someone I'd considered a friend, a member of our extended musical family.

Then fear gave way to fury. Whatever arsenal of curse words I had in my vocabulary at thirteen, Half-Pint heard them all as I pushed him away from me with every ounce of strength I possessed.

"Don't you EVER touch me like that!" I screamed, scrambling to my feet, my whole body shaking with rage and humiliation.

The other boys laughed, treating it like a joke, like it was all part of the game they'd been playing. Their dismissive laughter only fueled my anger, making me feel even more alone, even more violated.

In my fury, I threw the book I was reading, and it went flying across the room like a missile.

Right into Jerome's eye.

The sharp corner of the book cut his retina, detaching it entirely. The laughter stopped instantly as Jerome collapsed, screaming and writhing in pain. The atmosphere in the room transformed in an instant from playful chaos to actual emergency.

I stood there, horrified, my anger instantly replaced by remorse and fear. Jerome was hurt—seriously hurt—and it was all my fault. I started crying, my whole body shaking with sobs.

The boys, only now seeming to sense the gravity of the situation, ran to Jerome's aid, surrounding him with genuine concern.

Marques ran outside to get Chris, who took one look at Jerome's eye and rushed him to the hospital without waiting for explanations.

I sat on the edge of the couch, hugging my knees to my chest, replaying the afternoon over and over.

Jerome turned that injury into a fashion statement—an eyepatch that became his signature look, part of the group's evolving image. The story behind it became industry legend, though the truth was hidden beneath layers of male bravado.

I learned a hard lesson that day about boundaries, about speaking up sooner, about the complex dynamics that can develop when children work in adult environments. But I also learned something about my own worth, my own voice—not just the one I used for singing, but the one I needed to protect myself.

Immature would go on to find seismic success—without Half-Pint, who left the group shortly after the incident. The official story cited "creative differences," but those of us who were there suspected a different reason. And I went on my own way, too.

DROP-DEAD GORGEOUS

I NEVER WANTED to act.

Well, that's not entirely true. I very much enjoyed acting, but I didn't think I was good at it. Not until I met the man who would become my favorite teacher, Mr. Bialik, in the seventh grade.

The instant he swept into the classroom in oversized denim and with thick wire-rimmed glasses perched delicately on the bridge of his nose, the energy lightened. Mr. Bialik taught drama at Bancroft Middle School. His class was a portal to another world, one where I felt as free as I did when I sang. He had an aura that made the room glow.

Mr. Bialik exposed us to every style of acting there was. And he made it fun. Improv was where I felt most exposed. Most vulnerable. Most alive.

"Brandy, you're killing the scene again," he called out one class, his voice carrying across the room like warm honey with just enough edge to make me stand at attention. The other students froze, their eyes darting between us as I stood there nervously.

I twisted my hands together. "I just wasn't sure where to take it," I admitted, my voice barely audible over the hum of the ancient air conditioner.

Mr. Bialik stepped into our circle, his footsteps deliberate as he crossed the scuffed linoleum floor. He put both of his hands on my shoulders and lowered to meet my eyes the way my dad often did when he wanted me to really hear what he was telling me.

"Don't kill the scene . . . progress it," he insisted. "There are rules we need to learn, but once you understand them—" he snapped his fingers "—that's when you can start challenging. That's when the magic happens. Give it another shot?"

After class, when the other students had filtered out in a chorus of chatter, he pulled me aside.

"Don't overthink it," he told me, his voice softer now, meant only for my ears. The scent of his sandalwood cologne mingled with the strong espresso that wafted from an open Thermos on his desk. "You have a spark. A gift. When you get out of your head, it really comes out."

"Really?" I asked, taken aback. The word came out half-whispered, as if speaking it too loudly might make his belief in me evaporate.

"I see how hard you work. How much you care." Mr. Bialik leaned in, close enough that I could see the flecks of amber in his hazel eyes. "But you're a natural. Lean further into your instincts. Next class, I want to see you jump without looking. Trust yourself. Can you do that for me?"

For a young girl drowning in insecurities, Mr. Bialik's words were a life raft. Something inside me awakened.

"I'll try," I promised, clutching my notebook to my chest like a shield.

"Don't try," he said with a wink. "Do. And watch what happens."

One class, Mr. Bialik surprised us by having his daughter, Mayim, sit in. She sat atop her dad's desk, dressed in denim jeans and a chunky sweater, her hair in a neon scrunchie. Millions of Americans welcomed her into their living rooms every week, but what struck me most wasn't Mayim's fame. It was how normal she seemed—laughing at her dad's corny introduction, rolling her eyes when he mentioned an embarrassing childhood story.

"So," she began, her voice deeper and more thoughtful than her character's, "who here wants to ask me if Joey Lawrence's hair is as perfect in real life as it is on TV?"

The room erupted in laughter, the tension breaking like a fever. A dozen hands shot up, including mine—I couldn't help it. But Mayim didn't just offer gossip and glamour. She transformed before our eyes from TV star to mentor, her intelligence and passion evident in every gesture.

There wasn't a girl in my seventh-grade class who wasn't watching Mayim on *Blossom*, and now she was here . . . talking to us.

"The thing no one tells you," she said, leaning forward, "is that acting for TV is like running a marathon at sprint speed. You're there at five in the morning. The lights are hot. Your feet hurt. You've said the same line fifteen different ways. And then someone says, 'We need another take,' and you have to find a way to make it fresh all over again."

Like my classmates, my heart raced with fangirl excitement. When Mayim started walking through the technical elements of shooting a network show—the marks on the floor, the way the cameras moved in careful choreography, how the lighting changed the mood of a scene—I found myself hanging on her every word.

"So, you actually have to hit the same emotional note take after take?" I asked.

Mayim's eyes found mine, and a smile of recognition spread across her face.

"Exactly," she said, pointing at me with an enthusiasm that made my heart soar. "And sometimes it's the twentieth take, and you're exhausted, and the director wants just one more with 'a little more vulnerability but also more strength.' And somehow, you have to find it."

I probably asked Mayim a million questions about how it all worked—not even realizing that soon I'd get those answers for myself.

If it wasn't for Mr. Bialik, I probably would have focused entirely on singing. I was working with Marcus Aurelius, a local producer we met a few years earlier on the talent show circuit.

Marcus took me to every label he could. Warner. Arista. Elektra. Epic. It was a no. Every single time. It was all a spinning reel of boardrooms and men in stiff suits with even stiffer expressions, their eyes glazing over before I'd even finished my first run. Their faces are indistinct in my memory now, melded into one collective mask of indifference, but their words still cut like freshly sharpened knives.

One of those auditions still stands out as if it happened yesterday. I had just sung my heart out. And before you ask, yes, I sang "Greatest Love of All." Like Whitney, it had become my signature song. I'd poured everything into it—all my dreams, all my longing, all my passion. The last note still hung in the air, vibrating through my body like a prayer.

"Hmm. Does she need to do so many of those vocal *rolls*?" the executive asked, flailing his arms in the air as if tracing the words he was saying with his finger.

The question was posed as if I wasn't standing in the room, as if I was a product on a shelf rather than a fourteen-year-old kid. The man who asked it—a senior VP with salt-and-pepper hair and a tie—didn't even look at me as he said it. His eyes remained fixed on his notepad, pen tapping against the spiral binding in an arrhythmic beat that felt like code for "next, please."

Rejection was one thing. Questioning how I sang was another. It was like someone asking Picasso why he needed to use so many blues.

One evening, my parents sat me down in our living room.

"Bran, are you sure this is still what you really want to do?" my dad asked, his voice gentle but his eyes serious.

"More than anything in the world," I said, gripping my glass so tightly I was afraid it might shatter. "This is my dream."

"Well, your mom and I have been talking," my dad began, exchanging a look with my mother that contained an entire conversation in a glance.

I didn't know what was coming next, but I dug my feet into the carpet to brace for whatever it was. The fibers tickled between my toes, grounding me to this moment.

"I'm going to quit my job and manage you, and Ray," my mom said, her words landing like pebbles in still water, creating ripples I couldn't yet comprehend. "I'm going to take the principles I learned in my career and apply them to the entertainment industry. What I don't know, we'll learn quickly. Together."

I couldn't believe what she was saying. It sounded crazy, reckless, beautiful. I had seen how happy she was as she took on more at work, how her shoulders straightened and her smile widened with each new responsibility. My mom had started as a tax preparer for H&R Block and rose to district manager with a determination that seemed to bend reality to her will. She oversaw more than a dozen offices across the South Bay, her days a haze of meetings and reports and problems solved through sheer force of competence. I didn't know much about her work, but I did know I rarely saw other women who looked like her whenever she carted me along to one of the offices she oversaw.

"But, Mommy, your job," I said. "Don't you love it?"

"I do, yes. But it's just a career," she said. "My child's dream is *my* dream. You'll understand when you're a mother one day."

From my earliest memories, my mother's belief had been my foundation. But this—this was sacrifice in its purest form. And her resolve was unshakable. I would return from school to find her absorbed in study at our dining table, legal pads covered in her meticulous handwriting, or stretched across the couch immersed in books about show business, her reading glasses perched at the end of her nose. She devoted herself to mastering the industry with the same fierce focus she'd applied to rising through the ranks at H&R Block, and it inspired me to keep pushing myself.

So, when it came time for high school, I knew there was only one place I wanted to go: Hollywood High. Mr. Bialik had encouraged me to look into the school's performing arts magnet program, his eyes lighting up as he described the opportunities that awaited there. Being in an environment where my talents could be nurtured was appealing to my parents—and the opportunity to study dance, drama, and vocal was appealing to me.

The standards of beauty and desirability were well ingrained in me before high school, etched into my psyche with the permanence of hieroglyphs on ancient stone. Growing up, I endured commentary about my looks—about my body from both boys and girls, their words like small paper cuts that, over time, created scars no one could see but me. Before my breasts developed, I felt the unwelcome poke and jab of fingers on my chest to tease my lack of progress. And who needs a mirror when there's a bully waiting to point out your imperfections in singsong taunts?

Puberty would transform my body with the silent efficiency of time-lapse photography, but it didn't shift how the boys—and some of the girls—at school treated me. The boys responded to a certain type—a type I studied with the dedication of an anthropologist observing a foreign culture. The pretty girl with long straight hair, caramel complexion, and straight teeth. These were not qualities I possessed, and I felt both the ridicule of boys and the sting of the pretty girls icing me out, their backs turning to me in perfect unison whenever I approached the lunch table.

During the tough times, I remembered my mother's words.

"When I first laid eyes on you," she would say, "I told the doctor, 'I have just given birth to a star.'"

The way her eyes twinkled when she spoke of my destiny made me believe it, too. When she said I was meant for something bigger, I held on to those words.

I was confident in my voice. And my charm. But I believed that in order to be beautiful, you had to be thin, with long silky hair and light skin. And I was the girl with braces, short hair, and features that I didn't believe were beautiful. I hated that my eyes were as far apart as they were, and I didn't have the elegant nose, slender jawline, or any of the soft features I saw on television and in magazines.

Going to a high school full of starry-eyed kids lusting after Hollywood dreams was probably the worst thing an ambitious but insecure young girl could have done for her self-esteem. And yet, as I arrived for my first day at Hollywood High, the butterflies in my stomach felt more like excitement than dread. The thought of being around kids who were chasing the same dreams that kept me up at night was thrilling. Maybe here, finally, I would find my tribe.

Whatever apprehension I held about not fitting in evaporated fairly quickly. The students at Hollywood High were amazing to me. They made me feel welcomed, their acceptance wrapping around me like a warm embrace. I had classmates—peers—who embraced and encouraged my abilities. This was new terrain for me, and I relished it.

Although singing was my true passion—the thing that made my soul feel like it was hovering slightly above my body—I also loved to dance. Mr. Long taught dance at Hollywood High, and he exposed us to different styles. African. Classical ballet. Hip-hop. Jazz. Contemporary. Modern. Latin. Each style was a new language he was teaching us to speak, and I wanted to be fluent in all of them.

"Feel it here," he would say, pressing his hand just below my rib cage. "The movement doesn't come from your limbs—it comes from your center. Your power source."

He was a generous, patient teacher, and his compassion became a balm for the parts of me still raw from years of subtle rejection. I would practice even more when I got home just so that I could try to impress him in the next class, transforming our small living room into a dance studio, pushing the coffee table against the wall and using the reflection in our glass cabinet as my mirror.

Joining the choir at school was a no-brainer, as natural as breathing. The first day I walked into the choir room at Hollywood High, I felt an exciting tingle. The grand piano gleamed in the corner, its ivory keys worn from years of fingers coaxing melodies from their depths. I remember the way my heart swelled when I saw the risers, the way my palms dampened with anticipation. This was where I belonged. This was where my voice would soar.

But the solo assignments came and went, and my name was never called. At first, I thought maybe I just needed to prove myself, to show them what I could do. Then I thought it was maybe because I was a freshman. I stayed after class, perfecting harmonies, hoping the director would notice my dedication. I volunteered for the less desirable alto parts even though my soprano range was my strength. I arrived early to help set up chairs and stayed late to put them away. And still—nothing.

The day they posted the solo list for the winter concert, I practically ran to the bulletin board. My finger traced down the neat typewritten list once, twice, three times—searching for my name among the chosen few. It wasn't there.

That night at dinner, I pushed my food around my plate, the silence heavy between bites.

"You're awful quiet tonight, Bran," my father said, his voice gentle with concern. "Everything all right at school?"

I looked up to find both my parents watching me, their faces open and waiting. The dam broke.

"I don't understand it," I said, the words tumbling out like water over rocks. "I keep getting passed over for solos in choir. Ms. Tapper says that upperclassmen have seniority, but other freshmen are getting these opportunities. Stacey Miller got a solo, and she's a freshman, too. And she can barely stay on pitch!"

My mother paused her chopping, wiped her hands on her apron, and turned to face me fully. "Brandy, listen to me. Life isn't always fair. But you can't let that stop you."

"But—"

"No buts," she said firmly. "You focus on you. On your growth. On becoming the best Brandy Norwood you can be. The rest will follow."

But I couldn't help but notice the patterns forming in front of my eyes. I was a Black girl from a Black neighborhood going to a school where there were very few girls who looked like me, and even fewer who showed up with braids and twists like I did. My hair wasn't straight and silky like the girls who got solos. My clothes weren't from the expensive boutiques on Melrose. And while no one ever said it explicitly, the message was written in every rejection, in every opportunity that flowed around me like water around a stone.

I struggled with my suspicion that there was discrimination happening, the thought fluttering at the edges of my consciousness. One afternoon, sitting on the school lawn during lunch, I watched as Ms. Tapper personally escorted a talent scout over to Melissa Hayden, a senior with bone-straight blond hair and eyes the color of a summer sky. The two talked animatedly while Melissa beamed, her future brightening with each word they exchanged.

That evening, I brought it up to my mother as she braided my hair, her fingers moving entirely off muscle memory, each twist a meditation.

"Mom, do you think maybe the reason I'm not getting chances is . . . because I'm Black?"

Her hands stilled for a heartbeat before resuming their

rhythm. "Baby, listen to me," she said, her voice low and intense. "Never make being Black an excuse. You can do whatever you put your mind to. No matter what any of these teachers tell you, no matter how they treat you, just focus on your gift and your faith. Everything will happen for you as it should."

She tugged gently on my hair for emphasis, making sure I was really hearing her.

"There will be people that don't want you to succeed because of the color of your skin. But that's their burden to bear, not yours. You understand me?"

"Yes, ma'am." I nodded, even as part of me rebelled against her words. It wasn't that I wanted to use my race as an excuse—I just couldn't ignore what seemed obvious to me.

My mother had always taught me to rise above, to work twice as hard and be twice as good, to never give anyone the satisfaction of seeing me fail or give up. She believed in the power of determination and excellence to overcome any barrier. And I wanted to believe that, too. I wanted to believe that my talent would eventually shine so bright that no one could deny it, regardless of what I looked like or where I came from.

So, I never voiced those suspicions again, pushing them down where they couldn't touch my dreams. I channeled my frustration into music outside of school. If Hollywood High wouldn't give me opportunities, I would create my own. If they wouldn't hear me in choir, I would make myself heard elsewhere.

As the guidance counselor of Hollywood High's performing arts magnet program, Ms. D was closely involved in helping students navigate the industry. She was the gatekeeper who could open doors or keep them firmly shut. She was an eccentric lady with a collection of brooches shaped like exotic animals and hair that seemed to be starched into place. And she had a deep love of cats. You'd go visit her office and a cat would seemingly appear out of nowhere, materializing from behind stacks of old issues of *Variety* and the *Hollywood Reporter* or leaping down from top shelves with silent grace. And never the same cat, either, as if she had an endless supply of feline companions hiding in the shadows.

Ms. D had some experience with Hollywood. She was a day player, doing a few lines here and there on TV shows but nothing substantial. But she was the direct line to casting agents looking for young talent at our school. She was like the fairy godmother who could transform your dreams into reality with a phone call. You wanted to end up on the constellation of headshots she kept on a wall in her office—the former Hollywood High students she'd helped break out. Smiling faces, various shades of beige, looked down at you, showing you what was possible if she chose you.

When I found out about a particular audition—a role in a teen drama about an aspiring singer—I worked up the courage to ask her why I wasn't being sent out for it.

"You're not going because you're not drop-dead gorgeous," she said matter-of-factly, not even looking up from the magazine she was reading. The words fell from her lips with the casual cruelty of someone commenting on the weather. "They want a Vanessa Williams beauty, and you're *not* that."

"But what about my talent?" I asked, my voice cracking despite my best efforts to sound mature and professional. "What about what's inside my heart?"

Now she did look up, her reading glasses sliding down to the tip of her nose as she peered at me over them. "That's not gonna work in Hollywood."

Simple. Easy. End of discussion.

My face burned from her bluntness, the heat of humiliation crawling up my neck. I didn't yet have the wisdom to see beyond the rejection, to understand that one person's opinion wasn't the final verdict on my worth. A person simply decided I wasn't pretty enough and, in my fourteen-year-old mind, that became absolute truth.

I never forgot Ms. D's words. They would play on a loop when I went out to auditions, an unwelcome soundtrack to my efforts. Even as things started to happen for me with my career, those words would fill my head from time to time, a ghost that refused to be exorcised.

You're not drop-dead gorgeous. You're not drop-dead gorgeous. You're not drop-dead gorgeous.

Once my mom was officially my manager—armed with homemade business cards and a determination that could move mountains—she connected with an acting agent who had seen potential in me and Ray J, which was really exciting. The guidance counselor might not have sent me out for roles, but my agent did. One of the auditions was for a new family sitcom launching on ABC. The role was Danesha Turrell, a shy fifteen-year-old girl who took schoolwork, boys, and talking on the phone very seriously.

The hard plastic chair dug into my back as I reviewed the sides one last time, the script pages worn at the edges from my constant handling. I tried to ignore the dozen or so girls sitting in the waiting area, each absorbed in their own preparation ritual—muttering lines under their breath, applying lip gloss, or staring intently at nothing. Any one of us could have filled the role of Danesha.

I only got nervous when I noticed Amber Hart, a Hollywood High classmate, saunter in. She was incredibly talented and had a kindness to her that made you wonder if it was real or a put-on. If there was an audition calling for a young Black girl, she was there—and most often walked away with the part. She'd already had bit parts on a few sitcoms, and she was in a Coke commercial that had run every night for weeks over the Christmas season.

"Brandy Norwood?" The assistant's voice made me jump. "They're ready for you."

As I gathered my things, Amber caught my eye and offered a practiced smile, perfect white teeth gleaming against her deep brown skin. "Good luck," she said in that way that somehow felt both sincere and condescending at the same time, a master class in subtle shade.

Inside, four producers sat at a folding table beside the show's star, Thea Vidale. I recognized her from the headshot hanging in the hallway, though the photo didn't capture the magnetic intensity of her presence in person. Her eyes, sharp and assessing, flickered over me with the practiced evaluation of someone who had seen hundreds of hopeful young actresses come and go.

"Brandy for Danesha," announced the producer in the center, not looking up from her stack of headshots. Her cherry-red nails tapped against the glossy surface of my photo, creating a rhythm that matched my racing pulse.

"Yes, that's me," I said, willing my voice not to shake, fighting the urge to clear my throat.

"Let's start with Danesha's first scene. Ready?" The question wasn't really a question—it was a challenge.

I closed my eyes, took a deep breath, and remembered what Mr. Bialik once told me: *Don't kill the scene.* The memory of his voice gave me courage, a phantom hand on my shoulder steadying me.

"Ready!"

The audition itself became a time-slip—a montage of fragments where I inhabited Danesha's skin so completely I forgot my own name. Time stretched and compressed. I remember Thea's eyes widening slightly during one of my line readings. I remember a producer leaning forward, pen suspended above his notepad. I remember finishing the scene and the strange, suspended silence that followed—the kind of silence that feels like possibility.

"Thank you, Brandy," the producer with the red nails said, her face carefully neutral. "We'll be in touch."

The next forty-eight hours were the longest of my young life. I tried to lose myself in schoolwork, but algebra equations blurred before my eyes, transforming into dialogue from the audition. Had I been too animated? Not animated enough? Should I have worn my hair differently? I replayed every second of those fifteen minutes in the audition room, scrutinizing each word, each gesture, each breath.

"You're going to wear a hole in the carpet," my mother observed on the second evening, watching me pace the living room for what must have been the hundredth time.

"What if they never call?" I asked, the question that had been haunting me finally escaping my lips. "What if Amber got it?"

My mother patted the couch beside her. "Then you'll audition for something else."

"But this one felt right, Mom. Like it was meant for me."

"Then have faith," she said simply, smoothing a hand over my braids. "What's meant for you won't pass you by."

I sat in choir, mouthing the words to songs while my mind raced with possibilities. Every time a classroom phone rang, my heart leaped into my throat, certain it was the call that would change everything.

I was in history class, struggling to focus, when there was a knock at the door. Through the narrow window, I could see Ms. D standing in the hallway, and behind her—my mother? My stomach dropped.

"Mr. Reynolds," Ms. D said as she opened the door, her voice carrying that official school-administration tone. "I need Brandy Norwood to come with me, please."

The class turned as one to stare at me. My face burned as I gathered my books, certain that every student was thinking the same thing: What could she have possibly done?

Ms. D's face was unreadable as she led me into the hallway

where my mother waited, purse clutched tight against her side, her expression equally impossible to read.

"Mom?" I asked, my voice small in the empty corridor. "What's going on?"

My mother and Ms. D exchanged a glance—the only time I'd ever seen anything approaching warmth pass between them.

"I've signed you out for the day," my mother said. Ms. D nodded and retreated down the hallway, her heels clicking against the linoleum.

"Mom?" I repeated, panic rising in my chest. "What's happening? Did someone—"

"Come on," she said, taking my arm and steering me toward the exit. "Get in the car."

The walk to the parking lot felt endless. My mind raced with possibilities, each more terrible than the last. Paw Paw was sick. Dad had lost his job. Something had happened to Ray. We had to move.

It wasn't until we were in the car, the doors closed and the engine running, that my mother turned to me. I braced myself for whatever news was coming, gripping the edge of my seat.

She kept a straight face for what seemed like an eternity before her face broke into the widest smile I'd ever seen, her eyes dancing with a joy so pure it took my breath away.

"I figured the star of the new ABC sitcom didn't feel like spending the rest of the day in class!"

The words hung in the air for a beat before their meaning penetrated the fog.

"What?" I whispered, afraid to believe it.

"They called an hour ago," she said, reaching across to squeeze my hand. "You got it, baby girl. You got the role!"

I screamed—a primal, joyful sound that filled the car and probably carried all the way back to Ms. D's office. My mother laughed, and I threw my arms around her neck, nearly strangling her with the force of my embrace.

"Really?" I kept asking, tears streaming down my face. "Really, Mom? For real?"

"For real," she confirmed, her own eyes glistening. "They start filming in three weeks."

As we pulled out of the school parking lot, I looked back at the building. In a matter of months, I had gone from wondering why a guidance counselor wasn't sending me out for auditions to being cast on a network sitcom. It was surreal.

My time at Hollywood High was brief, a chapter that ended almost as soon as it began. Years later, the artist Eloy Torrez would paint a stunning mural across the school. It was a celebration of the talent that came through those doors and the dreams that began there, a visual testament to possibility. Stunning portraits of Dorothy Dandridge, Lana Turner, Cher, Ricky Nelson, and Judy Garland tower above the entry to the school auditorium, their faces gazing down on generations of hopeful students.

In between Dolores del Río and Selena is my portrait. The painting of me is based off a *Seventeen* magazine shoot I did a few months after my debut album was released. It was my first big magazine cover. "Brand New Diva" was written in bold letters next to my portrait. My braids are swept in a messy half updo. My makeup is a flawless, fresh-faced look. There hadn't been many Black artists to grace the cover of *Seventeen*, so this was a huge deal, a door I was opening not just for myself but for the girls who would come after me.

I still remember the camera lens pointed at me, the photographer's gracious encouragement as I found my light. One thought echoed in my mind as the shutter clicked, a whisper that would take years for me to learn to ignore: *You're not drop-dead gorgeous.*

MOTHER, MAY I?

THE AUDIENCE MELTED as my tears took them out of focus. All that was left was their laughter echoing in my head. The sound wasn't just bouncing off walls; it was penetrating my skin, seeping into my bones. The laughter was *at* me; of that, I was as certain of as the blood rushing to my cheeks. We hadn't even started filming when it happened—my first cycle, a hurricane of emotions sweeping through me without warning: terror shaking my core, embarrassment flooding my face, and, somewhere beneath it all, a reluctant sense of awe at my body's transformation.

"Look at our little Danesha becoming a woman," my TV mother had announced to the audience, her voice booming through the speakers. "Guess we'll have to adjust those costumes, huh? Make room for the changes!" She'd winked, and the crowd had roared.

I stood frozen, my feet cemented to the glossy floor, feeling the spotlight burn against my skin. The women who had gathered around me earlier that day had spoken in hushed, reverent tones, creating a sacred circle of protection. "Baby girl, this is your power coming in," Yvette Wilson whispered to me, squeezing my hand with a gentle kindness that made me grateful she was cast as my aunt Lynette on the show. "Every woman remembers her first. Now you'll remember yours was right here, on the show that's giving you your big break."

But that tenderness evaporated the second my TV mother seized upon my transformation and served it up for laughs. The crowd's thunderous response mingled with the cramps twisting through my abdomen. I felt the room tilt beneath me, the air suddenly thick and suffocating. As I blinked back tears that threatened to smudge the mascara I'd been so proud to wear, I knew with absolute clarity—my TV mom hated my guts.

Thea Vidale was a rising star in comedy when ABC approached her to lead a sitcom. The landscape of Black television was evolving but still tightly controlled. *The Fresh Prince of Bel-Air* and *Family Matters* offered audiences polished portraits of Black life, draped in upper-middle-class comforts and aspirational lifestyles that felt like beautiful fantasies to many viewers.

Thea was different. Raw. Real. A working-class single mother in Houston, Texas, balancing supermarket shifts by day and a beautician hustle by night—not a doctor or lawyer in sight. It was revolutionary in its ordinariness, a mirror held up to millions of households rarely seen on primetime. The vision was clear: create the Black *Roseanne*, unflinching in its portrayal of everyday, salt-of-the-earth struggles. Thea would shoulder the distinction of being the first Black woman comedian to headline her own sitcom.

I was cast as Thea's spirited teenage daughter, Danesha. Adam Jeffries, Jason Weaver, and Brenden Jefferson were cast as my brothers, forming a family unit that would, for better or worse, become a second home.

A few months before *Thea* began production, I walked the gleaming hallway of Atlantic Records once again, my heart drumming against my ribs. The last time I had stood before Darryl Williams, the label's A&R, I'd been a wide-eyed eleven-year-old with nothing but raw ambition. He'd looked at me then with kind eyes that saw potential still waiting to bloom and said words that would become a lifeline: *Come back to me when you're fourteen.*

Those seven words had tattooed themselves on my soul. They weren't a dismissal—they were a promise. A contract between my future self and the universe. Everything I did from then on—every vocal exercise, every late-night practice session with my dad at the piano, every song I dissected and reassembled in my bedroom—was preparation for this exact second.

The Atlantic Records offices hadn't changed much. Platinum and gold records still adorned the walls like constellations, mapping out a universe I desperately wanted to inhabit. Phones trilled in distant offices, and snippets of bass lines thrummed through closed doors—the heartbeat of the music industry pulsing all around me.

My mother sat beside me, her posture perfect, her eyes watchful. Her belief in my gift made me stand a little taller as the receptionist led us into a conference room.

The space was intimidating in its simplicity—a long table reflecting the overhead lights, leather chairs that seemed too big for my frame, and floor-to-ceiling windows framing the Sunset Strip. My palms were slick with sweat, but my resolve was ironclad. I was prepared to sing "Greatest Love of All" and Mariah's "Vision of Love."

When Darryl nodded for me to begin, I closed my eyes for just a beat. In that darkness, I gathered everything—the nerves fluttering in my stomach, the doubt whispering at the edges of my mind, the hunger gnawing at my core. Then I opened my mouth and let it all transform into sound.

I sang like my entire existence depended on the next note. I gave Darryl every fragment of emotion I'd ever felt or witnessed.

These weren't my songs, but every beat carried my interpretation. When the final note dissolved into silence, Darryl leaned back in his chair, fingers steepled under his chin, eyes narrowed in thought. Then he nodded—a small movement that shifted my entire world—and said, "I want you to come back . . . and sing for my boss, Sylvia Rhone."

It was as if someone pushed open the door to my dream just enough to peek inside. And now there was a second door.

Bigger.

Scarier.

But *right there*, waiting for me to turn the knob and enter.

The hours between singing for Darryl and returning to perform for Sylvia Rhone stretched like taffy, sweet with anticipation but pulling at my nerves. I knew what this second audition meant—it was binary. Yes or no. Deal or no deal. The culmination of years of practice or another lesson in patience.

By then, I'd sung in so many sterile record label offices that the routine was etched into my muscle memory. Me, dressed in my carefully selected outfit (a purple suede vest and matching skirt my mom had splurged on at the Galleria, despite my dad's protests about the price). Me, with my charm dialed up to maximum, smiling so hard my cheeks ached. Me, singing with every cell in my body vibrating with purpose. And always, always, the row of suits behind imposing tables. Men, mostly. White, mostly. Barely looking up from their legal pads.

But this time, when I walked into that conference room, at the head of the table sat a Black woman. Sylvia Rhone. She had presence. Her eyes—sharp, intelligent, missing nothing—watched me as I positioned myself in the center of the room. I stood tall, anchored by my mother's quiet strength beside me.

The energy crackled between us—a recognition, perhaps. Like each of us was exactly where we were supposed to be. All I had to do now was the one thing I knew how to do better than anything else in the world.

And so, I did. I shut out the conference room and transported myself back to our family room in Carson. Just me and Dad at the piano, with Mom listening from the kitchen, Ray curled up on the couch. I sang full-throated and free, the way I did when no one was judging, when music was just oxygen.

"Who do you want to be like?" Sylvia asked when the last note faded. Her voice was smooth, deliberate.

The question caught me off guard. No one had ever asked me that—or anything, really—after I performed for them. Most just nodded and said they'd be in touch, or worse, started discussing me as if I wasn't standing right there.

I didn't hesitate. The answer lived in my bones.

"I want to be like Brandy," I said. "There's not going to be anybody like me."

It wasn't arrogance speaking. It wasn't a line I'd rehearsed in front of my bedroom mirror. It was a knowing that had taken root in my heart from the very first time I found my voice in the choir. A certainty that had only grown stronger with each passing year.

Sylvia didn't break my gaze. A slow smile spread across her face, revealing perfect teeth and something more valuable—genuine interest. She turned to Darryl, a silent conversation passing between them. Then she looked back at us, her eyes resting on me with an intensity that made me stand even taller.

"Welcome to Atlantic Records," she said, the words simple but laden with meaning.

"Are you serious?" I asked.

"I'm serious," Sylvia said. She reached out her hand to shake mine. I leaped toward her and gave her the biggest hug.

"I promise I won't let you down," I whispered through sobs.

I had a record deal.

On the spot.

I wasn't waiting anymore. I wasn't hoping or praying or wishing on stars. I had crossed the threshold and stepped into the body of the person I had always known I would become. And it was only the beginning.

Walking out of the label and back onto the Sunset Strip, it was like the city had come alive. I was floating on a cloud, and to celebrate, I wanted two things: Del Taco and a day at Disneyland with Ray.

Darryl wasted no time lining up producers and writers. Meanwhile, I reported to a soundstage in Hollywood to go into production on *Thea.*

The first table read was when it all became real. I took my seat in front of a small stack of pages. My character's name—Danesha—was printed in bold black letters on a white paper tent folded neatly in front of me. I ran my finger over it, trying to absorb the reality that this was mine. This space belonged to me.

Still, I didn't feel like an actress. Acting wasn't instinctual the way singing was. When I sang, I disappeared into pure emotion. When I acted, I had to think. Had to try. Had to concentrate so hard my temples pulsed with the effort. I glanced around the table at my castmates, all so comfortable in their skin, their characters, this world. Jason, already a veteran at fifteen, flipped through his pages with casual confidence. Adam cracked jokes with the writers like they were old friends. And Thea was commanding and magnetic as she held court at the head of the table, her laugh carrying to every corner of the room.

Doubt danced on my shoulders, but excitement twirled alongside it. I had earned this seat. I belonged here just as much as anyone. I summoned the words of my favorite teacher, Mr. Bialik: *Don't kill the scene . . . progress it.*

The table read, as I would quickly discover, was the gentlest part of a shooting week. Once we were under those blazing lights, with a live studio audience reacting to our every move, the real work began.

Early in production, there was a scene I just couldn't land. A simple exchange with my TV brother, but the timing kept slipping through my fingers. I either rushed the line, stepped on his cue, or missed the beat entirely. Take after take, I felt myself unraveling, my confidence dissolving under the pressure and the weight of expectant stares.

"Cut!" The director's voice sliced through the set.

"Back from the top!"

"Cut!"

"Brandy, try to remember your cue is when he turns, not when he finishes speaking."

"Cut!"

"Cut!"

"CUT!"

My TV mom turned to me with eyes that could have cut diamond.

"Little girl," she snapped, her voice low but sharp enough to reach me across the set. "Is it that hard for you to remember a fucking line?"

The air evaporated from the room. The crew froze, eyes darting everywhere but at us.

I sat motionless, heat flooding my face. If I could have dissolved into the floorboards, I would have. But there was nowhere to hide under those merciless lights.

The one place I still felt whole—still felt powerful—was in my music. So, I sang. Between takes, in my trailer, under my breath while walking down hallways. I sang because it kept me anchored and kept my instrument conditioned. My dad's voice was always in my ear: *Your voice is a muscle, baby girl. You don't use it, you lose it.*

But my singing wasn't always welcome on set. One afternoon, as I hummed absent-mindedly, Thea turned to me with a sharpness that made me flinch.

"When you get your own show, you can sing," she said. There was no mistaking the tone. This wasn't playful teasing between castmates. She was not feeling me. At all.

The space between us started to widen after that. Co-stars noticed. PAs whispered. The easy warmth we had developed at the beginning had curdled into something prickly and suffocating. I dreaded the days we filmed our one-on-one scenes.

It got to a point where I couldn't hide my frustration anymore, and I finally broke down after a day of filming. "Mom, she hates me," I cried, tears falling hot and fast.

My mother's hands tightened on the steering wheel. She didn't say much. Just "Mmm-hmm" and "I see." But the very next morning, instead of dropping me at the studio entrance like usual, she parked the car and walked me to set. She grabbed a metal chair and pulled it up to the director and took a seat—all without breaking gaze of my TV mother.

"Okay, I'm going to just sit *riiiiight* here today," she said, drawing out her words nice and slow. Her Southern drawl came out thicker than usual. Her voice was as sweet as apple pie, but she had a fire in her eyes that could have melted the Antarctic Plateau.

Thea stared back, surprise flickering across her face before settling into a tight smile. "Suit yourself," she said with a small shrug. After that, the barbs became less pointed and the coldness thawed just enough to make the set bearable again.

Thea lasted one season. Just nineteen episodes. It was a smart, funny, sharply written show that deserved a wider audience than it received. Getting Black stories greenlit was an uphill battle then. Still is. So, I hold that show close to my heart, not because it was easy—Lord knows it wasn't—but because it meant something. It added a vital voice to the conversation, even if that voice was silenced too soon.

I respect Thea Vidale and the crucial role her show played in my career trajectory. My feelings toward her were complicated. I feared her sharp tongue, resented the stiffness of our interactions—but I wanted her to like me. Not just because I was cast as her daughter, but because we were creating something that reflected lives rarely seen on those glossy network schedules.

I was ambitious, insecure, maybe a little arrogant. Definitely not a walk in the park myself. I own that. But I give my younger self some grace, too. I was a hormonal teen navigating body changes and the crushing pressure of dual careers simultaneously taking flight. Between takes, I struggled with our strained dynamic, but when the cameras rolled, we found harmony. Thea and Danesha offered a relatable portrait of mother-daughter complexity. The friction between us somehow translating into authentic family chemistry on-screen.

When it had become clear that Thea and I were oil and vinegar, I adopted a silent mantra that burned in my chest with each workday: *You may not like me, but you will not deny my talent or my voice.*

I don't know if I still carry it with the same intensity now. But back then, it was all I had, and it pulsed through me like lifeblood, keeping me upright when I wanted to crumble.

In one of my favorite episodes, my character and her brothers perform Aretha Franklin's "Respect" as a surprise for their mother. When I saw that written in the script, I recognized it immediately for what it was—an opening. A chance to prove something not just to the audience or the network, but to my TV mom.

The day we filmed, I channeled every ounce of hurt, every side-eye, every dismissive comment into that performance. I sang right to her, my eyes never leaving hers—no flinching, no shrinking, no holding back.

You may not like me, I thought with each note, *but you cannot deny my talent or my voice.*

As the last note hung in the air and the audience burst into applause, I saw something flicker across Thea's face. Her eyes softened. Her smile—wide and genuine—transformed her completely. For just a second, the wall between us turned transparent, and I glimpsed what might have been if things had been different.

The audience's cheers washed over us like a wave, but it was that brief connection with my TV mom—that flash of pride in her eyes—that meant the most. In that single instant, we weren't Thea and Brandy with all our off-screen baggage. We were simply a mother seeing her daughter shine, and a daughter basking in that recognition.

It was just a moment. But sometimes, a moment is enough.

THE KIND OF GIRL YOU COULD BE DOWN FOR

WHEN I FIRST stepped into that studio to record my debut album, my relationship with my own voice was . . . complicated. There I was, fourteen years old, a record deal to my name, yet still wincing whenever I heard my vocals isolated on the four-track. Did I really sound like *that*?

In my bedroom, I'd spent hours layering harmonies, building voice upon voice until the sound made the hairs on my arms rise. But strip those layers away, and I'd cringe, convinced I sounded like a chipmunk singing into a tin can.

My years with Immature had given me a taste of studio life, but this was the real thing. A team of producers and writers had been assembled just for *me*. The weight of that reality pressed against my chest. Now, as Darryl Williams, the A&R director who believed in me enough to sign me, was laying out a game plan for my album, I was terrified.

"We're gonna start you with Damon Thomas and the guys from Somethin' for the People," he told me, his eyes bright with expectations I desperately wanted to fulfill.

From the outside, the studio was a plain, unremarkable white building on the corner of a busy stretch of Santa Monica Boulevard. Inside, the walls were lined with artifacts from some of the iconic artists who had recorded there. Fleetwood Mac, Smokey Robinson, the Jackson Five, and Roy Orbison had all recorded music inside these booths.

The studio door swung open, and there they were—Damon and the trio from Oakland: Curtis, Rochad, and Jeff. I remember thinking they looked so *cool*, so at ease in this sacred space, while I felt like an impostor waiting to be found out.

"Little sis," Damon said, giving me a fist bump that somehow made me stand taller. "We've been waiting for you."

The smell of incense lingered from an earlier session, mixing with the scent of the pizzas Darryl had waiting for us.

Damon leaned against the console, arms crossed, studying me as I picked at the veggies on my slice.

"Who inspires you the most—and why?"

That final word—*why*—struck something deep inside me. In all the label meetings, all the auditions, all the conversations about my "sound" and my "brand," no one before Sylvia had ever asked me to explain myself, to reveal the reasoning behind my musical obsessions. I looked up at him, and whatever anxiety I'd been nursing melted beneath the warmth of his genuine curiosity.

"Whitney," I said, my voice barely above a whisper. Then stronger: "Whitney Houston."

"Mmm." He nodded, waiting for more. "Tell me why . . . and not because her voice is amazing. We all know that."

"Because . . ." I paused, searching for words big enough to hold what I felt. "Because when she sings, it feels like she's hugging you with her voice. Like she's not afraid to open herself up to you. And Mariah . . ." I closed my eyes, feeling bolder now. "Mariah builds these castles in the air with her harmonies. Her songs are like tales from faraway places. I like the way I feel when I listen to them."

When I opened my eyes, Damon was grinning, nodding like I'd just confirmed something he already knew.

"That's what we're gonna find for you," he said. "Music that makes you feel like that. Your own kind of magic."

My dad was there for every session, my constant guide. We'd developed our own musical shorthand over years of practice—a slight tilt of his head when I was going flat, a subtle lift of his finger when he knew I had more to give, a nearly imperceptible smile when I hit a note that impressed him. In the studio, he never tried to take control. Never tried to tell these seasoned professionals their business. He was just . . . there. My foundation as my vocal coach.

I remember watching Damon and my father exchange a look during that first session—a silent acknowledgment of their shared purpose: me. They weren't competing for authority; they were combining forces. The relief of that realization washed over me like cool water.

Damon slid behind the boards, fingers dancing across faders with practiced ease. "Let's see what you got, baby girl. No pressure. Just vibe with it."

The beat dropped, thick and syrupy, wrapping around me like a velvet cloak. I closed my eyes, let it seep into my bones, and when I opened my mouth to sing, something unexpected happened. The voice that emerged wasn't the chipmunk I feared. It was fuller, richer, drenched in something I hadn't heard before. Something that sounded almost like . . . confidence.

As the weeks unfolded into months, I clung to one thing with a fierceness that surprised even me—my background vocals. Those stacked harmonies I'd crafted in my bedroom weren't just sounds to me; they were my signature. I needed them to exist on this album exactly as I heard them in my head.

But I was fourteen. Unproven. A voice with potential but no track record. Creative control wasn't even in my vocabulary, let alone my contract. I was being presented with records—timeless records that would have sounded amazing with anyone on them because they were that good. I was asked my opinions, sure, but I wasn't fully convinced those opinions would have carried any real weight if push came to shove.

Until one afternoon when Damon brought an unfamiliar face to the studio.

"This is Robin," he said, gesturing to the boy beside him. He looked as if he'd been plucked straight from a wholesome family sitcom, all clean lines and gentle features, and maybe just a few years older than me.

Robin nodded shyly, settling himself at the piano bench like it was home. His fingers found the keys—tentative at first, then with growing assurance as a melody took shape beneath his touch. When he opened his mouth to sing, the contrast was startling—this sweet-faced boy with a voice steeped in soul:

Memories of yesterday
Loneliness my way to say
I needed you, and all you do
To come and rescue me

It was gorgeous. Painfully so. The kind of song that could crack you open if you weren't careful. "First song I ever wrote," he told me afterward, a hint of pride coloring his voice.

As he played through it again, I couldn't help myself. I started humming a harmony line that unfurled in my mind like a ribbon of silver, soft and instinctive.

Robin's hands stilled on the keys. "What was that?"

I froze, heat rising to my cheeks. "Just . . . how I heard it in my head."

His eyes widened. "Do it again."

So I did, and he started playing along, his fingers finding

chords that cradled my harmony like it had always belonged there.

"I like that," he said, a grin spreading across his face. "Why don't you try it like that?"

I felt something bloom inside my chest—pride. Even though I wasn't writing much of what I was singing, producers like Robin were bringing me into the process, making me feel like a collaborator rather than just a vessel for their ideas. And that lessened the sting of having backing vocalists and minimal creative control.

We spent hours that day fine-tuning "Love Is on My Side," a beast of a record with lush instrumentation and verses that built like waves before crashing into a foam of runs and riffs. Vocally, it was like climbing a mountain—steep, demanding, glorious. It took more than a few attempts to get it right.

My father stayed tucked into his corner, headphones half-on, occasionally scribbling notes, offering the gentlest corrections. "Try that last line one more time, sweetheart," he'd murmur. "But open up the vowel here." He'd shape his mouth to demonstrate, and I'd mimic him, finding the sound he knew was hiding in me.

Robin was just seventeen then, as green as I was and years away from becoming Robin Thicke, the R&B-pop star, but I absorbed his self-assuredness like a sponge. The gentle encouragement he offered wasn't just validating; it gave me courage to speak up more in the studio, to believe that my instincts might actually be worth something.

A year into recording, Darryl introduced me to Keith Crouch. There was something different about Keith from the second he walked in. The nephew of legendary gospel singer Andraé Crouch, Keith had been crafting songs since his teens and had just wrapped a stint writing for Michael Jackson. The weight of that lineage, that experience, hung over him.

But Keith didn't come in with stacks of demos or prepackaged ideas. Instead, he sat across from me, eyes locked on mine, and asked:

"So . . . what do you want to sing about?"

The simplicity of it stunned me into silence. At fourteen, my emotional palette was still developing, but there were themes that consumed me: Boys. Crushes that swept me off my feet. Heartache that felt earth-shattering even though it was barely a paper cut. I spilled everything to Keith that day. Every lingering glance in the school hallways. Every flutter in my stomach when the phone rang. Every tear shed over someone who never knew they held my heart in their hands.

Keith just smiled, jotting notes, nodding encouragingly as I rambled. When I finally ran out of words, he told me to take a walk with my dad, while he disappeared into a corner with his notebook and a keyboard.

Days later, Darryl summoned me to the studio, practically vibrating with excitement. "Keith made something," he said, his eyes dancing. "And I think it's your first single."

I had recorded a handful of songs by then, but none had pulled this kind of reaction out of Darryl. I propped myself up on the console, pressing as close to the speakers as I could get when he hit Play on the demo.

The beat dropped, and it was unlike anything I'd heard before—laid-back yet bubbling with urgency. It was soulful with a hard edge, and smooth like honey but with enough kick to rattle your speakers.

Everyone in the room was nodding, bodies swaying unconsciously to the rhythm. My dad. Ray, who had come with me, was standing on a chair dancing. Everybody was feeling the record.

Everyone except me.

"I don't like it," I said, my voice barely audible over the playback.

Darryl's jaw dropped before he composed himself. "Um, you don't?"

I shook my head, a knot of worry forming in my stomach. "I just . . . I don't hear my voice on it."

I expected argument. Dismissal. What I got instead was a smile and a challenge:

"That's fair. Well, how about this. You work with Keith to come up with your take on it. Sing it however feels good to you. That's your homework," he said.

For the next two days, I worked with Keith and his collaborator, Kipper Jones, recording what would become "I Wanna Be Down." The guys were patient, collaborative, asking questions that made me feel like we were building something together rather than them simply directing me. When I heard the playback of my first take, I felt magic pouring out of the speakers. This would be my introduction to the world. That much was certain.

We refined and polished until the record was perfect. When Darryl returned to the studio, Keith hit Play. The voice blaring from the speakers was mine and yet somehow not mine—fuller, more assured, wrapped in a production that felt like it had been crafted specifically for the texture and tone that was uniquely my own:

I would like to get to know if I could be
The kind of girl that you could be down for
'Cause when I look at you I feel something tell me
That you're the kind of guy that I
should make a move on . . .

I felt the energy in the room shift like a tide. This was *my* song. There wasn't anything like it on the radio. I felt it as my vocals filled the space around us, bouncing off the walls and seeping into our skin.

Darryl went wild, jumping up and down, pointing at me with a gleeful vindication. His intuition had proved true. We kept at it, and Keith brought in stellar collaborators: Rahsaan Patterson, Glenn McKinney, and his brother, Kenneth. I can still feel the exhilaration that coursed through me while recording "Baby" and "Best Friend," knowing the lyrics were drawn from my own heart, my own experiences—especially "Best Friend."

My little brother, Ray, was—and remains to this day—the other half of my heart. I wanted to honor our bond, to celebrate how much his spirit fueled mine. Even at twelve, Ray had an ear for music that was nothing short of extraordinary. Having him with me in the studio, watching his face light up when certain lines hit just right, was one of the purest joys of the entire process.

Keith and Glenn captured our sibling connection in "Best Friend," and the first time I heard it, tears sprang to my eyes. I knew immediately it would be my favorite track on the album. Time hasn't changed that feeling one bit.

As I recorded my album, Usher and Aaliyah made their debuts. Watching them break through gave me hope. I was particularly drawn to Aaliyah—her angelic spirit, the way she balanced street edge with sweet innocence. Her voice seemed to float above the beat, untethered by gravity but never disconnected from the rhythm.

I wanted to bring something equally fresh to R&B, to carve out my own space. R&B was merging more deeply with hip-hop, creating something that honored tradition while pushing boundaries, and I was thrilled to be part of that evolution. I wanted my album to show I was worthy of standing alongside my contemporaries.

Somethin' for the People brought a sonic palette that provided the foundation for the album—a smooth blend of hip-hop sensibilities and contemporary soul that felt more relaxed than the aggressive punch of New Jack Swing, which was still very much the nucleus of Black pop music.

The guys loved that I was willing to experiment in the studio, that I never backed down from a vocal challenge. With my father there to guide me, I felt safe taking risks, stretching beyond what I thought possible.

I remember the day they brought in "Sunny Day," an upbeat, midtempo record that evoked summer cookouts and block parties. It had this breezy, boom bap groove with the nostalgic energy of a throwback rap record. But the key was stratospheric. The verses and hook soared so high I knew I'd have to push myself to the absolute limit to get anywhere near the demo's feeling.

But I welcomed the challenge. My natural voice sits in the alto-tenor range, but in those days, I didn't yet appreciate the subtle power of my natural register. I wanted those sky-high money notes that made crowds erupt, so I pushed and squeezed and reached for every note beyond my comfort zone.

I never attempted these vocal acrobatics onstage—too much could go wrong, and the memory of freezing in front of my church congregation as a small child still haunted me. The promise I'd made to myself then—to never let fear silence me again—was sacred. But in the studio, protected by the possibility of multiple takes, I could play, experiment, fail without threat of humiliation.

The producers recognized my determination and developed techniques to push me even further once they had me venturing outside my comfort zone. Keith knew my admiration for SWV's Coko and wielded it like a magic spell.

"You want to be as cold as Coko?" he'd challenge, a glint in his eye. "Do another take."

It worked every time, sending me back to the booth with renewed fire.

We were nearing the end of recording when Sylvia Rhone

requested one more song—a ballad to balance the album's energy and showcase my range. Keith and Kipper went to the notebook of our old conversations and whipped up a tender composition reminiscent of Whitney's early heartbreakers. "Brokenhearted," they called it. I fell in love with it the second they played me the demo.

But there was a catch: we had exactly one day to record it to meet our deadline. In order to keep the album's release date, we had a single day to cut "Brokenhearted" if we wanted it for the album, and I had already made plans, weeks before, to go to Six Flags Magic Mountain amusement park with my friends. After months in the studio, I was desperate for just one day of normal teenage life—roller coasters, cotton candy, screaming until my voice was raw for reasons other than singing.

"Can I record the day after tomorrow?" I asked Keith.

"We've only got tomorrow," he said.

"Well, that's not gonna work," I huffed.

He played his trump card without missing a beat: "You want to be as cold as Coko? Well, Coko ain't picking Magic Mountain over the studio!"

"Well, maybe Coko doesn't like roller coasters," I shot back, arms crossed defiantly.

"Fair point," he conceded with a laugh. "Look, Sylvia really believes in this record, and you love it, too. I saw it in your eyes. If we want this record, we *have* to do it tomorrow. Let's just knock it out, and then you can ride all the roller coasters you want."

Keith was right, and deep down, I knew it. But I was still unmoved. It was just one afternoon—one afternoon to be Brandy the teenager instead of Brandy the recording artist.

My father, who had remained quiet throughout this exchange, finally spoke. "Well, it sounds like today is the day you have to decide whether you want to go to Magic Mountain with your friends or be a recording artist."

The simplicity of his statement cut through my resistance like a hot knife through butter. This was a time—the first of many—where I would have to choose between normalcy and the extraordinary path I'd been fighting for since I was seven years old. I wanted this more than breath itself. It was just one more afternoon in the studio.

When I returned the next day, I knocked out the lead vocal for "Brokenhearted" in a single take. As the last note faded, I looked out from the booth to see Kipper wiping tears from his eyes, my father laughing with pride, and Keith nodding with satisfied approval.

I was both exhausted and exhilarated—and intensely aware that Magic Mountain awaited me on the other side. But more importantly, I had just completed my debut album. And I celebrated by riding coasters until dusk.

I am sitting in an old, dilapidated barn, golden-hour sunlight filtering through cracks in the wooden slats, casting honeyed streaks across my face. A cameraman circles me like a satellite, his lens capturing every blink, every subtle shift in my posture. My braids are styled into a delicate bob that brushes against my shoulders when I move. The artificial breeze from a wind machine provides blessed relief from the heat as I lip-synch "I Wanna Be Down" for what feels like the hundredth time.

Just weeks earlier, I had been sitting in my mother's car at a Del Taco drive-through when the unmistakable opening beats of my song spilled from the speakers of the car ahead of us. A stranger—a complete stranger—was listening to my voice on the radio.

My voice. On the radio.

I exploded out of our car, heedless of my mother's startled yell, and began jumping up and down in the drive-through lane, pointing wildly at the car ahead.

"That's me!!! That's me on the radio!!"

It was an out-of-body experience. A tsunami of pride washed over me as I thought about all the rejections, all the doors slammed in my face, all the times I'd been told I wasn't pretty enough, wasn't talented enough, wasn't *enough*—and how I had never, not for one second, given up on myself.

Now here I was, on a video set, about to share my face and my music with the entire world in cinematic form.

Having done television for a year on *Thea*, I was accustomed to cameras. But recording a music video was an entirely different beast. On the sitcom, I was playing a character, one small piece in an ensemble puzzle. Here, there was nowhere to hide. I was selling myself as an artist—my voice, my image, my essence.

I had made one thing clear from the beginning: I didn't want to pretend to be someone else. The Brandy you see in that video is who I was—a sweet, sometimes naive fifteen-year-old girl with unwavering faith in her gift and her purpose, but still wobbling occasionally on the tightrope of self-assurance.

What I knew without question was that the music felt right in my soul. It spoke to me as a teenager who loved R&B, soul, hip-hop, and gospel with equal fervor.

I had secretly hoped that "Best Friend" would be the first single—you rarely heard upbeat anthems celebrating the sacred bond between siblings. But I understood why "I Wanna Be Down" was chosen as my introduction to the world. It was a sweet, flirty, and innocent song about that universal flutter of first attraction, but it didn't matter. Those butterflies of new romance? Whether you're fourteen or forty, they dance the same delicate patterns in your stomach and the record captured that feeling.

I would like to get to know if I could be . . .
The kind of girl that you could be down for . . .

I loved how those lyrics made me feel—young, free, and full of hope about the woman I was becoming. After the bullying, and the rejection, I was determined to show everyone who had ever dismissed me how unwise they had been to underestimate Brandy Norwood.

This was my time. I felt it in my bones. But with that certainty came a shadow of worry: Would people like me? At fifteen, I had already developed an awareness that every move I made was no longer entirely my own. The world would be watching, judging, deciding who I was based on what they saw in this video. I needed to make a perfect first impression.

Director Keith Ward wanted me to feel at ease. The concept was deliberately simple: just let people see Brandy as she is. We invited my friends to be in the video. My brother was there. It should have been pure joy.

But as I sat in that barn, the camera circling like a hawk, I sensed a subtle shift I couldn't quite articulate. I didn't realize it then, but in those instances, I was etching an image into stone—creating an expectation that would follow me for years to come. Right there in that barn, surrounded by hay bales and filtered sunlight, I was becoming a brand as much as a person. I was creating a box that would both shelter and confine me.

In the version of me that still believed, I thought I was just being myself. I couldn't have known how that "self" now belonged to the world. How every deviation from the sweet, innocent girl in braids would be met with resistance. How difficult it would eventually become to grow up in the public eye.

But that afternoon, as the director called "Cut!" on the final take, all I felt was exhilaration. I had done it. My song was on the radio. My music video would soon be on television screens across America—and the world. Everything I had dreamed of since I was a little girl singing in church with my dad and my brother was unfolding before me like a miracle.

I just didn't yet understand the cost of miracles. Or how completely they change the person who receives them.

BROKENHEARTED

ANTHONY WAS THE sun in my teenage galaxy, everything else merely planets orbiting his gravitational pull. He was devastatingly handsome. Tall, with skin the warm brown of autumn leaves, and a smile that could power a lighthouse. He was from the valley, and we met on the audition circuit, just two young kids who loved to sing. Anthony was in a singing group, along with his older brother. While they hadn't yet broken out, everyone recognized that they were stars waiting for the right night sky.

Anthony and I lived for our duets. It was all we wanted to do—find empty rooms with good acoustics and fill them with melodies that were half his, half mine. I had desperately wanted him to play my love interest in the "I Wanna Be Down" video, to immortalize our connection on film, but he couldn't because of a family trip that took him out of town during the shoot. Our relationship existed in that sweet, innocent terrain of first love—we were young, our hearts simultaneously devoted to our craft and to the delicate bloom growing between us.

We both shared an almost religious devotion to Boyz II Men. We considered them untouchable when it came to their harmonies, their intricate vocal arrangements leaving us breathless with admiration. We would spend hours deconstructing their vocal choices. Anthony's group had even performed Boyz II Men songs at talent shows—that's how deeply their influence ran. We were each other's most dedicated cheerleaders, our support for one another second only to that of our parents. Anthony's elation when I got a record deal rivaled my own, his pride palpable enough to touch. Whenever there was a hard day on the set of *Thea*, he'd sit with me at the park and be a shoulder. "Keep your eyes on the prize," he'd say. The prize, we both knew, was the music. Knowing he was just a phone call away provided a lifeline once newfound fame accelerated my life, and my schedule, beyond comprehension.

One morning, my mother's hand on my shoulder gently pulled me out of my slumber, her touch familiar even through dreams.

"Wanya's on the phone," she announced, her tone almost deliberately casual, as if she were telling me it might rain later.

I stared up at her, disoriented. "Wanya?" Surely this was some elaborate joke, a prank she'd constructed to brighten the morning.

But there was no mischievous smile, no "gotcha" hovering on the horizon. Just the cordless phone extended in her outstretched hand and a stillness on her face that whispered: *This is happening. This is real.*

Sure enough, Wanya Morris—my favorite member of my favorite group—was on the other end of the receiver, his voice traveling through invisible waves to reach my ear.

He congratulated me on the success of "I Wanna Be Down," and made a joke about it knocking his group's record off the top of the R&B chart—something I still couldn't believe, considering their hit "I'll Make Love To You" had dominated radio waves for months.

"I want to meet you," he said.

"WHAT! Are you serious?" I demanded, launching myself from beneath the covers.

"Yeah," he laughed, the sound warm and rich even through the phone's tinny speaker. "It's the least you could do after your record knocked us out of No. 1."

I glanced up at my mother, who remained stationed in my bedroom doorway, hands planted firmly on her hips. From the ear-to-ear grin stretching across her face, breaking through her normally composed demeanor, I could tell she'd already been privy to the purpose of this call. We waited until I'd ended the conversation before releasing twin screams.

"I Wanna Be Down" was huge, but I wasn't used to stars reaching out to me—and certainly not to hang out. An older family friend's house was the hangout spot. That's where I was whenever I wasn't at home or on the road doing promotion, hanging and singing with my crew. Of course I invited them all over to meet him. Ray was there, so was Anthony and his brother, their faces a mixture of excitement and disbelief. None of us thought he was actually going to show, but he pulled up—all smiles and charm. It was like the most popular senior had invited us sophomores over to the cool table. That's what it felt like to be hanging out with him.

A connection was forged. He would call to give me advice about navigating the industry. He became one of my closest friends, a confidant who understood the surreal life that had become my reality.

In the five months after my debut album dropped, my life spun by like a carousel—bright, otherworldly, a bit dizzying. "I Wanna Be Down," the song I once second-guessed, soared beyond anything I'd imagined—right to the top of the R&B charts. Then we released "Baby" as my second single and it was as if the universe split wide open for me. The dream I'd held close since childhood was no longer a fantasy—it was unfurling in front of my eyes.

It was as if I had been swept up in a tornado, spinning through a firestorm of photo shoots, radio interviews, studio sessions, video shoots, TV appearances, performances.

It was work—beautiful, exhausting, exhilarating work. I had a responsibility to be *on* from sunrise to sunset, and I was savoring every second, letting each experience coat my tongue like honey.

So much of my life was just beginning, but deep in my heart, I could feel all that was ending. Doing simple things like hitting a Del Taco or going to the mall with my brother was getting tougher, each public excursion a performance I hadn't auditioned for. Seeing friends on the regular was getting harder. And then there was my relationship with Anthony. This sweet puppy love was now competing with a world that demanded everything I had to give.

In the beginning we maintained our connection with relative ease. We had a window of time after his school day let out and before I had to rehearse where we could talk. Though I awakened in different cities each morning, the rhythms of our phone time brought me great comfort.

Gradually, however, those patterns eroded. Sporadic at first. Eventually the missed calls between us accumulated like fallen leaves. It was both of us. Days of silence stretched between conversations. And when we did manage to connect, his voice seemed to reach me from increasingly greater distances.

His interest in my professional journey and personal well-being never wavered, but I sensed a widening gap separating us far beyond a few missed calls—a chasm that geography couldn't explain and time couldn't heal.

I was in some city, feeling homesick after a show. I did my usual round of calls—Mom, who then passed the phone to my dad, who then passed it Ray. Then I called Paw Paw. Then Anthony. I could hear something in his voice that night. He told me he'd been keeping something from me, and it was eating him up. He'd given his virginity away to another girl, despite our shared promise. I had been saving myself for him. Apparently, his patience had worn thinner than mine. It happened on the trip that kept him from being the love interest in the "I Wanna Be Down" video. The irony stung far more than what felt like a betrayal did, but my life was moving so fast, the idea of sitting brokenhearted was a luxury I knew I didn't have.

It was my final hours as a fifteen-year-old. The last seconds before crossing that mythical threshold into Sweet Sixteen. And I wasn't celebrating in typical teenage fashion—I was ringing it in at a Hard Rock Café that pulsated with energy, walls vibrating with music, the space packed wall-to-wall with faces that once only glimmered on my television screen through the glow of my family's living room. Faces that had lived in my imagination suddenly breathing the same perfumed air as *me.*

I was in Phoenix, Arizona, for NBA All-Star Weekend. I was set to perform the next day alongside Mary J. Blige, Queen Latifah, the Fresh Prince and Boyz II Men. I was still getting used to being invited to the same places I used to catch glimpses of on TV.

But here I was, stepping into a glitzy All-Star Weekend party being thrown by MTV, my heartbeat keeping rhythm with the bass rumbling from the stage as Shaquille O'Neal performed his new single, his massive frame commanding the stage like a gentle giant with a microphone.

"Oh my God, Ray J," I gasped, my fingers suddenly tightening around his arm with enough force to leave crescent moons from my nails. "That's *Leon.*"

Above the Rim was my favorite movie at the time. I think I watched it a hundred times. I nearly squealed at the sight of him, the sound bubbling up from some girlish place that no amount of fame could polish.

"Ray, you have to introduce me," I whispered urgently, my words tumbling over each other in their rush to escape.

Ray merely nodded—so casual, so unbothered. It didn't matter that he'd never actually met Leon either; Ray's charisma was currency. He strolled over with the ease of someone who slid through MTV soirees on the regular. Ray dabbed Leon up and guided him right to where I stood. My heart was hammering against my ribs like it might break free.

Leon embraced me with arms that seemed to envelop my entire being. "Brandy, congratulations on all your success. Your voice is something else—been playing that album nonstop."

I felt myself dissolving into the floor, my bones turning liquid with joy. An actor I admired knew my music. In the span of five minutes, I met Paula Abdul, Magic Johnson, Treach from Naughty by Nature, and MTV VJ Bill Bellamy—and they all seemed as excited to meet me as I was to meet them. Every few steps it seemed we were bumping into royalty. I encountered so much enthusiasm about my music my heart was beating at triple the rate.

It was one thing to be ushered beyond the velvet rope, but to be among the stars and hear my name and music on their lips? It transcended surreal and entered the realm of divine fantasy.

And remarkably—impossibly—every single day of my life had begun to feel this way, extraordinary becoming my new ordinary.

Right before the stroke of midnight, my parents grabbed me from VIP and started moving me toward the front of the restaurant.

"Mom . . . what's happening?" I asked, confusion creasing my brow as we moved through the crowd.

"Just wait. It's a surprise," Ray answered in my mother's place, exchanging a knowing wink with my father as they continued guiding me forward, my heartbeat accelerating with each step.

When we reached the front, the lights suddenly intensified—brighter, hotter, bathing everything in a golden glow that made the party shimmer. And then a voice—a hauntingly familiar voice that had serenaded me through countless afternoons—

resonated behind me, sending electric currents racing along my spine.

"Tonight is a special evening," the voice announced, rich as velvet and smooth as caramel. "It's Brandy's birthday."

I turned slowly and found myself to standing before Boyz II Men—in the flesh. I hadn't seen Wanya since he dropped over my friend's house, and I'd never met the rest of the guys. Now here they were, surprising me.

Like a scene from a teenage drama, the guys began to sing Happy Birthday—their voices blending in that signature a cappella harmony that had made them legends, every perfect note directed at me as a towering cake adorned with sixteen dancing flames was wheeled forward, its glow illuminating their faces in flickering amber light. This feeling, this memory—I wanted to preserve it forever. And that became my silent wish as I closed my eyes, the flames flickering through my lashes.

Then he looked directly at me, his gaze intense, and proclaimed to the crowd: "She's one of the baddest singers of the '90s. She's gonna be out there for a long time."

His words felt like an anointing I hadn't known I was waiting for. It was, without question, the coolest surprise of my young life—that was until he called me at home shortly after with an invitation:

"Wanna open for us on tour this spring?"

Just that casual, and nonchalant, as if he were asking how my weekend was.

The question jolted every cell in my body.

Before the tour started, he began calling regularly—gradually becoming my anchor, the only person who truly understood the strange metamorphosis happening in my life. He became indispensable.

That first night opening for Boyz II Men, terror coursed through my veins. My hands were clammy, my mouth desert-dry, my stomach performing acrobatics as I watched a steady stream of cars pour into the parking lot of the Tacoma Dome arena. I'd never been to Washington before, and didn't see much of the city outside of the Seattle-Tacoma airport, the hotel, and now the arena where I was pacing around, killing time before I went out in front of eighteen thousand people who'd come to see Boyz II Men. I wore white leather pants and a matching bomber with chunky white patent leather boots; my braids were pulled into two buns high atop my head like Princess Leia. I looked in the mirror and muttered the advice I received at a talent competition years ago: *"People need to feel you as much as they hear you."*

There was a soft rap against my dressing room door. I looked at the clock . . . was it time? Already? I swallowed . . . okay, more like gulped. And went to the door.

It was Wanya, standing there with a dozen long-stemmed white roses.

"You ready, superstar?" he asked, handing me the flowers and pulling me in for a quick hug.

I offered a noncommittal shrug, attempting to project more confidence than I felt. "As ready as I'll ever be!"

He smiled, a slow unfurling like a rare flower blooming. "Are these nerves I'm seeing? Where's that girl I saw All-Star Weekend? You were on the bill with us, Mary J. Blige *and* Queen Latifah, and you came out and killed it. On your birthday, no less. This is your time!"

"Do you think the audience will like me?" The question escaped before I could contain it, my deepest fear finding voice.

"I listened to your whole album on the plane last night," he revealed.

My eyes widened, disbelief replacing anxiety. "You did?"

He nodded with quiet certainty. "Front to back. Twice." A pause, his gaze holding mine steadily. "You really are something, Brandy. The crowd is gonna love you. I promise."

His words hung suspended between us. I found myself speechless, gratitude forming a knot in my throat.

"You know," he added, as if the thought had just occurred to him, "we should do something together. I've been thinking . . . that 'Brokenhearted' joint? I could hear it as a duet. Our voices together would be dope, don't you think?"

I swallowed hard, wondering if I'd misheard. "Are you for real?"

"For real."

Two simple words would reshape my entire reality.

The anxiety that was blossoming into full-blown panic receded. I strode out onto that stage, every fiber of my body vibrating with purpose as the beginning bars of "Baby" blasted out of the loudspeakers. I lifted the microphone to my lips and heard pockets of the crowd shouting the lyrics back to me. I hadn't really understood the power of a No. 1 record before that night. The crowd went crazy. And out the corner of my eye I caught him off to the side of the stage. When our eyes met, he flashed a thumbs-up and ducked off to get ready for his own grand entrance.

During a day off from tour, we flew to Philadelphia to record the "Brokenhearted" remix at Boyz II Men's studio. A feeling burned within my chest as we sang together. I knew this sensation, like butterflies taking flight in your stomach.

At one point in the day, he turned toward me, his eyes softened with something unspoken.

"This is a smash," he declared, his smile slow and knowing.

I was excited he believed that . . . but my mind was also cloudy with this new feeling.

I floated out of that studio as if gravity didn't exist.

After that day, everything between us evolved with the silent inevitability of seasons changing.

Every glance he cast in my direction, every embrace that lingered a heartbeat longer than the one before, every preshow pep talk, every time I caught him watching from the wings. Suddenly it all felt . . . different. What had begun as admiration had transformed into something else. It seems to me that he weaponized my admiration, shaped my friendship into dependence, my respect into desire. I felt swept up in a current I couldn't control.

On the tour bus during long stretches between cities, I'd find myself drifting into daydreams—tracing the contours of his laugh in my mind's eye, wondering how it might feel if his fingers ever interlaced with mine and refused to let go. My journal pages began filling with the confusing thoughts that swirled in my mind.

We filmed the video for "Brokenhearted" not long after the studio session. By that point, the unspoken energy between us had intensified. We moved around each other like opposing magnets—as if actively trying to maintain distance even as we kept finding ourselves drawn into each other's orbit.

The attraction was subtle yet undeniable. It lived in the pauses between conversations, and it lingered in the charged atmosphere surrounding us.

"My girlfriend is sixteen." I don't remember when he first said it. But those four words started rolling off his tongue whenever we were alone. I couldn't tell if this refrain was meant to soothe his own conscience or temper the questions shimmering in my gaze. Perhaps it was his way of tethering himself to a boundary, even as he quietly edged past it. Or maybe it was simply a reminder to himself, a whisper to keep the illicit nature of our connection in view.

Regardless, I was under the impression that we were madly in love—or at least what I believed love to be at sixteen. A grown man's version of love, designed to serve his needs.

Your first real love, your first experience with sex—these

are a natural part of our youth, rites of passage that should unfold with tenderness and care. Mine unfolded under the influence of a man who seemed to know exactly how to make me question my own beliefs and boundaries. And I hung in this strange balance. I was navigating that time in full view of the world, every move scrutinized, every choice dissected by people who didn't know my heart. Part of me wanted to retain some semblance of "normalcy," but also I knew full well that what was happening between me and him was wrong. And yet, my attitude was, *"This was special. This was real. People just can't understand."*

I was young and inexperienced, and thought that following my heart meant following his lead, that what we shared transcended ordinary rules and limitations. I had wanted to wait until marriage and had shared those beliefs with him. But I also believed that having sex with him would cement our bond. Would prove I was mature enough for our relationship. Would make him happy. And so, I told myself I was ready. That this was my choice. But the truth is I felt like I had no choice. I felt like saying no meant losing him.

My first time lacked the specialness I had painted in my mind because it wasn't about me at all. Looking back, in my mind it was about him getting what he wanted from someone too young to recognize she was being used. There was no magic. No romantic tenderness enveloping us. All the passion he expressed through song felt absent because it wasn't lovemaking. I had wanted that milestone to be sacred, and I wanted to feel cherished in his eyes and in his touch. I was too naive to realize that deep down inside he did not see me as special. I think he saw me as conquerable. As someone whose boundaries could be negotiated away.

I was in over my head. Sneaking around and hiding things from my parents had become a constant. They barely liked the idea of me dating at all, and telling them about us was out of question. But it wasn't just about upsetting—or disappointing—my parents. He and I understood, with diamond-cut clarity that public knowledge of our relationship would ignite scandal, potentially threatening everything we'd both worked for. So he and I opted for elaborate fiction: we would pretend patience and claim we were waiting until my eighteenth birthday before pursuing any romantic connection.

I was foolish enough to believe I could successfully maintain this charade. That I could whisper breathlessly with him during late-night phone calls, could blush like a schoolgirl whenever he entered a room, could allow my eyes to linger on him during performances . . . and somehow these telltale signs would escape notice.

My parents confronted me in our living room one evening, their gazes sharp enough to cut through stone.

"What's going on with you and Wanya?"

I told them it was nothing.

Just friendship.

Just music.

Something fundamental fractured between us during this period—a fissure that would gradually widen as I hungered for greater autonomy going from sixteen to seventeen to eighteen.

My mom approached me one afternoon, her voice low with unmistakable gravity: "Are you willing to sacrifice your dream for Wanya?"

"Mom, I love him," I said, finally admitting the truth.

She sucked her teeth and snorted.

"You're not in love!" she shouted. "You don't know what love is . . . you'll see it for yourself."

I lacked vocabulary then for what I was experiencing—the suffocation of existing between the young woman I was becoming and the brand I was building. I rejected the premise that I had to choose between professional fulfillment and emotional connection.

I simply wanted to experience my feelings without apology or justification.

Whatever existed between he and I—it felt real.

I genuinely believed it was true love.

It was a quiet Friday night in. Take out from the Thai spot off Sunset Boulevard that we loved, and a stack of movie rentals awaited us. I was a few months shy of eighteen, and we could stop living in the shadows. For now, spending what time we had together at Wanya's apartment would do. Faith Evans's "Soon as I Get Home" poured out of the sound system in his kitchen as I set out plates, humming along. *I love this song*, I thought. I could connect with the message. He and I spent so little time together. I wanted more than whatever this was, but I figured it would all be easier once I was eighteen.

"You hear that?" he asked me as I dipped a crispy spring roll in neon orange duck sauce. I turned to see him swaying in the corner, eyes closed in concentration.

"Hear what?" I asked, confusion clouding my expression.

He paused the record, then rewound it and hit Play, knocking the volume up a few notches. Faith's voice filled the room briefly before he hit Pause.

"There. Right before the bridge. You hear that melody? Why don't you sing like that?"

"Excuse me?" I asked. I could hear the edge in my voice. This was an unfamiliar tone for me to have taken with him. Maybe I'd misheard him. I didn't understand.

We did this a lot, listen to music together. But that was the first time he'd made a comparative comment. At first, I dismissed it. I gave him the benefit of the doubt. I assumed good intentions, because I couldn't fathom that someone who claims to love you would try to tear you down. Maybe it was his way of encouraging growth and I was misreading his intentions.

But the critiques kept coming. Looking back, I now see them as deliberate—I see them as designed to keep me insecure, to maintain his power, to ensure I stayed grateful for his attention even as I diminished. We could be enjoying a drive, lost in conversation, when a woman's voice floating through car stereo speakers would prompt him to increase the volume and, like clockwork, some comment was made.

"This is how you should approach your lower register."

"You should try emulating her technique . . ."

"Why haven't you done a record like this yet?"

It started to eat at me. As if my own voice perpetually fell short of some invisible standard. I already faced constant comparison from journalists, critics, and radio hosts. All of us girls were placed side by side like collectible dolls on display. I shared this with him and how much the comments and the ridicule hurt me. And it seems to me now that he weaponized that pain, used it to keep me dependent on his approval. .

These little criticisms stacked up. All those insecurities blasted away by growing success suddenly came rushing back.

There were male singers that we both adored, voices that moved and inspired us, but I simply couldn't imagine doing to him what he was doing to me. It made me question everything—my talent, my instincts, my worth. It made me question myself in ways I'd never experienced before, planting seeds of doubt that would grow like weeds in my garden of confidence.

I never shared the discomfort, not out of fear—but simply because I didn't understand what it was, didn't have the language to articulate what was happening to me. Why was he doing this? What was the purpose?

There were all these red flags I couldn't see. I was blinded to the obvious. I used to think I was just so enamored by him, so hungry for his approval, that I ignored them like warning signs written in a language I refused to learn.

Another glaring red flag? I had to page him first. I could never just call him directly. He dictated when and how we communicated. He kept me waiting. This kept me uncertain and grateful for whatever scraps of attention he offered. At first, I reasoned it was to keep our relationship secret, another necessary sacrifice for love. But it went on for longer than I'm proud to admit, this digital leash that kept me tethered to his schedule, his availability, his whims.

These are the things that with hindsight you realize are wildly obvious signs of something wrong, neon warning signs that I chose to ignore because I didn't know what the hell I was doing, or what he was doing with me. Just that I was in love—or what I believed was love.

Then came the ache one afternoon, and I was forced to confront our reality.

I was heading back to set, sitting at a red light, about to make a left onto Sunset Boulevard, when I spotted his car waiting in the opposite lane. In the passenger seat sat his assistant. The way he ran his fingers through her hair said all that needed to be said.

The light turned green and I peeled off, catching one last glimpse of my broken heart in the rearview mirror.

Later that night I asked him: "Are you with her? Have you been with her?"

I could see it all over his face.

He confessed that he'd been sleeping around with other women but denied the assistant was one of them. I was sixteen years old, dealing with the infidelity of a grown man who I believe had pursued me, took my innocence, and was now revealing he'd not been faithful.

I may have been young, but I was wise enough to know I had been played. And that wasn't love.

For years, I struggled with how I was treated in this relationship. He saw a fifteen-year-old girl with rising fame and admiration for his talent, and I believe he deliberately took advantage. This was a twenty-two-year-old man who I believe knew exactly what he was doing when he pursued an underage girl. Looking back, it seems like he chose his moment carefully—reaching out to me when I was young, newly successful, and vulnerable to the attention of someone I idolized. At the time, it felt like a fairy tale. Now I see it as the beginning of a calculated courtship of a teenage girl by a grown man who knew exactly the effect his attention would have.

The shame I have carried over this relationship ends here, buried in these pages like ashes scattered to the wind. I have grown more resentful at his insistence on reframing that time, his continued attempts to rewrite history with himself as the misunderstood romantic lead rather than the adult man he was. His refusal to acknowledge what I believe he did, to take responsibility for the power I believe he wielded and abused, feels like its own form of continued abuse.

Over the years, I've seen him talk about our relationship in interviews and on social media, spinning tales that grow more elaborate with each telling. He's so convinced of the version he's told himself, but somehow can't keep his story straight, the details shifting like sand depending on his audience, his mood, his need for sympathy or admiration.

It's all the more infuriating because the narrative around us thrives, almost entirely, on the cliché of the young ingenue having a schoolgirl crush and getting her heart broken—poor little Brandy, so naive, so dramatic, so unable to handle adult relationships. This framing erases his culpability entirely. It centers my naivety instead of his manipulation. It asks why I didn't know better instead of why he didn't do better.

This idea that I was head over heels in puppy love and he had to let me down gently, like he was doing me a favor by breaking my heart, like I should be grateful for the lesson in disappointment he provided.

I was fifteen and he was twenty-one when we first met—old enough to know better, old enough to understand the power dynamics at play. We were in a different time, culturally, when men were seen as boys being boys, their seemingly predatory behavior excused as natural instinct, and we were seen as young, "fast" girls with crushes, our pain dismissed as dramatic over-reaction. It takes the responsibility off of the men and places it squarely on the shoulders of girls who were never equipped to carry such weight.

I have struggled not just with the shame I hold like a stone in my chest, but with the extent to which I have been left to hold it alone. I have taken responsibility for my feelings, for disrespecting my parents' wishes and getting involved with an older man despite their concerns. But shame wasn't the only reason for my silence all these years. Consideration was—for myself, for my daughter, for my family, for him and his family, for the complicated web of relationships and reputations that would be affected by the truth. I hope, from here on out, I'll receive the same consideration from him."I was young too. I wasn't 38 years old or nothing like that," he says, his voice carrying the practiced innocence of someone who's told this lie so many times he almost believes it himself. "She was old enough to get it... We didn't do it in states where it was illegal."

That last line says so much. This wasn't love. This was a man who knew exactly how to stay within the technical boundaries of the law while in my view completely obliterating the moral ones.

"It was a relationship, and it grew, and it un-grew." That's how he describes it, like we were plants in a garden that just naturally bloomed and withered with the seasons. As if he had no agency. As if he didn't cultivate it. I don't think a grown man pursuing a teenage girl just 'happens' naturally. As he tells it, my mother reached out to him because I was a fan, and I became his protégé. Again, this places the onus not just on me, but on my mother, painting her as complicit.

This is a difficult subject for me to write about, to excavate these memories that I've kept buried like bodies in a graveyard. Interrogating this time in my life has been profoundly painful, like performing surgery on myself without anesthesia.

I believed I was making decisions I wanted to make, that I was in control of my own story. That belief protected me from the truth: I wasn't in control. Looking back, I believe he was. Every decision I thought was mine seems to have been shaped by his influence.

Our brains are remarkable at protecting us from truths too painful to bear, convincing us we are autonomous in our decisions even when we're being systematically manipulated. That we are in control even when someone else is pulling all the strings. This is why we can't blame victims for not recognizing their abuse in real time.

I thought I was dating a person I wanted to be dating, not recognizing that my wants had been carefully cultivated, my desires shaped by someone who knew exactly how to make a teenage girl feel special, chosen, mature beyond her years.

There may have been some part of me that believed I would get in trouble or be judged, but being with him felt worth the risk because he'd convinced me that what we shared was rare, special, worth any sacrifice. And there's a heightened sense, when you are young and suddenly famous, that you're different from other teenagers, more mature, more worldly, more capable of handling adult situations.

It was not about rebelling against my parents, nor was I thinking this was someone who is older and taking advantage of my naiveté. This was me believing an idea of love that had been carefully constructed and fed to me by someone who knew exactly how to manipulate a young girl's understanding of romance, affection, and her own worth.

There have been plenty of cruel jokes at my expense over the years, each one a fresh wound on scars that never fully healed. Being taken advantage of as an immature teenager and then having it thrown in your face for the next 30 years is a kind of cruelty only reserved for women.

The shame ends here. The silence ends here.

I was not a fast girl with a crush. I was not a dramatic teenager who couldn't handle rejection. I was not an unstable obsessive fan.

I was a child. He was an adult. And it's time the world understood the difference.

A NEW DAY IS DAWNING

MOESHA SHOULDN'T HAVE been groundbreaking when it debuted on January 23, 1996. The television landscape was already saturated with coming-of-age series. Between *Saved by the Bell, Blossom, Beverly Hills, 90210, Clarissa Explains It All*, and *Boy Meets World*, America had feasted on teenage angst served through a particular lens: white, middle-class, and polished to a suburban shine.

Black girls rarely existed in these worlds, and when they did, we did not always get a full view of them. Sara Finney-Johnson and Vida Spears understood this reality when they began developing *Moesha* in 1993. They wanted to give young Black girls their own *Blossom*, their own *Clarissa Explains It All*. And so, they built a world around the character they longed to see on-screen—a girl named Moesha Denise Mitchell.

Sara and Vida were rarities—one of the few Black female writing teams who had managed to carve out space in writers' rooms where they were often the only women of color. They'd cut their teeth as program consultants on *The Jeffersons*, penning an episode before moving on to *The Facts of Life*. By the time *Moesha* was forming in their minds, they were writing and producing *Family Matters*, weaving stories about the Winslow family that the nation devoured every Friday night.

To sharpen their concept, they brought in Ralph Farquhar, a veteran writer who'd walked the halls of *Happy Days* and weathered the raunchy terrain of *Married . . . with Children.* After producing *The Sinbad Show*, Ralph had co-created *South Central*, a sitcom that dared to show a struggling single mother without sanitizing her reality. When Sara and Vida envisioned Moesha as a fourteen-year-old navigating adolescence in South Central Los Angeles, it was one of Ralph's writers who whispered my name into the mix.

Having worked with Ray J on *The Sinbad Show*, Ralph was no stranger to my family. He slipped the script to my father.

I was in the studio when my mom floated in. Her eyes sparkled with that particular maternal knowing, the kind that sees around corners and through walls. Under her arm was a binder, clutched like it contained state secrets.

"So, Bran," she said, her voice casual but her eyes intense, "there's this pilot that came our way." She settled beside me. "It's about this young girl growing up in Leimert Park. Her name's Moesha and—" she paused, letting the significance sink in "—the creator wants to meet you. He wants *you* to play Moesha."

The name caught in my ears like a familiar melody. "Her name is Moesha?" I asked, suddenly invested.

"A smart Black girl finding herself," she continued, her eyes never leaving mine. "There isn't anything like this on TV right now." Her fingers tapped the binder lightly. "It has you written all over it."

I glanced down at the script but didn't reach for it. The weight of what she was suggesting felt heavier than I could grapple with. "My own show?" I shook my head, the memory of *Thea* still raw. "I don't know about all of that. I don't think TV is for me."

She sat down next to me then, taking my hands in hers. Her palms were warm, soft from the cocoa butter she religiously applied.

"Don't let one bad experience keep you from doing what we both know you love," she said, voice gentle but firm. "I wouldn't have rushed over here if I didn't think this was worth considering."

"You really think I could do it?" The question came out smaller than I'd intended, a child's voice emerging from a teenager's body.

There was no hesitation from her, not even a blink. "She reminds me so much of you—especially the girl you turn into when we get to McComb. Bran, I'm telling you, it's not just a part—it's *you.* The way she sees the world, how she's trying to find her place in it, trying to hold on to who she is while everything around her is changing . . ."

She slid the binder toward me, her fingernails—painted a deep burgundy that week—tapping it for emphasis.

"Just read the first few pages. If it doesn't move you, I'll drop it. But . . ." She stood up, smoothing her dress, confidence radiating from her like heat. "I think you're going to see what I see when you read it."

That night, I crawled into bed—binder in hand. The day's exhaustion clung to me like a second skin, my muscles aching from hours in the studio. But my mother's certainty, her unwavering belief that this story would speak to me, made me flip to the first page despite my heavy eyelids.

I was sold from just the cold open.

```
INT. MOESHA'S BEDROOM-NIGHT

                    MOESHA (V.O.)

          They say the first love is
         the perfect love, something I
        won't know for two more months
         because my Amish father won't
        let me date or use electricity
         until I'm sixteen. But what's
           the difference? With this
          gigantic zit on my face, no
           boy would want me anyway.
```

The world of Crenshaw High School unfolded before me—a Black girl with a rich interior life, navigating the turbulence of adolescence while dealing with the complexities of her identity. Moesha was confident but vulnerable, wise but wonderfully naive (to a fault, at times). The strict father, the well-meaning stepmother who disrupted the family's balance, the annoying little brother who somehow always found his way into Moesha's business—these weren't just characters; they were a reflection of a modern family.

I could see Moesha flopped across her bed, writing furiously in her diary, the glow of her desk lamp casting shadows across her braided hair. I could hear her laughter as she traded jokes with her friends in the hallway, their voices a symphony of Black girl joy. I could feel her frustration as she pushed against the boundaries her father set. I could *see* her, right on the page.

A realization came over me.

This wasn't just about acting. It wasn't even just about the story. It was about showing girls like me that their stories mattered. I wasn't entirely convinced I was ready—but I was starting to feel like maybe I had to be.

The pilot was refreshing, but meeting with Ralph was what sold me. The world around Moesha would be honest to the culture and environment she inhabited. Her family lived in Leimert Park, a historic Black middle-class enclave of Los Angeles that's long been a hub of Black cultural expression. The community and culture of the neighborhood would be an integral part of the show, and we'd explore provocative subjects young people were navigating: Premarital sex. Teen pregnancy. Drug use. Inequality. Racism. Sexuality. Gender prejudice. Poverty and food insecurity. Sexual violence. Mental health. Abandonment. *Moesha* wouldn't be afraid to go there.

I had no idea what a show pitch was—or even looked like. We were escorted into a boardroom that stretched before us like a football field. What caught my eye, though, were the photographs scattered across the table like confetti—my face staring back at me from photo shoots that already felt like a distant memory.

They placed me at the head of the table, the room humming with expectation.

I didn't know what to say, so I said the first thing that bubbled up from my nervous throat:

"I understand you all wanted to talk with me?"

The room erupted in laughter. Ralph shot me a wink from across the table, his eyes twinkling with approval. Then he launched into the pitch, his voice painting pictures in the air between us.

Ten minutes into his pitch, one of the suits—a man with salt-and-pepper hair and glasses that caught the light—threw his hands up in a gesture of surrender.

"I don't know about the rest of you," he said, his voice cutting through the room like a blade, "but I think we've heard enough. We're in."

Moesha was greenlit for a pilot.

With no time to prepare, Ralph took me to read lines for the network and my worst fears were confirmed. I was . . . absolutely terrible. There's no other way to describe it. Maybe it was jitters vibrating through my body. Maybe it was the self-doubt that had taken root during my time on *Thea* or the painful memories from Hollywood High. Whatever the cause, the result was clear: I adored this character on the page, but I could not breathe life into her when the spotlight turned on.

Ralph, in a move that changed everything, reached out to Kim Fields, who had played Tootie on *The Facts of Life* and Regine on *Living Single.* She understood what it meant to grow up on camera, to carry the weight of a show on young shoulders. She also knew the added pressure of stepping into a role that little Black girls across America would look up to.

Ralph made an extraordinary request—would Kim accompany me on tour and help me prepare for the table read? It was asking for the moon and stars, but Kim, in an act of generosity I still can't fully comprehend, said yes. Ten years my senior, Kim became my mentor. She came from entertainment royalty; her mother, Chip, was a legendary actress, and her younger sister, Alexis, was starring on *Roc*, one of the few hit Black series on air back then. In a beautiful twist of fate, Alexis's character on *Roc* had actually served as an early inspiration for Moesha when she was conceived of as a fourteen-year-old. Years later, Alexis would join our cast in a recurring role as Alicia, a vapid mean girl who clashed with Moesha and her friends with delicious regularity.

Kim approached acting as a sacred craft. If we had ten minutes between sound check and performance, she was running me through an exercise. After one of my shows, Kim handed me a hardbound journal, its cover a rich burgundy leather.

"Write out Moesha's world," she instructed, her eyes serious. "Who is she? What motivates her?"

As America flashed past the windows of my tour bus, I filled those blank pages with the soul of a girl I was coming to love. I wrote about her yearning for independence, her search for identity, her awkward, beautiful journey toward womanhood. I detailed her hopes and fears, the music that made her want to dance, the dreams that kept her awake at night. I mapped the geography of her friendships, the complex terrain of her family dynamics, the uncharted territory of first loves and heartbreaks.

By the time I arrived at the table read, Moesha wasn't just a character I was playing—she was living inside me, her heartbeat synced with mine. Thanks to Kim Fields, I nailed it.

While touring with Boyz II Men, Wanya helped me develop an idea for the show's theme song—something youthful and vibrant, a clever nod to my own musical journey. Ralph's younger brother, a genius who had composed themes for some of the most beloved Black sitcoms of our time, came on board to bring the melody to life. As a young songwriter still finding her voice, I felt empowered, assured, and deeply connected to the words:

Up in the morning
A new day is dawning
It's me, it's me
Now am I realizing my responsibility?
It's me
My best friends are always on my mind
If you wanna be down, come on
Gotta do what I gotta do
I gotta move on

In *Moesha*, I found a portal to an alternate reality where I could experience normal teenage life. Behind the cameras, I could be just a regular girl with friends and crushes and homework. In that strange paradox, I found escape and peace, a respite from the relentless demands of being Brandy.

Whatever self-doubt had plagued me melted away after the pilot taping. The cast that surrounded me wasn't just talented—they were family. Theater legend Sheryl Lee Ralph embodied Moesha's stepmother, Dee, with such warmth and complexity that I often found myself turning to her for motherly advice even when the cameras weren't rolling. Countess Vaughn and Shar Jackson, perfectly cast as Moesha's best friends Kim and Niecy, sharpened my comedic timing with their razor-sharp delivery and infectious energy. William Allen Young, who played Moesha's father, Frank, became a true father figure, dispensing wisdom and corny jokes in equal measure. Lamont Bentley took on the role of protective big brother both on- and off-screen, while young Marcus Paulk reminded us all of our responsibility as role models. The set became a sanctuary, a place where I felt safe to try, to fail, to grow.

The physical act of transforming into Moesha was simple but effective: wardrobe dressed me in pleated, high-waisted pants, a cropped long-sleeve top, and an embroidered vest that captured the essence of '90s teen fashion. My braids were gathered into two high ponytails, and a touch of rouge warmed my complexion.

When I stepped onto the soundstage for the first time, the audience erupted like a volcano. That breath in time is etched in my memory more vividly than anything else from those early days: the roar, the pulse, the pure, unbridled energy of that crowd. I had more lines in the first five pages of the pilot than I ever did in a whole episode of *Thea*. During the table read, I felt like a sprinter trying to keep pace with Olympic champions.

There's a pivotal scene in the pilot where Moesha learns a hard lesson about trust and heartbreak. She sneaks out to meet a boy she's crushing on, only to discover he's seeing someone else. She returns home, her pride in tatters. Dee attempts to clear the air, but Moesha crumbles under the weight of her humiliation.

"It's just this stupid boy," she says, tears streaming down her face.

I had never mastered the art of crying on cue. In private, my emotions flowed freely, but in front of cameras, they seemed to freeze. So, I approached Sheryl, hoping she might share some of her theatrical wisdom.

"Crying isn't just sadness," she told me, her voice low and melodic. "It's truth. The body doesn't know the difference between real and imagined—if you believe it, the tears will come."

She led me to a quiet corner of the set, away from curious eyes and listening ears.

"Close your eyes," she instructed. "Think of something you've truly lost. Not what you think should make you cry—something that actually did."

I followed her guidance, feeling awkward at first, then slowly slipping into memory.

"Now," she whispered, her voice floating through the darkness behind my closed eyelids, "don't run from it. Walk straight into it. Let it fill your chest until there's no room left."

The first tear slid down my cheek before I even registered it was forming. Warm. Heavy. It contained a sorrow I hadn't acknowledged, a loss I'd been carrying like a stone.

"There it is," Sheryl said softly. "The most powerful thing you can do is not pretend—but reveal. That's the gift we give. Our truth."

We were proud of the pilot. The audience had laughed and gasped and applauded in all the right places. But at the network, the response was mixed. Some executives saw the vision, understood the potential. Others hesitated. CBS passed on the show. The producers began shopping it around to other networks, and we encountered a quiet resistance that spoke volumes. No one said *Moesha* was too Black—not in those exact words. Instead, we heard euphemisms: "too ethnic," "too specific," "not universal enough."

Then UPN came into play.

The fledgling network was hungry for content that would attract an underserved audience, and they saw in *Moesha* a portal into a world that television had largely ignored. With their green light, *Moesha* would become a flash point for Black girlhood on television.

As a midseason replacement, *Moesha* debuted in the second half of the traditional TV season. The show caught fire quickly, and by the end of our first season, we had become a genuine sensation. While the overall ratings weren't shattering records, the show was dominating in key markets. In Atlanta, *Moesha* brought the UPN affiliate its highest ratings in its fifteen-year history. In Los Angeles, we ranked second among teen viewers during sweeps, beaten only by the juggernaut that was *The Simpsons*. We produced fourteen episodes that first season, and the network ordered twenty-two for the next—our renewal coming a full six weeks before any other show on the slate.

With acclaim and success came crushing pressure. *Stay low and keep moving.* That became my mantra, the words my parents had whispered to me when things began taking off. It was advice meant to keep me grounded, focused, humble—and it helped. Having my family beside me made the impossible feel manageable. It was why, even after turning eighteen, I wasn't rushing to move out on my own. Instead, I indulged in a different kind of freedom: I bought the gold Lexus I'd been coveting since seeing it in a music video. Driving through Los Angeles with the windows down and music pulsing through the speakers was the closest I got to being a normal teenager. I cherished those rare slivers of liberty—taking Ray J shopping at the Beverly Center, grabbing dinner with my best friend Joi, pretending for an hour or two that I wasn't "Brandy" but just Brandy.

But balancing *Moesha* while recording my second album nearly broke me. As number one on the call sheet, I carried the heaviest load—scene after scene, week after week. During shooting weeks, we'd begin with a table read at dawn, move into blocking, then rehearsal, and finally filming. When the director called wrap, I'd head straight to the recording studio, often working until the early hours of the morning before grabbing a few precious hours of sleep and starting the cycle again.

When it came time to promote my music, my days stretched beyond what seemed humanly possible. Makeup at 7 a.m., hair at 8 (unless my braids needed redoing, which was an hours-long process in itself), styling at 9, interviews at 10, radio appearances at 11. A hurried lunch, then back to the *Moesha* set for the afternoon. Exhaustion became my shadow. I hid it well, plastering on smiles for cameras and interviewers. I was living a dream bigger than anything I'd imagined—and I didn't want to seem ungrateful.

But beneath the surface, I was barely treading water.

A few weeks into production for season three, I walked into my mother's office, my body heavy with fatigue, my mind clouded with something close to despair.

"I need to pull back from the show," I said without preamble.

"What do you mean, 'pull back'?" she asked, setting down the papers she'd been reviewing.

"I just . . . I need a break. Can't they write me out for a few episodes?"

She gave me a look that I knew all too well—one that told me I wasn't about to hear what I wanted.

"Bran . . . it doesn't work like that."

"No one told me it would be like this," I said, my voice cracking, betraying emotions I'd been bottling up for months. "You said if I didn't want to do this, I didn't have to."

Her voice softened but remained firm. "Once you sign those contracts, you do."

"Why can't you just be my mom right now?" I stormed out of her office, slamming the door behind me.

What I'd said was unfair. I knew it as the words left my lips. She was right—and we both knew it. I had agreed to another season of *Moesha* because, deep down, I wanted to do it. The issue wasn't the show—it was that I said yes to everything. I wanted the superstar career, the name in lights, the face on billboards. I wanted music and television and film and endorsements. I wanted it all.

So, during hiatuses, when I should have been recharging, I kept pushing. I said yes to *Cinderella*, to *I Still Know What You Did Last Summer*, to *Double Platinum*. I kept moving, even when my body and spirit begged for stillness.

But on Friday nights, after a grueling week of filming, nothing felt more luxurious than stretching out on my own bed with a movie and a large box of hot, crispy McDonald's fries beside me. Those slivers of solitude became sacred in a life that felt increasingly out of my control.

I also found sanctuary in braiding sessions. They remained rare shimmers in time when I could let my mind wander without agenda or expectation. It wasn't until that first season of *Moesha* that I truly understood the power my hair carried. At a promotional photo shoot with Countess, we both wore our hair in braids—mine styled into two high ponytails that crowned my head, hers gathered into a sultry bun. We looked beautiful, stylish, authentic—and most importantly, we looked like average Black girls. Time and again, I heard stories from young viewers who felt seen for the first time, who finally had someone on TV who looked like them and their friends.

Between filming and promoting my music, I wore every style of braid imaginable, each type telling its own story, carrying its own history. Some echoed the crowns worn by African queens centuries before. Others were modern reinventions, maps of identity and belonging. Cornrows following the curves of my scalp in delicate patterns, box braids with their perfect geometric precision, micro-braids fine as silk threads.

During production, the braiding sessions were marathon affairs. What had begun as an intimate ritual between my mother and me expanded to include a team of skilled hands working in perfect harmony. They would gather at my home, four to six people working simultaneously to create tiny, intricate braids that would take hours to complete. I would doze or study lines or listen to demo tracks as they worked their magic, transforming my hair into Moesha's signature style.

I never considered my hair revolutionary. But I now understand that braids connect us across time and space, linking past to present to future. They are an homage to those who came before and a promise to those who will follow. And I take immense pride knowing that my hair created space in popular culture for Black girls to see their own styles celebrated, elevated, and adored.

As much as I appreciated the writers' commitment to crafting provocative stories about teenage life, I struggled with Moesha's worldview. She was refreshingly headstrong, assertive, and outspoken—qualities rarely allowed for Black girls on-screen. She pushed back against sexism and misogyny, fought for agency over her body and dating life, and never wavered even when her father took an adversarial stance against her choices.

And yet there were times when Moesha could be incredibly judgmental, even cruel, especially to those who loved her most. She could be regressive, contradicting her own feminist principles. Nothing grated on me more than how she sometimes treated her best friends, making jokes about their bodies, their socioeconomic status, their intelligence. How could a show meant to empower young Black girls feature a protagonist who engaged in body-shaming or slut-shaming? The true magic of the series, in my opinion, was the sisterhood between Moesha, Kim, and Niecy—and I worried that we sometimes undermined that magic with cheap jokes.

I understand it was a product of its time, with writers trying to balance traditional sitcom humor with authentic teenage dynamics. But there were moments when I worried we were undercutting our own potential.

I gave so much of my childhood to Moesha, and the irony wasn't lost on me that this character's life was so different from my own. Moesha got to make mistakes, to stumble and fall and pick herself back up. She dated freely, explored her feelings about sex, made her own choices about her body. She wore what she wanted, said what she thought, enjoyed freedoms

I could only dream about. The life Moesha led was a universe away from what I could be as Brandy.

Between the success of my debut album and *Moesha* becoming a hit, I was catapulted to a level of fame that left me disoriented. I began to lose sight of myself beneath the layers of expectation and performance. I struggled to reconcile normal teenage desires with the complications of celebrity and the responsibilities that came with it. Everything in my personal life became classified information, buried beneath secrecy and discretion. I couldn't do anything that might tarnish the image of Brandy or Moesha—the music and the show would suffer, and so would everyone who depended on their success.

Brandy was a persona; Moesha was a persona. And somewhere beneath it all was me—the real me, who just wanted to sing and go to the mall, ride roller coasters at Magic Mountain, date boys without worrying about ending up in tabloids.

I deliberately kept music separate from Moesha; it was an intentional choice that the character couldn't sing. But even with this boundary in place, it became impossible for audiences to separate this fictional character from the real Brandy. They were watching both of us grow up simultaneously, and in their eyes, we might as well have been the same person. I knew the show had truly penetrated the cultural consciousness when people stopped calling me Brandy altogether and addressed me only as Moesha.

Although I loved losing myself in this complex character, the blurred lines between us left me increasingly uncertain of my own identity. Where did Moesha end and Brandy begin? It was only a matter of time before the weight of these questions, of the punishing schedule, of the relentless expectations, came crashing down around me.

But that's a story for another chapter.

R&B

RAY J AND I were born just twenty-five months apart. We've always been each other's compass, pointing true north when the world spins chaotic. And we still are. In my most precious memories of childhood, Ray is right there beside me. Riding bikes under the summer sun. Singing in the choir. Learning music with our dad. Searching for pennies with our Paw Paw. Shuttling to talent shows.

I can still feel the scorching asphalt beneath our bike tires as we raced down Carson streets, the summer heat shimmering above the pavement like dreams made visible. I can hear our voices blending in church, his tenor finding the spaces between my soprano, creating harmonies that made the stained-glass windows tremble. I remember Paw Paw whispering "Y'all gonna be worth more than these one day, remember that."

But there were shadows, too—times when Ray disappeared from view, wandering paths I couldn't follow. Before Woodland Hills and its manicured lawns welcomed us, the South Bay held us in its complicated embrace. And Carson? Carson had its teeth in Ray.

I'd come home from dance practice to find his room empty, window open, the curtains dancing with night air.

"Mom," I'd say, my voice deliberately casual as I helped her fold laundry. "You might want to check under Ray's bed. Just saying."

Or over breakfast: "Dad, did you look in on Ray last night? I thought I heard something."

I never outright snitched, but I left breadcrumbs. And when those breadcrumbs led our parents to Ray's empty bed or to friends they'd never heard of, I felt no remorse. Love doesn't always wear a smile. Sometimes love is the voice that raises the alarm.

When Ray was thirteen, gang colors started appearing in his wardrobe—subtle hints of affiliation that made my stomach knot with fear. Our family moved with the swiftness of a tornado. Within days, Ray was living with our mother's closest friend in a different neighborhood. Carson wasn't just dangerous for him anymore; it was hungry for him.

Then came television. Working with Immature. Record deals. Our family's address changed to Woodland Hills, and suddenly, we were Ray J and Brandy. R&B.

When we joined Immature on tour, I watched Ray's talent unfold like a rare flower. There was something magnetic about his style—raw, unfiltered, touched by something divine. But it was his attention to detail that really made him special. Ray studied music intensely. He'd fixate on arrangements and melody and developed quite the ear long before he started writing his own lyrics. He'd listen to my songs late at night, cross-legged on hotel room floors, nodding with his eyes closed.

"That's it, B," he'd say, snapping his fingers to an invisible beat. "That line right there? That's the one that's gonna make 'em cry."

"Best Friend," my favorite record from my first album, started as our song—a duet that would tell the world what we meant to each other. I can still see us in the studio, sharing a microphone, giggling between takes.

"You're flat," I'd tease.

"You're sharp," he'd counter.

But the truth was, Ray's voice wasn't ready. His gift was still ripening. The day I had to tell him he wouldn't be singing on the track, we sat at a park near the studio, the Los Angeles skyline glittering in the distance.

"They said no," I whispered, unable to meet his eyes.

Ray was quiet for so long I thought he might be angry. When I finally looked up, he was smiling—a smile tinged with disappointment but not defeat.

"It's all good, B. I'll be in the video, right? Besides—" he nudged my shoulder with his "—I ain't ready to share a stage with the great Brandy Norwood yet anyway."

But I heard the catch in his voice. I felt the weight of his sacrifice.

The finished song became something precious to us. Families across the world embracing the record as their own has been one of my life's greatest joys. At cookouts and weddings, I've seen siblings sway to the words I sang for Ray, and my heart threatens to burst from my chest.

Don't know what I'd ever do without you
From the beginning to the end
You've always been here right beside me
So, I'll call you my best friend

To this day, some of my favorite recordings carry Ray's invisible signature—his suggestion for a harmony change here, his background vocals there. We've sketched plans for a joint album on napkins and in late-night text messages, but neither of us has pulled the trigger. That duet version of "Best Friend" still exists, locked away in a vault somewhere. Maybe someday, when the time feels right, we'll share it with the world.

There's a particular kind of heartache that comes from watching someone you love be overlooked. It cuts deeper than your own disappointments, burns hotter than your own failures. This is what happened when Ray released *Everything You Want* in 1997.

I remember him pacing the kitchen the week before recording began, his energy electric, contagious.

"I'm ready, B," he said, gesturing with hands that couldn't stay still. "Got the best team. Darryl's overseeing everything. Keith Crouch is handling production. This is it. This is my moment."

He'd spent months finding his voice—not mine, not our father's, but purely his. I'd visit the studio and lean against the wall, watching him work with a rigor that both surprised and moved me. The music they created was incredible—simultaneously rooted in R&B tradition while pushing against its boundaries. Funky. Soulful. Forward-thinking.

When they played me the rough mix of "Let It Go," I grabbed both Ray's and my mother's hands.

"This is it," I whispered, my eyes wide with certainty. "This single is going to change everything. You're about to take off."

My mom nodded, her eyes glistening. "My baby," she said simply, squeezing his fingers.

Ray just smiled—confident, ready.

And initially, we were right. "Let It Go" rocketed up the charts, cracking the top 25 on Billboard's Hot 100 and becoming one of the year's bestselling singles. The cassette and CD singles flew off the shelves. Ray was everywhere—radio interviews, television appearances. The buzz around his debut album was deafening.

But when *Everything You Want* finally dropped, something inexplicable happened. Or rather, didn't happen. The album, despite the huge success of its lead single, stalled. Radio stations that had kept "Let It Go" on rotation didn't pick up the follow-up singles. The anticipated sales never materialized. The momentum didn't pick up.

One night, it was just us at home, lounging and watching old reruns.

"B?" Ray's voice was smaller than I'd ever heard it.

"Yeah," I said, sitting up on the couch.

"I don't get it," he said after a long pause. "I gave them everything. I gave them me. Why don't they see me?"

The vulnerability in his voice shattered something in me. Ray—my fearless, irrepressible baby brother—sounded lost.

"They're blind," I said fiercely. "And deaf. And stupid. Your album is brilliant, Ray. Time will prove it."

But even as I spoke, guilt was taking root in my chest, spreading its tendrils around my heart. I began to wonder if my success had inadvertently cast a shadow over him. If "Brandy's brother" had become both his introduction *and* his limitation.

I started praying differently at night. Instead of asking for my own blessings, I begged God to redirect them to Ray. I would gladly take second place, third place, no place at all—if only he could have his fair chance to shine.

Watching our mother during this period nearly broke me. Sonja Norwood, the woman who could sell us "to the ocean, and the ocean would buy us," as she often joked, was struggling to mask her heartbreak. But around Ray, she maintained her fortress of strength.

"It's just the first album," she'd assure him, her voice steady as bedrock. "We're playing the long game here."

But I caught the stolen seconds when she thought no one was watching. One evening, I came home after a recording session ended early. The house was quiet, and I found my mother sitting alone at the table, her normally immaculate makeup streaked down her cheeks, shoulders curved inward like wilting flowers.

She flinched when I touched her.

"Mom," I whispered, fear climbing my throat.

"I'm fine, baby," she said too quickly, straightening her spine. "I'm just tired."

I sat beside her and took her hand. We didn't speak much. We didn't need to. These weren't tears shed over chart positions or sales figures. These were tears of frustration at media outlets that insisted on making every success a comparison.

Ray and I never subscribed to that narrative. We'd hear stories about famous siblings tearing each other apart over record releases or film opportunities, and we'd shake our heads in disbelief. That darkness never found purchase between us.

A few months after Ray J's album came out, Disney came calling. A concert series aimed at younger viewers was being launched on the Disney Channel, and they wanted Ray J to headline a special. When he asked if I would join him, it was an easy yes. I would have helped my brother in any way I could, *but* this was extra special for me. I loved singing with Ray, and any excuse to work together, we always took it. And now we were doing a TV special, *together*, and it was going to be filmed at Disneyland? This was yet another one of those times when I needed to pinch myself, just to know I was standing in my body and this was my life.

Hidden deep inside the happiest place on earth was a nondescript production facility that was base camp for our rehearsals. Ray had the focus of someone with everything to prove and nothing to lose. His stage presence was electrifying, and it made me so proud to watch him come alive with the band the way I'd seen him in the studio.

Our Mississippi summers, those carefree days riding bikes under the thick Southern heat, seemed impossibly distant from our present reality. Now we were, quite literally, walking through a fairy-tale castle on our way to work.

Between rehearsals for the Disney special, Ray and I stole an afternoon for ourselves, just brother and sister—and a park escort that would sneak us to the front of the lines.

Main Street U.S.A. unfurled before us, a pastel-colored fantasy of turn-of-the-century America that never actually existed.

The morning sun caught the fresh paint on the Victorian facades as cast members rushed to their positions. The scent of waffle cones and brewing coffee collided with the artificial butterscotch pumped through hidden vents, creating that signature Disney perfume.

"Remember that commercial we used to see?" Ray said, his eyes scanning the storefronts. "The one with the jingle?"

"'I'm going to Disneyland!'" we sang in unison, then dissolved into laughter.

Ray grabbed my hand, suddenly solemn. "We made it, B. Look at us. We used to beg Mom and Dad to bring us to Disneyland on the weekends, and now we're here filming a concert special! Me and you." His voice caught on the last word, and I squeezed his fingers in mine.

"I hope you know how proud I am of you," I said. "Of us."

The afternoon passed in a sun-drenched dream state. The guide took us on a giant loop around the park. We conquered Big Thunder Mountain Railroad, crashed down Splash Mountain at the precise second a park photographer captured Ray's face contorted in what can only be described as elegant terror, and wandered through Adventureland as the shadows lengthened across the pavement. We took countless photos and signed autographs for every kid who ran up to us.

As dusk descended, turning the sky the color of bruised plums, we found ourselves back on Main Street. The nightly electrical parade was hours away and people were staking claims along the route, spreading blankets and unpacking snacks with the serious focus of settlers claiming Frontierland.

"One more ride?" I suggested, though my feet were throbbing in protest.

Ray pointed toward the Matterhorn, its faux-alpine peak now glowing softly in the twilight. "For old times' sake."

The Matterhorn bobsleds were exactly as I remembered—jerky, ice-cold, and leaving bruises in places you didn't know could bruise. We screamed our way through the mountain's twists and turns, past the glowing red eyes of the Abominable Snowman, and back into the warm California night.

As we staggered off the ride, Ray threw his arm around my shoulders. "Best day ever?"

"Top five, at least," I conceded, leaning into his embrace.

We walked back to the rehearsal studio, both pretending we weren't limping slightly. The day's perfect bubble was thinning; tomorrow would bring cameras and expectations, interviews and obligations. The Disney special, Ray's next single, my upcoming project—all waiting for us beyond the park gates.

But for these stolen hours, we'd been just Ray and Brandy again.

The night of the concert, magic hung in the air. Under a canopy of stars, with Sleeping Beauty's castle illuminated behind us, we took the stage. Ray moved like electricity in human form. The crowd didn't see "Brandy's brother"; they saw Ray J, star in his own constellation. They screamed his name. They knew every word to "Let It Go."

We closed the show with our duet, "Thank You"—a song about unconditional love and unwavering support. As the final chorus approached, the lights dimmed everywhere except on us.

Thank you for the good times
Thank you for the ups and downs with you
Glad it's you that's on my side
Any way it goes I thank you

As we sang the last line, Ray turned to me—not playing to the cameras or the audience, but looking directly into my eyes. We weren't performers but simply siblings who had traveled an improbable road together.

"Thank you," he mouthed, just for me.

And I whispered back, "Always."

Bathed in spotlight and stardust, I realized something: maybe my success wasn't overshadowing his path, but illuminating it. Perhaps I wasn't a barrier, but a bridge.

Ray will probably read this and shake his head, telling me I'm being too hard on myself—again. He's been telling me that for years, but my struggle with self-worth often made his reassurances sound like distant echoes. Feeling undeserving of my opportunities and accolades, I would have traded it all to see him celebrated equally.

Yet what makes me proudest of my brother isn't his accomplishments—though they are many—but his resilience. His ability to reinvent himself. To build his own empire on his own terms. To remain fearlessly, unapologetically Ray J.

We are still each other's best friend. We are still each other's biggest fan. We are still Ray J and Brandy—R&B—finding our way through this complicated world, together.

THE FAIREST OF THEM ALL

AS A LITTLE GIRL growing up in Carson, California, I harbored three dreams that burned like constellations across the midnight sky of my imagination: to be a star whose light reached the farthest corners of the world, to have a band whose harmonies would echo through time, and to meet my North Star—Whitney Houston.

The first time her voice found me, she was performing (you guessed it) "The Greatest Love of All" on television. The memory lives in my body like muscle memory. Our living room bathed in the blue-white glow of the screen, Mom and Dad settled into our worn couch, while Ray and I sprawled between their feet on the carpet, the fibers tickling our elbows. But when this woman—this vision—appeared on-screen, something magnetic pulled me forward. I rose without thinking, drawn by some invisible force, and positioned myself mere inches from the screen, so close I could feel the static electricity kissing my cheeks.

Whitney stood there in a delicate white cocktail dress that cascaded like moonlight down to her knees, her hair styled into a halo of tight, bouncy curls that framed her face like God had personally sculpted each one. It was just her onstage, a microphone clutched in her elegant fingers, a row of spotlights bathing her in divine light, as though heaven itself had opened up to illuminate her.

I couldn't have been more than seven, my body still all knees and elbows, my hair in careful braids my mom had stayed up late to perfect the night before, but the experience was close to spiritual awakening. And that voice. Lord, that voice. Even now, decades later, I struggle to find words capacious enough to describe what hearing Whitney Houston sing did to me that night.

Her voice seemed to erupt from within, vast and untouchable, like some force of nature that had chosen her as its vessel. Her tone flowed like a clear river—deep and steady in its course, yet capable of sudden, powerful swells that could lift you clean off your feet and carry you away. She could soar high and hit these angelic notes that sliced through the air like shards of glass, yet her lower register held a warm, velvet tone that invited you into the most tender parts of her soul.

It wasn't just me who fell under her spell. When we gathered as a family to watch Whitney sing the national anthem at the Super Bowl, I witnessed firsthand how her voice transfixed everyone it touched. Mom and Dad sat there, eyes glistening, hands clapping so furiously you'd have thought they were right there in the Tampa stadium instead of our living room in Carson. My dad let out a long, low whistle after her final note—his highest form of praise.

"That's what greatness looks like, baby," he said. "Remember this."

Watching how Whitney wielded her instrument, how her voice reached into people's chests and rearranged things inside them, flipped a switch deep within me. I knew with bone-deep certainty what I wanted—no, what I was born to do. I was born to sing like Whitney. I was born to make people feel the way she made me feel.

"Mom," I whispered that night as she tucked me in, my heart still racing with revelation. "I'm gonna be just like Whitney Houston when I grow up."

She smiled that knowing smile of hers, the one that creased

the corners of her eyes. "Baby girl, you ain't gotta be like Whitney." She smoothed my forehead with her cool palm. "You gotta be Brandy. The world's waiting on Brandy."

But in my child's mind, Whitney became my North Star. If I could make someone—anyone—feel even a fraction of what she made me feel, I'd have succeeded. Using my stuffed animals as my adoring audience and a reading lamp as my spotlight, I would perform her songs in my bedroom. I'd stand as tall as my small frame allowed, elongating my spine as if reaching toward some divine light, focusing on each note like Whitney did.

Whitney was such a careful, intentional singer. She was moved by spirit, yes, but she understood her voice as an instrument. My dad showed me how to study Whitney's technique and pull elements from it without merely mimicking her. He'd sit with me, his patient hands beating time on his knee.

"Listen to how she breathes here," he'd say, rewinding the cassette tape. "That's control, baby girl. That's knowing exactly what your instrument can do."

When I was twelve, with my dream of meeting Whitney burning bright as ever, fate handed me an unexpected opportunity that I seized with both hands. My mom took me to a taping of *The Tonight Show* in Burbank. When it was announced that BeBe & CeCe Winans were going to be the musical guest, I was desperate to get to them. BeBe & CeCe had a record with Whitney, "Hold Up the Light," that I loved singing with my dad and Ray. If I could get to them, they could get me to Whitney. I hatched a plan.

If you've ever attended a live television taping, you know there's precious little for you to do besides sit, wait, and clap when the glowing signs demand it—the literal definition of a captive audience. I was a charming kid with big eyes, bigger dreams, and a voice that belied my small stature. With a bravery I can scarcely believe I possessed, I stood up and began to sing "Hold Up the Light."

People turned in their seats, first with confusion, then with surprise that melted into delight as my voice filled the studio. The crowd's energy shifted; they cheered me on, their unexpected applause propelling me forward. Their attention carried me from the rafters all the way down to the soundstage floor, past security guards who couldn't quite bring themselves to stop this little brown girl with the big voice, all the way backstage to where BeBe and CeCe stood in conversation.

They seemed genuinely tickled by the pint-sized dynamo who had sung her way down from the audience just to meet them. I told them about singing at church with my dad, how their music had become part of my studies.

"Now, what do you know about BeBe & CeCe Winans?" Bebe asked.

I put my hands on my hips and sang a little bit of "Hold Up the Light" like I had in the audience.

"Well, I'll be!" BeBe shouted.

Gathering every ounce of courage in my twelve-year-old body, I confessed my deepest hope—the real reason I had tried so hard to get close to them.

"Is there any way you could call Whitney so I could just talk to her?" I asked CeCe, my voice barely above a whisper, before adding with the sweetest plea I could muster, "Pleasssssseeeeeeee."

CeCe just giggled, her eyes warm and kind beneath her precisely styled bangs. She regarded me with a gaze that seemed to take the full measure of my yearning soul. The silence stretched between us, elastic with possibility, until finally, without a word, she moved toward her purse, extracted a small leather-bound address book, and picked up a nearby phone.

My heart forgot how to beat as she dialed.

"Nip! Hey, girl," she said into the receiver, her voice casual as Sunday afternoon. "I'm here with this little young lady dying to talk to you . . ." A pause, a melodic laugh. "Girl, she sang her way from the audience to get back here."

Another pause.

"Yeah, she got a voice on her, too," CeCe said.

I felt the ground shift and tilt, as if the green room was being tipped on its side. Disbelief rattled through my limbs as CeCe, calm as still water, extended the receiver toward me with a playful smile. She nodded gently, urging me forward. The seconds stretched between us, thick and heavy with promise.

My fingers hovered inches from the plastic, reluctant to touch this lifeline that would tether me to a world I'd only visited in dreams. Then, trembling like autumn leaves, I reached for the phone and pressed it to my ear.

"Hel . . . ll . . . ooo? Whitney?" My voice emerged as a nervous whisper, trembling like the flutter of hummingbird wings.

A soft pause, a gentle rustle on the other end, and then . . . a laugh. A low, sweet laugh that sent electricity racing through my veins.

"Speak up, baby, I can hardly hear you," the voice coaxed, breathy and warm, unmistakably hers—Whitney Houston, the woman whose voice had reshaped the geography of my dreams.

I clutched the receiver tighter, my fingers now slick with perspiration. The world around me—the bustling backstage area, the hovering studio personnel, even CeCe watching with amusement—all of it fell away.

"Whitney . . . I . . . I . . . Oh my God, is this really you?" I stammered, my free hand pressed against my racing heart.

"Yes, baby, it's me," she purred. "And I gotta say, you sound too nervous to have sang all the way backstage to meet BeBe and CeCe."

I laughed nervously, trying to anchor myself in reality. "I . . . I didn't expect . . . I mean, I never thought . . ." The words tangled on my tongue, refusing to form coherent sentences.

"Well, we all get a little surprised sometimes, don't we?" Whitney teased, with an intimacy that made it feel like we were the only two people in the universe.

I swallowed hard, unable to contain the smile that threatened to split my face in two. "I love you and I'm your biggest fan. I want to be just like you when I grow up."

"Little ole me?" she asked with a melodic chuckle that I wanted to bottle and keep forever. "Now, tell me, what's your name?"

"Brandy," I said quickly, almost breathlessly, as if I needed to remind myself who I was.

"Well, Brandy," Whitney said, my name in her mouth sounding like poetry, "I hope you're enjoying your day. It's a pleasure to meet you."

The call lasted barely a minute—sixty precious seconds that altered the trajectory of my life. CeCe gently reclaimed the receiver from my grasp, her smile knowing and warm. "There you go, baby girl," she said softly.

I stood frozen in place, the phantom weight of the phone still pressed against my ear. It was as though the telephone line had carried me to a place where dreams could touch down and leave their imprint on ordinary life.

Like a match to kindling, that brief connection had sparked a fire that would light my way forward through every dark night of doubt.

A year later, my face pressed against the cool glass of an airplane window, I watched Los Angeles disappear beneath a blanket of clouds, the city transforming into a sparkling grid that grew smaller with each passing second.

My mom sat beside me, her fingers laced with mine, both of us barely containing the electricity that hummed between us. We were flying to New York City for a meeting with Whitney Houston. Not the poster on my wall or the voice in my cassette player, but the flesh-and-blood woman. She'd recently launched a management company with her friend and business partner, Robyn Crawford, and Marcus Aurelius, the producer we'd been working with, had somehow—miraculously—arranged this meeting. This was before my first record deal with Atlantic, when I was still auditioning for label executives every chance I could.

Whitney had gone all out to welcome us—booked a plush hotel suite, arranged for a limousine to escort us through Manhattan's concrete canyons. I remember stepping out of the hotel lobby that morning, nerves dancing through my veins like lightning, clutching my mom's hand as a sleek black limousine—longer than any car I'd ever seen—pulled smoothly to the curb outside. Of course, I was dressed for the occasion: my favorite denim jacket meticulously covered in Whitney pins that I'd collected over the years, and beneath it, a Whitney concert T-shirt that I'd begged my dad to buy me when her tour came through LA.

We had driven perhaps five blocks, the New York streets rushing past in a smear of yellow cabs and pedestrians, when the car phone rang—its shrill tone slicing through our excited chatter.

Marcus answered, his voice warm and friendly as always.

I watched his face change as he listened to whoever was on the other end. The corners of his mouth dropped, flattening what had been a reassuring smile into something altogether different. My stomach twisted into a knot before he even opened his mouth to speak.

I already knew before he uttered a single syllable.

"I'm so sorry," he said finally, his eyes finding mine with genuine regret. "Whitney's water broke. She's being rushed to the hospital."

Just like that, my dream meeting dissipated into the gray New York sky like morning mist. So close—close enough to taste—and then gone.

My little heart ached with disappointment, but there was something else there, too—a strange, sweet joy bubbling up beneath the surface. Because even with this missed connection, an undeniable truth remained: Whitney Houston knew who I was. She had been waiting to meet me.

"Remember what I told you," my mom whispered, squeezing my hand in the hushed sanctuary of the limousine's back seat. Her eyes were fierce with certainty. "Cream rises to the top. And that's when you're going to meet her."

My mom spoke those words into existence. Two years later, having ridden the bloom of sudden fame following my debut album, I received an invitation to perform at the 1995 Nickelodeon Kids' Choice Awards. And guess who was hosting?

Whitney Houston.

By then, I'd done enough interviews gushing about my love for her that it no longer felt like a question of if our paths would cross. It felt inevitable.

I lingered at rehearsals all day, trying to appear casual and professional while every minute stretched into an eternity. The butterflies in my stomach had transformed into a flock of wild birds, and I could barely stand still.

And there she was.

Walking straight toward me across the soundstage, her presence commanding the room.

"Heyyyyy, baby girl," she sang, her voice the same honeyed velvet I remembered from the phone but now accompanied by her luminous smile, those famous cheekbones, those expressive eyes fixed directly on me.

My body betrayed me instantly. This was Whitney Houston—standing before me, calling me "baby girl." A scream erupted from somewhere deep in my chest. And then, inexplicably, I ran. I couldn't explain the impulse then, and I can't explain it now. It was as if my brain short-circuited from the overwhelming voltage of emotion—anticipation, excitement, disbelief, joy—all colliding at once. I crumbled into tears, my composure dissolving like sugar in tea.

Whitney followed after me, her laughter floating in the wind behind her. "Where are you going!" she called, tender amusement in her voice. "Don't you start crying and carrying on."

Before I could gather myself, she enveloped me in her arms—the very arms I'd seen grace countless magazine covers. The scent of fresh-cut flowers mingled with vanilla wafted from her hair as she pulled me closer. She wasn't an image on my television screen or a voice in my cassette deck . . . She was right here, solid and real, her warmth radiating through me.

"I'm so proud of you," she murmured into my ear.

She pulled back slightly, her hands—soft and warm, with perfectly manicured nails—coming up to cup my tear-streaked face. Her eyes locked with mine, and she asked me a question that revealed how deeply she saw me:

"How are you handling it all?"

In a room crowded with lights, cameras, and industry personnel, Whitney created a bubble around us—a sacred space where she was no longer the superstar and I the fan; instead, we were two kindred spirits navigating the same tumultuous waters of fame. She was one of the few people alive who truly understood the disorienting whiplash of newfound celebrity, who knew what it was to have the world suddenly turn its gaze upon you, expectant and hungry. She saw me, not just as a young singer, but as a human being trying to find her footing on shifting ground.

Whitney wore a chic, oversized denim jacket. I gasped audibly when she shrugged it off and draped it over my shoulders, the weight of it both substantial and symbolic. The fabric still held her warmth, and I fought the urge to bury my nose in the collar to capture her scent. She kept me at her side for the remainder of the afternoon, her arm casually draped around me, including me in her conversations as if I had always been part of her inner circle.

They say you should never meet your heroes—that the reality will inevitably disappoint the dream. But on that day, mine was everything I had imagined she would be.

Everything and then some.

"*Heyyyyy*, baby girl," Whitney sang into the phone, her voice enveloping me like a familiar embrace.

This was how our calls began now. *Our calls.* After spending that transformative afternoon together during the Kids' Choice Awards, Whitney had taken it upon herself to check in on me. She'd call to compliment me on a performance she'd seen, to offer advice on navigating the industry's treacherous waters, or just to see how I was doing—how I was really doing, beneath the smiles and the spotlight.

The first few calls followed the same pattern: her melodic greeting flowing through the receiver, me screaming like I'd touched a live wire, and Whitney having to talk me back down to earth. But how exactly was I supposed to act when Whitney Houston—the woman whose voice had soundtracked my childhood dreams—was calling me up on a random Tuesday afternoon as if we were old friends?

I had manifested mentorship through years of fervent wishing, and now it was here, tangible and real, on the other end of the receiver. I never fully adjusted to the miracle of Whitney being just a phone call away, but I did eventually learn how to contain my fangirl hysteria when she called.

One crisp fall day, my phone rang with her distinctive "Hey, baby girl," but this time, it wasn't just to check in. Whitney was calling about work—my work. She wanted me to contribute to the soundtrack for her next film, *Waiting to Exhale*. She was personally curating the album along with Kenneth "Babyface" Edmonds and had me in mind.

Babyface! The mere mention of his name was enough to send my stomach into somersaults. He was the architect behind some of the most influential R&B of his generation. I'd been mesmerized by how frequently I'd encounter his name while poring over album liner notes. Hit after timeless hit bore his distinctive imprint. He represented a level of musical mastery I dreamed of working with "someday"—when I was established enough, accomplished enough, worthy enough.

Whitney rattled off the lineup of artists she'd assembled for the project, her tone casual, as if she weren't listing musical royalty: "Toni Braxton. Aretha Franklin. Mary J. Blige. TLC. SWV. Patti LaBelle. Chaka Khan. CeCe Winans . . ." And Whitney wanted me in the mix. Me.

I was still processing this honor when I found myself at Babyface's gorgeous home studio in Beverly Hills. The space was immaculate—state-of-the-art equipment gleaming under soft lighting, platinum records adorning the walls like precious artifacts. I was a barely contained bundle of nervous energy, trying desperately to appear professional.

"I have this idea," Babyface said, his voice gentle and measured as he settled into his producer's chair. "It's different from anything you've done before. I want something youthful, fun—but with a bit of maturity that shows your growth."

Babyface pressed the play button on the console with long, elegant fingers, and out poured this laid-back, infectious groove that immediately set my body swaying. The funky bass line transported me straight back to the Sly Stone records my dad would play around our house on Saturday afternoons. The hook was deceptively simple but undeniably captivating: *"Be sittin' up in my room, back here thinkin' 'bout you . . . I must confess, I'm a mess for you."* It was fire—the kind of record guaranteed to ignite dance floors from LA to Atlanta the second the DJ dropped the needle.

I couldn't wait to get into the booth. Rushing past Babyface with barely contained excitement, I positioned myself behind the microphone, headphones hugged against my ears, determined to impress this musical genius who had crafted hits for New Edition, Tevin Campbell, Whitney, Madonna, and countless others. In my eagerness, I overshot the mark spectacularly. Too many runs, too many ad-libs, too many vocal acrobatics—I was all over the place, trying to showcase every trick in my arsenal at once.

Babyface paused the track, his voice floating through my headphones as soft and gentle as falling snow.

"Brandy," he said, "you don't have to do too much. Less is more here."

Babyface patiently steered me toward a more restrained approach that unexpectedly pulled out the lower octaves of my range—territory I typically avoided. I had always believed my power resided in belting, in those high notes that made audiences gasp. But Babyface helped me embrace another dimension of my voice, showing me that sometimes the most profound impact comes from holding back, from suggestion rather than declaration. The swinging, understated groove of "Sittin' Up in My Room" proved the perfect showcase for this newfound vocal restraint.

I was floored when Whitney later told me it would be the second single from the soundtrack, right behind her own "Exhale (Shoop Shoop)," which she had also recorded with Babyface. My singles "I Wanna Be Down" and "Baby" had already established me with platinum success, but "Sittin' Up in My Room" propelled me further into the stratosphere. The record crossed over to pop charts, where it remained for thirty-three weeks—the longest-charting song of my career.

Meeting Whitney had been the fulfillment of a childhood dream, but what I received from her was infinitely more valuable than a mere handshake or photo opportunity. It was a genuine investment in my future.

And she kept investing.

I was home, enjoying a rare day off from taping *Moesha*, when the phone rang, pulling me away from a mindless afternoon of channel surfing.

"Baby girl."

That voice—warm, raspy, unmistakable—flowed through the receiver.

"I have this project that I'm working on with Debra Martin Chase," she continued. "What do you think about playing Cinderella?"

My brain struggled to process her words, certain I had misheard. "Cinderella-Cinderella?" I stammered, my head beginning to spin as if I'd stood up too quickly.

She laughed softly. "Yes, girl. I think you would be great in this role."

"Wait—I thought *you* were gonna be Cinderella," I said, still trying to bridge the gap between her words and my comprehension.

"No, honey. I want you to do it . . . I'm gonna be your Fairy Godmother."

I screamed. No, really—full-out, top-of-my-lungs, running-in-circles-around-my-living-room screamed. I actually put Whitney Houston on hold—can you imagine the audacity?—while I completely lost my composure, unfiltered joy coursing through me like electricity.

When I finally returned to the phone, cheeks aching from smiling so wide, I took a deep breath and said with all the dignity I could muster, "I would be honored. Of course."

Inside, though, I was spiraling through a storm of thoughts. *This is Whitney Houston. I have to be good—no, better than good. I have to be perfect.*

What I would come to learn was that Whitney and Debra were developing a fresh take on Rodgers and Hammerstein's classic *Cinderella* with producers Craig Zadan and Neil Meron.

When Disney greenlit the project for ABC, they envisioned something revolutionary—a fairy tale that reflected the world's beautiful diversity, one that transcended the limitations of traditional casting.

What none of us fully grasped then—what we couldn't possibly have known—was how profoundly this single casting decision would challenge an industry still clutching tightly to outdated traditions.

One network executive, who enthusiastically supported Whitney as the Fairy Godmother, expressed reservations about the prospect of two Black women in the central roles.

"If you're coming up with someone like Brandy as Cinderella," this executive suggested, "why can't you go and get Jewel instead and have a white Cinderella and a Black Fairy Godmother?"

Craig and Neil—bless their conviction—didn't flinch in the face of this suggestion. "Absolutely not," they responded firmly. "The whole point is that Cinderella is Black and so is the Fairy Godmother. We weren't interested in a white Cinderella when we started working on this. Still aren't!"

The memory still raises goose bumps along my arms. Because it would have been so painfully easy to compromise, to smooth out the edges and label it "diverse" while still centering a fair-skinned Disney princess. But they refused to dilute their vision. They recognized what this representation could mean to millions of little girls who had never seen themselves reflected in fairy-tale royalty, and they stood firm in their commitment.

Debra, Neil, and Craig arranged to meet with me and my parents over lunch on the *Moesha* set. As we gathered around a table laden with platters of fried chicken, waffles, macaroni and cheese, and yams from Roscoe's, they outlined their vision for an inclusive reimagining of the beloved fairy tale: Victor Garber and Whoopi Goldberg as the King and Queen. Bernadette Peters as the wicked stepmother. The cast would be deliberately multicultural—a revolutionary concept for mainstream television at that time—which left me breathless with excitement.

When they walked us through the production schedule, reality hit me like a tidal wave. Eight weeks of intensive rehearsals and studio recording sessions before filming would even begin. I would need to master ballroom dancing, operatic singing techniques, and a completely different performance style than what I was accustomed to in R&B and sitcom work. It felt overwhelming yet exhilarating—a once-in-a-lifetime opportunity that required diving headfirst into uncharted waters at a time when I was already juggling multiple demanding projects.

Rehearsals were grueling—more demanding than anything I had experienced before. We trained with Broadway-level rigor: blocking, singing, dancing for hours that stretched into days and weeks. Eventually, we reached a point where we could run the entire production from start to finish as if it were a live Broadway performance. With each passing day, each blister on my feet, each vocal exercise that stretched my range, I began to feel less like an impostor and more like I truly belonged in this rarefied creative space. Surrounded by such extraordinary talent—stage legends and screen veterans—it became impossible to sink beneath my own doubts. There was always someone there, lifting me higher than I thought I could reach.

My greatest anxieties centered around the ballroom dancing sequences and the studio recordings. Both required technical precision and formal training that lay well outside my comfort zone as an R&B artist and television actress.

We recorded the musical numbers at the iconic Capitol Records studio in Hollywood, where legends like Frank Sinatra and Nat King Cole had once stood before the same microphones. Chris Montan and Arif Mardin, our music producers, sought to honor Broadway tradition while infusing it with contemporary sensibilities—updating the original orchestration with modern rhythms and fresh arrangements to bridge classical and pop styles.

I was initially paired with Paolo Montalban, the Broadway-trained actor cast as my Prince Charming. The contrast in our vocal styles created an interesting challenge—Paolo possessed formal theatrical training that I lacked, while I brought a contemporary pop sensibility he wasn't accustomed to. The producers guided us toward a creative middle ground: they encouraged me to playfully exaggerate operatic vocals—to make light of it rather than fear it—while directing Paolo to channel the soulful pop stylings of George Michael. Somehow, through this musical alchemy, we found the fusion of two distinct worlds. What audiences hear in the film is precisely that—two voices stepping into each other's territories, creating a sound that belongs entirely to our Cinderella.

The night before my scheduled studio session with Whitney, my phone rang just as I was climbing into bed, exhausted from a full day of dance rehearsals.

"Baby girl." Her voice was warm and familiar in my ear. "You ready for tomorrow?"

"Oh my God," I confessed, nervousness bubbling up despite my exhaustion. "What if I crack—"

"Stop all that," Whitney interrupted firmly but kindly. "You're exactly where you're supposed to be."

By then, I had grown somewhat accustomed to our telephone conversations, but the prospect of standing beside Whitney in the studio—rehearsing a duet with the voice that had shaped my childhood dreams—sent fresh waves of anxiety and excitement coursing through me. "Impossible; It's Possible" marks the climactic crescendo of act one, when Cinderella's Fairy Godmother encourages her to attend the royal ball, transforming a humble pumpkin into a magnificent carriage and tattered rags into a ball gown. It had always been my favorite number in the musical, and now, in yet another surreal twist of my charmed life, I was about to record it with Whitney Houston herself.

Once the initial starstruck jitters subsided, I found myself

Photo provided by author

Photos provided by author

Left: Raymond Boyd/Getty Images | *Right:* Raymond Boyd/Getty Images

Left: Getty Images | *Right:* Paras Griffin/Getty Images

Left: Kevin Winter/BET/Getty Images | *Right:* Getty Images

Left: Kevin Mazur/BBMA2020/Getty Images | *Right:* Andrew H. Walker/Getty Images

Left: Alberto E. Rodriguez/Getty Images | *Right:* Vince Bucci/Getty Images

Walter McBride/Getty Images

relaxing into a natural rhythm with her. There was something disarmingly genuine about Whitney's presence that made it impossible to maintain pretense. I wasn't performing for her—I was simply there with her, learning, growing, singing. It was the most exhilarating professional experience of my young life.

"Now, why are you down there?" she asked during one take, placing one warm hand on my shoulder and guiding me gently toward a higher register. "Come up here with me, baby. That's where your power is."

We filmed *Cinderella* across two sprawling lots. Universal's European Village provided the exterior world—cobblestone streets, castle walls, and village squares—while our interior scenes unfolded across MGM's historic soundstages, the very same ones where Judy Garland had once clicked her ruby slippers in *The Wizard of Oz*. There was something profoundly poetic about walking the hallowed ground where Hollywood magic had been created for generations, now being transformed for our groundbreaking vision.

Every inch of our set exploded with color—bold reds, royal blues, emerald greens—creating a vibrant, fantastical world that celebrated life in all its hues. As extras in elaborate costumes filled the ballroom scenes, I began to fully appreciate the brilliance behind the production's approach: by focusing on the joy and magic rather than drawing attention to the varying skin tones, we created a world where no one was an outsider. In this fairy-tale kingdom, everyone belonged simply because they existed.

But beneath the glitter and glamour, I was dangerously close to burning out completely. From the time my debut single had climbed the charts, I hadn't stopped moving—recording, touring, filming *Moesha*, promoting, rehearsing. The demands of multiple projects had stretched me paper-thin. What I craved more than anything was balance—a precious afternoon with friends at the mall, a movie night, a few hours to just be a normal teenager rather than "Brandy the Brand."

When one morning's shoot ran hours longer than scheduled, my hopes for an afternoon of normalcy evaporated into the studio lights. I retreated to my trailer and collapsed into tears of exhaustion and frustration.

Debra, our producer, with her characteristic blend of compassion and pragmatism, found me curled into a ball on the small sofa, streaks of mascara mapping rivers down my cheeks.

"I just want a normal afternoon," I whispered, the words catching in my throat. "Just once."

She knelt beside me, her presence soft but steadying. "I know," she acknowledged, her eyes reflecting genuine understanding. "And I know we promised you'd have the afternoon . . . but this is what you signed up for. And there are hundreds of people waiting out there—extras, crew, lights, cameras. They're all ready for you."

And so, I wiped my tears away, fixed my makeup in the tiny trailer mirror, and walked back onto the set with my head high and shoulders back—not just an actress playing a princess, but a professional honoring her commitments.

Whitney's time on set was limited by her packed schedule—just a handful of precious days amid our weeks of filming. But when she was there . . . the very air seemed to shimmer with possibility. She would glide onto the set wrapped in her magnificent gold Fairy Godmother costume, an ethereal vision that hushed conversations and turned heads wherever she moved.

On one particularly dreamlike day, it was just Whitney and me, nestled inside an ornate carriage for hours as we filmed our duet scene. This was when I felt most like Cinderella. Not because of the breathtaking powder-blue gown with its impossible waistline, or the pumpkin carriage transformed by movie magic, or the perfect lighting that bathed everything in golden warmth—but because of the way Whitney Houston looked at me. She hadn't merely handed me a role; she had gifted me a legacy.

Sitting in that carriage beside Whitney, my mind drifted back to the little girl I once was. The wide-eyed child who stood transfixed before a television screen, watching Whitney Houston perform and wishing with every fiber of her being to be just like her someday. That girl never would have dared to dream that one day she'd not only meet her idol, but that Whitney would pick up the phone just to check in on her—to see how she was really doing beneath the spotlight's glare. And she certainly couldn't have imagined that together they would make history by giving generations of little girls an image of representation to hold on to, to dream through.

But, as Cinderella learned from her Fairy Godmother in our film, impossible things happen every day. Sometimes, if you're very lucky, they happen to you.

TRUTHFULLY

I WAS READY to make a different kind of record. Something deeper. Something that would crack open my soul and let the world see all the jagged pieces inside. Not just catchy hooks and polished harmonies—but something that felt like the truth. *My* truth.

I was now eighteen—technically grown but still caught in that space between girlhood and womanhood, where everything feels both terrifyingly permanent and impossibly fleeting. I wanted this next album to reflect that tension—the coming-of-age ache, the invisible bruises blooming beneath my skin, the desperate fight to be seen and heard in rooms where money talked louder than talent.

The pressure hung in the air around me, thick and suffocating against the Los Angeles summer smog. I didn't need anyone to spell it out for me, though Lord knows they did anyway. My debut album had landed four Top 40 hits, two No. 1's on the Billboard R&B chart, and spent eighty-nine weeks on the charts. Eighty-nine weeks of my fifteen-year-old voice floating through car speakers and department stores and high school dances across America.

Now came the test. Prove it wasn't a fluke. Avoid the sophomore slump.

The label came to me with the idea of sitting with David Foster. David was classically trained. A true piano man who built skyscrapers out of melodies. He was behind ballads that have defined generations—records that are staples in the Great American Songbook, the kind parents dance to at weddings and children learn to sing at recitals. He did "I Will Always Love You" for Whitney. "The Power of Love" for Celine. "Unbreak My Heart" for Toni. "Earth Song" for Michael. And so on. When he reached out to my label, it wasn't even about me—it was to ask who sang the background vocals on "Sittin' Up in My Room" because he wanted to work with whoever that was. When he found out I'd done all the vocals myself, he asked if I'd be interested in coming by his studio.

That was a yes. An easy yes.

When I got to David's studio in Malibu—perched on a cliff where the Pacific stretched blue and endless beyond floor-to-ceiling windows—he was sitting at the piano with Diane Warren, who had a petite parrot perched atop her clavicle. From the doorway, I thought it was a little stuffed animal—until I shuffled into the room and the little guy turned and looked at me, letting out a little coo.

"He likes you," Diane said with a smile as I stood there feeling like an impostor invited to a master class.

Diane is a legend on her own. The queen of power ballads. She had a way of writing about love and heartbreak that felt like confessional poetry. She didn't just write songs—she exhaled them, as if they had been sitting deep in her chest all along, waiting for the right voice to bring them to life.

She had a song she wrote the previous Christmas that she'd been sitting on, protecting like a hushed secret. It was about unrequited love, and that aching need to know if the other person shared the same feelings that keep you staring at the ceiling at 3 a.m.

She played me the rough demo that she cut herself, her voice raw and unpolished, but the emotion was pure crystal.

Have you ever loved somebody so much it makes you cry?
Have you ever needed something so bad
you can't sleep at night?
Have you ever tried to find the words, but
they don't come out right?

It hit like a truth you didn't know you needed to hear. The corners of my eyes welled up. I thought about the in-between space I'd been living in, and I knew I had to sing this song. Let it live in me. Let myself feel every word.

I was supposed to sing this song. It was waiting on me and *my* voice.

But feeling it and nailing it were two different things entirely. David leaned over the piano, his fingers still hovering over the keys, and gave me a look. A kind one, but also serious. The look of someone who had pulled career-defining performances out of many a legend.

"This is the kinda song that requires you to go for those money notes," he said, voice gentle but unwavering.

"Money notes?" I asked, smoothing my hands down the front of my jeans.

He smiled, and tiny lines appeared at the corners of his eyes. "The ones that make people jump out of their seat. The notes that make them feel something in their marrow. That's what makes songs memorable."

His words lit a fire in me, sparks catching along my spine. I was intimidated, standing there in my platform sneakers and baby tee in front of musical royalty, but the one place I've always been completely fearless is inside the vocal booth. That's my church. My confessional. My battleground.

I looked at both of them, these titans of the industry, and whispered, "If I crack, don't laugh. But I'm gonna try."

And I did. I cracked a few times, sure—notes fracturing

halfway up my throat. But I wasn't afraid to embarrass myself. I'd rather miss a note than not try to find the right one. I kept going, pushing harder, reaching deeper, until I found the sound that matched the feeling Diane had put into those lyrics. I wanted to impress David and Diane—not from ego, but from admiration.

These were giants who made signature records, songs that became the soundtrack to people's most intimate moments. I knew "Have You Ever?" would be mine before I even sang it.

David pulled so much out of me in the studio that day—wisdom pouring from him like water from a spring. We cut more songs together after that. Even covered a Bryan Adams record, "(Everything I Do) I Do It for You," transforming it with my voice until it became something new altogether. He stretched me out of my comfort zone, into places I didn't know I could go vocally. And that's what I needed.

But not everything hit like that.

As the label kept sending me producers and tracks, the sparkle started to dull. A lot of the songs didn't feel like me. They didn't speak to where I was—emotionally, artistically, spiritually. They felt like they were written for someone else, or worse, for some focus group's idea of what I should sound like. Empty calories that might taste good going down but leave you hungry an hour later.

And if I can't feel it, I can't sing it. That's not just a cute saying; it's my truth. The microphone catches everything—especially the lies.

So, I took a break. *Moesha* was heading into its third season, and I needed to shift my focus.

One morning, I was driving to set when a Mary J. Blige record came on the radio. The beat sampled the piano movements from a Lil' Kim track I remembered, with strings added underneath.

I cranked the volume up because it sounded so left of center, yet also like classic Mary. She was evolving without losing her essence. I reached out to my label A&R, Paris Davis, and he told me a young up-and-coming musician named Rodney "Darkchild" Jerkins had produced it. He thought it might be a good idea for us to meet—as did I.

Every Friday night, Rodney and his crew hit this soul food spot tucked deep in the heart of Hollywood. Crowded booths burst with laughter and the clatter of silverware played percussion beneath old-school R&B and hip-hop joints spilling from hidden speakers.

When I arrived, I spotted Rodney nestled in a corner booth with his brother, Freddie, and their friend LaShawn Daniels. The three of them could have easily passed for a rap group—they just had style oozing out of them. Even from across the room, they caught my eye.

Platters of candied yams, buttery corn bread, smothered chicken, and fried fish perfumed the air. The food looked divine—but the volume inside the restaurant swallowed my focus. Every surface seemed to amplify sound—the hard floor, the wooden tables, the low ceiling. Trying to connect with the guys was like swimming through sound, catching fragments of sentences that floated past me like driftwood.

"Can we leave here?" I asked gently, hoping I wasn't making a bad impression by disrupting their weekly ritual. "I'm having a hard time hearing y'all."

But they didn't hesitate. We slipped out into the night and ended up at Jerry's Deli in Studio City. No savory soul food, no hip vibes—just thick leather booths the color of tobacco, sterile diner lights that buzzed faintly overhead, and the hum of cars cruising down Ventura Boulevard. I could hear myself think again. And more importantly, I could hear them.

We sat for hours, the world rolling past the windows. Coffee refills turned into dessert orders turned into late-night breakfast platters. We talked about growing up in the church—how the choir shaped our ears, how those Sunday-morning harmonies lived inside us still. About our inspirations. About our favorite music. About our ambitions—the dreams we whispered to ourselves when no one else was listening.

Rodney leaned forward, elbows on the table, eyes bright with passion. "I'm inspired by producers like Jimmy Jam and Terry Lewis for what they did with Janet Jackson," he said, "and what DeVante Swing did with Jodeci. They didn't just make hits—they built worlds."

I nodded, feeling the conversation sink into that honest place where artists recognize each other. "I want to use my voice differently in the studio," I told them. "I want to be more than just the singer who shows up and sings what's given to her."

Maybe a year or so after my debut came out, Quincy Jones, the legendary producer and composer, invited me to contribute vocals for his latest compilation album, *Q's Jook Joint*. We did three songs together, including a cover of "Rock with You," a record he produced for Michael Jackson the year I was born. Quincy truly encouraged my vision. He didn't just tell me what to do—he asked me what I heard in my head, then helped me find a way to make it real.

"You know what Quincy told me?" I said to Rodney, stirring my coffee even though I hadn't added sugar. "He told me how Michael would stack his vocals to make his voice bigger. Layer after layer, until it sounded like something otherworldly.

"That's the secret to making records sound magical," I continued, repeating Quincy's words like scripture. "Presence and power. If you trust your instincts, the payoff will be tenfold."

When I shared that story with Rodney, Freddie, and LaShawn, they all lit up like Christmas trees, energy crackling between us like electricity.

"Okay, let's make that happen," Rodney said, without hesitation, without doubt. Just pure belief.

"Really?" I asked, voice smaller than I'd intended, years of being told to stay in my lane making me cautious.

"My dad once told me, 'Just create. Don't chase what's already been played. Compose your own,'" Rodney said, his voice carrying the weight of inheritance, of lessons passed down. "Let's build your sound from the ground up. Something that only you could sing."

But there was something else Rodney told me that left the biggest impression, that echoed in my mind long after we'd paid the bill and gone our separate ways.

"I don't want to be one of those producers who is just known for making hit records," he said, eyes serious. "I want to be known for creating whole bodies of work with artists. Stories. Journeys. Albums that people live with."

Those words—that frame of thought—intrigued me. At least enough to spend a few days in the studio with Rodney and his crew. What could it hurt? The worst that could happen was that nothing came of it. The best? Something new. Something real.

The following week, the label set us up at Pacifique Recording Studios in North Hollywood. It was me, Rodney, Freddie, their sister Sybil, and LaShawn, all huddled together in a room talking—really talking—about life. Not just surface-level conversations, but excavating the kind of ugly, hard truths that make great songs. We were all fairly close in age and clicked so instantly that I let my guard down entirely, the walls I'd built in self-protection crumbling like sand.

"I don't want to just sing someone else's story," I said, hugging my knees to my chest on the studio sofa. "I want to help shape the sound. I need to be part of the process."

"The music has to be yours. It has to sound like your soul," Rodney said, nodding, understanding the yearning in my voice because he felt it, too. "Otherwise, what's the point?"

"You are the paint, we are the canvas," LaShawn added, a

poet's soul in a producer's body. "We're just here to help you express what's already inside you."

A thick, dusty book lay on the coffee table between us. The title kept catching my eye, bold letters on a faded cover. *The Dictionary of Clichés.* Something about it pulled me in, made my fingers itch to touch it. I started flipping through it while we brainstormed. But then certain phrases started jumping out at me.

Opposites attract.

Love is blind.

You don't know what you've got 'til it's gone.

Clichés can feel lazy, like shortcuts to emotions we haven't yet earned. But they persist in our language because they are lived. By all of us. You tell yourself you'd never fall for someone like him—and then you do. *Opposites attract.* You see their flaws and think love will fix it. *Love is blind.* You take the little things for granted until the silence stretches too long, and suddenly, the absence says more than any fight ever did. *You don't know what you've got 'til it's gone.*

Suddenly, like a match to dry paper . . . a fire lit in me.

"What if we used clichés as inspiration for titles? And build songs around them," I said, holding up the book, my voice quickening with excitement. "Everyone knows these sayings, but what if we made them personal? Made them *ours*?"

There's that saying, a hit dog will holler (which was in the book, by the way). Well, flipping through these pages, seeing some of these phrases, and reading about their origins was like being woken up by a splash of ice water. Each cliché felt like a key to a locked door inside me.

Learn the hard way.

Put that on everything.

Never say never.

Angel in disguise.

I saw little pieces of myself reflected back at me from the yellowed pages. And I wanted to pour them into a microphone—

confess everything I was feeling about the years I'd spent with Wanya. I was still carrying the pain of that sweet first love morphing into something else—distance, silence, and then, worse, betrayal. The wound was still so fresh I could touch it, feel it throb beneath my fingertips. So, I opened up about my heartache. The years of wondering if this man loved me as deeply as I believed I loved him, and the hurt of learning (the hard way) that his heart was elsewhere by catching him at a stoplight hugged up with the girl he said was just his assistant.

My voice cracked as I spoke, and I didn't try to hide it. "I was sixteen when we started dating. Sixteen. I thought he hung the moon and all the stars. He was my first, in all ways—and he was cheating on me the entire time."

"Did you confront him?" Sybil asked, her eyes soft with understanding.

I nodded, remembering the scene like it was yesterday—the taste of tears and rage burning the back of my throat. "Well, I had to page him first. And wait for him to call me back."

"Girl," Sybil said, sucking her teeth. "That's your *first* sign. So, what did he say?"

"That I was being dramatic. He said nothing was going on. That she was just his assistant. But I noticed her clothes started getting better, and he found all these reasons to have her around me," I said.

"Oh, that's dirty as hell," LaShawn yelled.

Shame spoke first. Then clarity. It was like a dam broke. Next, Sybil shared a story about discovering her husband was having an affair.

"Two months into the marriage, I get a phone call in the middle of the day asking if she can speak to my husband . . ." She paused, swallowed hard. "The woman tells me she's in labor and on her way to the hospital. Two months in, and he had a baby on the way with someone else. I was totally blindsided and so embarrassed."

The room went quiet for a beat, the kind of silence that feels sacred. The kind that comes before something important.

"Why don't we write something to that," Rodney said finally, not a question but a declaration. "Let's put all of this—everything we've been talking about—into the music."

Our first day together was alchemy in motion. We all felt it. That one conversation birthed "Learn the Hard Way," and once the dam cracked, the music came flooding like a river breaking through ice.

I still get goose bumps thinking about how instant the chemistry was between me, Rodney, Fred, Sybil, and LaShawn. It was as if we had known each other long before our paths crossed at that soul food restaurant. One day together turned into five. In those five days, we cut "Learn the Hard Way," "Never Say Never," "Happy," and "Put That on Everything." Just pure creative juices overflowing inside the studio, spilling out of us faster than we could contain them. We were feeding off each other, a feast of ideas and experiences turned into music. Rodney would tell me to trust myself more. My instincts. My choices. It wasn't just encouragement—it was liberation. Permission to be fully myself in the booth.

"We have something here," Rodney said on day five, eyes bright with the knowledge of discovery. "You should let me executive produce your project."

"You're right," I said, "we do," and agreed to continue working with him. I believed in Rodney the same way he had believed in me at Jerry's Deli.

Just like that, a creative partnership was born. A musical marriage of minds.

I was the paint. Rodney, Freddie, and LaShawn gave me a canvas.

LaShawn and I would be in one room working on the vocal arrangement of a song we'd finished writing the day before, perfecting harmonies that floated like ghosts around my lead vocal, while Rodney would be in the next room at the boards creating the wildest beats I'd ever heard—sounds that seemed to come from the future or some parallel dimension where music had evolved beyond what our ears were accustomed to.

One day, he played me this haunting record he'd been tinkering around with. It was dreamy, like a lullaby whispered in the dark, but it had an intoxicating bass line that gave a sultry undercurrent of desire. And he built it around a vocal of Joe singing *"And I love you baby."* Joe is an incredible vocalist. His debut album came out a year before mine, and he was currently riding the wave of back-to-back R&B smashes, including "Don't Wanna Be a Player," which Rodney produced. That echo of *"And I love you baby"* reminded me of all the times I'd heard those same words from my ex while he was secretly sleeping with someone else—and all the times she smiled in my face, knowing she had what was supposed to be mine.

"I was thinking this could be like an interlude or something," Rodney said, watching my face as the music played, gauging my reaction.

"No," I said, already hearing melodies forming in my mind, lyrics bubbling up from the memory of the pain. "We should turn this into a real song. This is too good to be just an interlude between songs."

The studio felt electric—no ego, just flow. Rodney gave me space to lead. To explore. To be messy. He never tried to control it or shape it into something it wasn't meant to be. Rodney pushed me to trust my pen as much as I trusted my gut. "You're a writer," he'd say. "A real one. Stop doubting that."

The studio became my catharsis. I was finally grieving not just the end of my relationship, but the young girl whose first experience with love had left her broken. And I channeled that pain in the studio, let it flow through me and into the microphone. That entire album was about that relationship, and about me not recognizing my own worth.

I made that album, primarily, to reclaim my power. I also made it to heal. I was hiding behind a mask, doing my best trying to get through each day. My mother knew I was heartbroken. A few friends knew. But I found solace in the recording booth. I found it in work. That's what coping looked like to me then: work, work, work. And I ran myself into the ground.

You can hear my anguish all throughout *Never Say Never.* The pain in every run, every high note, every whispered confession.

But you can hear something else, too.

You can hear me becoming. Not just an artist, but a woman. Not just a singer, but someone with something to say. I was finding my voice—not the one shaped by producers and label expectations, but the one that had been waiting, quietly, inside me all along.

Never Say Never wasn't just an album. It was my metamorphosis. My soft unfolding. My truth.

VS.

SO THERE MONICA and I stood, all draped in elegance and glamour, yet barely concealing the ice in our eyes.

It was the 1998 MTV Video Music Awards, and the air was charged with anticipation. Universal Amphitheatre hummed with the collective breath-holding of an industry waiting for what everyone hoped would be a spectacular collision.

It would be the first-ever live performance of "The Boy Is Mine," the song that had dominated radio for thirteen straight weeks, the duet that had launched a thousand tabloid headlines.

This should have been our coronation. "The Boy Is Mine" was making history as the first No. 1 pop hit for either of us—two young Black girls who'd dreamed of Whitney Houston–level crossover success since we were singing into our hairbrushes. Instead of savoring this crowning achievement together, we spent the performance slinging daggers with our eyes, our voices intertwining in perfect harmony while our spirits remained galaxies apart.

I tasted the irony, metallic and familiar. How could we sound so divine together yet be so disconnected? The very song protesting ownership of a man had somehow taken ownership of us, defining a relationship that hardly existed beyond industry functions and brief encounters.

Versions of the story have been told by everyone from MTV VJs to radio hosts to our own entourages—everybody but us.

The world loves a juicy rivalry, especially between women, and this one had all the ingredients of an epic saga: two rising R&B princesses with similar trajectories, distinct personalities, and a hit song about fighting over the same man. But beneath all the manufactured drama pulsed something far more insidious: an industry obsessed with pitting women against each other, forcing us to navigate waters where collaboration was viewed as an anomaly and comparison was the only constant.

Within the span of ten months, Aaliyah, Monica, and I came onto the scene with our first singles. Aaliyah's debut came out in the spring of 1994, five months before my first single, "I Wanna Be Down." "Back & Forth" was a smash, but it was really Aaliyah's vibe that made you fall in love with her. She had this allure—precocious and angelic, yet mature and mysterious. I was a fan of her album, *Age Ain't Nothing but a Number.* It was edgy but still girly. Aaliyah's voice was light and silky, effortlessly cool. And her album landed at a time of tremendous musical innovation. TLC updated the girl group model into something fierce and groundbreaking. Mary J. Blige used hip-hop to create a new take on the blues. Janet Jackson explored her sensuality through adventurous, paradigm-shifting R&B. Whitney Houston and Mariah Carey were at the top of their game and only getting better. I was excited to jump into the mix. But the comparisons were harsh and immediate.

"An album that seems based on the philosophy 'if Aaliyah can do it, why can't I?' except that in singing about best friends, heroes, and puppy love instead of about making love, teen actress Brandy Norwood acts her age. A premature effort, at best." I read the words over and over, hoping they'd somehow morph into kinder sentences. In the photo for my album cover, reprinted next to the review, I'm sitting cross-legged in front of a white backdrop, wearing combat boots, a baggy jumper, and a newsboy cap—my braids pulled into pigtails. I'd loved the image, but now, seeing it printed alongside the review, it felt juvenile. My album had been out for a couple of months and was mostly getting great reviews. But this one bothered me, not just because it was negative, but because I'd been reduced to a lesser version of Aaliyah. A sanded-down imitation.

Like Aaliyah, Monica was an invigorating voice in R&B. She was a Southern girl with a palpable authenticity. I loved her debut, *Miss Thang.* Her voice was so versatile. She could give you vulnerability and softness, and sass and attitude. And she was also incredibly inspired by Whitney.

Each of us—Aaliyah, Monica, and I—brought something distinctive to the scene. We were representing Black girlhood in our own unique ways: Aaliyah with her mysterious sensuality, Monica with her around-the-way realness, and me with what the press called my "wholesome charm." We existed in different lanes, created different sounds, presented different aesthetics. And yet I'd heard enough radio chatter and read enough magazine columns to know that in the popularity contest, I wasn't the favorite. I lacked the sex appeal of Aaliyah and the exciting street edge of Monica. It didn't matter that we were all being embraced by fans who saw themselves in our varied expressions; drama was far more enticing than celebration.

The questions started innocently enough during interviews:

"What do you think about Aaliyah's sound?"

"Do you like Monica's style?"

"How would you compare your image to theirs?"

"Are you all friends or . . . ?" The trailing off was always loaded with implication.

The truth was simpler and more beautiful than any fabricated feud. Aaliyah was a genuine source of inspiration for me, and when I stepped onto the scene, she not only embraced me but actively championed my success. After I won a handful of statues at the inaugural Soul Train Lady of Soul Awards in

1995, the most extravagant bouquet of white lilies and orchids arrived at my hotel suite. The card read simply: "I'm so proud of you. Keep shining. Love, Aaliyah."

We were both grinding so hard, trying to carve out our paths while navigating the disorienting maze of sudden fame. We crossed paths often—at photo shoots for magazines eager to feature the "new generation," at award shows where we were pitted against each other in the same categories, at radio stations where DJs would awkwardly ask us about the "competition." In those spaces, we always found a quiet corner for girl talk, those precious stolen seconds where we weren't rising stars but just two teenagers processing the surreal nature of our lives.

"Girl, did you hear this mess?" Aaliyah whispered to me backstage at a radio show. "Apparently, we're 'locked in a bitter battle for R&B supremacy.'" She air-quoted with slender fingers adorned with rings I would later try to find in every accessory shop in LA.

"Battle? I'm just trying to remember my choreography and not fall offstage in these boots." I laughed, and she joined me.

"One day," she said, "we should do something together. Really give them something to talk about."

Our refusal to feed into some sort of contrived feud only seemed to rile up the media more. It was painful to hear the fabricated rumors—that I was jealous of her movie deals, that she thought my acting career made me less authentic as a singer. Aaliyah carried herself with such grace through it all. I often wonder what magic we might have created together had we been given the chance. It breaks my heart that we never got to see all that she had to offer this world, that her light was extinguished so soon.

When Monica first burst onto the scene, I immediately felt a kinship with her, too. The depth and power of her voice told me she was raised on gospel, just like I was. It wasn't just her music; it was her entire demeanor. Both Monica and Aaliyah were girls you wanted to spend time with—magnetic personalities. The first time I crossed paths with Monica was backstage at the Lady of Soul Awards. We practically ran toward each other with open arms, enveloping one another in the kind of hug that says, *I see you, I get what you're going through.*

But solidarity isn't a story the industry wants to sell.

A radio station in LA decided we needed to be rivals, and so "Brandy vs. Monica" became their thing—their golden ticket to ratings heaven. They crafted these ridiculous skits where the DJs, with their carnival-barker voices, pretended to be us, bickering and clawing at each other like alley cats fighting over scraps. My persona—the character they invented that wore my name like an ill-fitting costume—was portrayed as fake, obnoxious, a saccharine-sweet facade hiding something sinister underneath.

I was sixteen. Sixteen and watching my identity being sculpted by strangers who had never even had a conversation with me.

I'm sure they all thought it was just pure, innocent fun—just entertainment, just business, just the game we all signed up to play.

The same station, with the audacity that only comes from complete disconnection from consequence, invited me to present at their Summer Jam event. I remember standing backstage in this fitted white outfit I thought made me look sophisticated, my stomach already in knots, when I heard it start.

"Coming up next . . . but first, let's check in with Brandy!"

Through the speakers, one of those stupid skits played. My character's voice squeaking through the stadium speakers like nails on a chalkboard. I could hear the whooping and hollering cascade through the crowd like a wave—thousands of people united in laughing at this caricature of me. The sound rattled through my bones. I still had to walk out there.

Legs wooden, mouth dry, I stepped onto the stage, only to be greeted by a tsunami of boos. The entire stadium—faces twisted, mouths open, hands cupped around lips—letting me know exactly what they thought of the Brandy they believed they knew.

Time froze. I stood there, microphone in hand, watching faces contort. Front row, a girl with box braids and a crop top was looking at me like I'd personally stolen something from her, like she wanted to climb up on that stage and beat my sixteen-year-old ass right there in front of everybody. Her eyes burned into me—real hate, not the playful kind. That's what fame gets you sometimes: real hate from strangers.

I couldn't shake it.

My existence seemed to upset people. What could I have possibly done at sixteen to warrant this level of hating? To deserve this public flogging? Was it the success? The singles? The way I wore my hair? The way I sang? The way I didn't sing? What was it about my child-self that had offended so deeply?

Somehow, I moved my lips, sound came out, and I got through it. But something crystallized in me that night—hardened like amber trapping an insect. What once was nerves and jitters before performances became full-blown stage fright, a monster that lived in my chest and clawed at my throat whenever I had to face a crowd.

"You were so professional up there," my mom said afterward, squeezing my shoulder in the green room as I stared into a mirror, trying to collect myself for the meet and greet I was scheduled to do. Even though I was embarrassed and wanted to leave, there was still a long line of kids waiting with their parents to meet me.

For days, the station replayed the audio of me getting booed by the audience. I was in the car with my dad, aimlessly changing the tuner, and there it was. The chorus of jeers and giggles.

"Why does the world hate me so much?" I broke into tears.

My dad pulled over. He rolled the windows down. It was one of those days when the valley was so hot it felt as if the sun was dancing on your skin.

"Bran, the world doesn't hate you. And you know that. People are gonna talk crap and start mess. And what do you do?" he asked.

"Stay low and—"

"And what?" he asked, waiting.

"Keep moving."

"That's right, baby girl. Stay low and keep on movin'," he said, before turning our family mantra into song.

"Stay low and keep on movin' . . . Keep on movin' . . ." he sang, nudging my shoulder to join in.

"Stay low and keep on movin' . . . Keep on movin' . . . Stay low and keep on movin' . . . Keep on movin . . ." we sang in unison.

My dad always knew how to cheer me up. But that day lives in me, still haunts me. I feel it before every performance, fear it might happen again.

The experience was nasty, but it gave me inspiration to toy with the speculation and play into it. I wanted to capitalize off the conversation around Monica and me and create a moment that showed the world, *Look, we get along. There's no issue.*

Monica and I were both working on our sophomore albums, and the stakes couldn't have been higher. Aaliyah had linked up with a then barely known Timbaland and Missy Elliott and created *One in a Million*, an album that transformed the sound of R&B when it dropped in 1996. The beats were unlike anything I'd ever heard—futuristic, disjointed, hypnotic. Her vocals floated over them like smoke, creating an otherworldly experience that left me both inspired and intimidated.

But it was never about competition. Aaliyah's evolution lit a fire under me. It motivated me to push boundaries and explore new sonic territories. I wanted to create something fresh, provocative, unexpected. The first album wasn't entirely my vision—I was only fifteen when it was recorded, still finding my voice, literally and figuratively. Now at eighteen, working through a heartbreak that felt apocalyptic and the constant pressure of performing perfection both on set and onstage, I was finally expressing my truth on *Never Say Never.*

One of the songs that emerged from those early sessions with Rodney and the crew was "The Boy Is Mine." The original version was stripped down, almost mournful in tone. The mood and tempo were completely different, with only my voice carrying the story of betrayal and territorial love. We all loved the record but knew it needed something to elevate it, to make it more than just another track on my album.

I immediately thought of Monica. The song could be a clever way to subvert all the speculation and gossip swirling around us. Our voices and personalities contrasted so beautifully that they would explode with delicious back-and-forth tension. I could already hear it in my head—her rich, robust tone playing against my lighter, breathier delivery. I thought it was a brilliant idea, a power move that would benefit us both.

Everyone around me hated it.

"You're fanning the flames," my mother warned.

"People will blow this out of proportion," my brother said.

"It's a mistake," one Atlantic executive said flatly during a meeting, not even bothering to hear me out.

The pushback shook my confidence. There was so much noise in my ear that I grew nervous about reaching out to Monica directly. What if she thought I was trying to amplify the rumors? What if she took it as an insult? I asked the label to make the initial contact, to present it as a business proposition rather than a personal request.

I got a call from my A&R manager, Paris, his voice carrying a mix of amusement and exasperation: "She told us to tell you to call her yourself."

By then, the resistance had only strengthened my resolve. I was fully committed to my creative vision, and part of that vision was recording this song with Monica. Nobody else. So,

I picked up the phone, my heart racing as I dialed the number her team had provided.

"Girl, why didn't you pick up the phone and call me yourself?" she said, repeating the same message we'd been delivered, no hello, no preamble. "I thought somebody was playing on my phone when your label called."

We both erupted in laughter, and just like that, the ice was broken.

"So, I really want to do this song with you," I said, twirling the phone cord around my finger like I was gossiping with a school friend. "I think we could have the last laugh with this one."

"Okay, how about this," she proposed. "Why don't you come down to Atlanta to hang out? I heard you like Six Flags. We got one down here."

"Oh word?" I perked up at the mention of roller coasters—my secret obsession. "I'm there!"

Little did I know that from that point forward, things would get considerably more complicated.

Before we recorded "The Boy Is Mine," Monica and I hadn't spent significant time together outside the manufactured environments of award shows and industry events. The pleasant smiles and brief exchanges weren't enough to build a real friendship, but I had always felt a genuine connection with her, the same way I did with Aaliyah. There was an unspoken understanding between us—we were navigating the same treacherous waters of fame at the same tender age.

I hoped the three of us could eventually form a true sisterhood, a support system against the isolating nature of celebrity. But the persistent rumors that we were secretly at odds had triggered old wounds from school days—times when girls I thought were friends turned out to be anything but. I'd grown wary, suspicious of people's intentions, reluctant to trust too quickly. At the same time, I still desperately wanted to be liked, to be accepted. I know I tried—perhaps too hard—to win Monica's friendship. Her invitation to visit her hometown felt like an open door, and I was eager to step through it.

True to her word, our first real hangout was at Six Flags Over Georgia. I was practically shaking with excitement—not just for the thrill of roller coasters, but for the rare chance to breathe without expectation. Days off had become precious commodities in my life. I was juggling late-night recording sessions with the grueling schedule of *Moesha,* often running on fumes and determination. An afternoon being a regular teenage girl with someone who understood the weight of the spotlight felt like medicine for my soul.

"I ain't been here in a minute," Monica said as we approached the entrance, a childlike glee softening her usually composed features. "Not since I started blowing up."

"Well, today we just two girls having fun," I said, linking her arm through mine. "No entourage, no cameras—just us."

We spent hours screaming our lungs raw on every coaster the park offered. We indulged in cotton candy that turned our tongues blue, hot salty pretzels, and frozen lemonades that gave us brain freeze. Between rides, we gossiped about industry boys we had crushes on, compared tour horror stories, and laughed until our sides ached. For the most part, we went unnoticed—baseball caps pulled low, oversized shirts disguising our frames.

But our anonymity was shattered as we climbed into the front of Ninja, the park's tallest roller coaster. A group of young girls spotted us, their eyes widening in recognition. They waited patiently at the ride exit, practically jumping up and down with excitement as we stepped off the ride, still laughing at each other's terrified expressions during the loops.

One girl asked Monica for an autograph, extending a park map and pen with trembling hands. We smiled and played along, adrenaline still buzzing in our veins from the ride.

"Is it weird having people call you by your TV name?" Monica asked later as we shared a funnel cake dusted with powdered sugar that kept floating onto our clothes in the gentle breeze.

"Honestly . . . yeah. It kinda bothers me," I admitted, surprised by my own candor. "I mean, I love playing Moesha, but sometimes it feels like Brandy is disappearing."

She raised one perfectly arched eyebrow. "So why didn't you correct that girl?"

I shrugged, using my finger to trace patterns in the powdered sugar. "I don't know. I guess I don't want to spoil the fantasy for them."

Monica studied me for a second, her eyes searching mine. Then she grinned and deliberately enunciated, "Well . . . BRANDY," drawing out my name like a melody line. "What you wanna ride next?"

The connection we forged at Six Flags carried over into the Atlanta studio we'd booked for the following day. Rodney and LaShawn had flown down with me, and my instincts told me our duet had the potential to be world-stopping before we even laid down our vocals. The original version I'd recorded solo had a haunting quality to it, but something shifted in the atmosphere, quiet but undeniable, when our voices intertwined.

We gathered in the dimly lit recording room—just Monica, Rodney, LaShawn, and me. No label executives, no managers, no entourage—just four creatives playing with sound. The intimacy fostered a rare environment where we could experiment freely, bouncing ideas off each other without judgment.

"Let's try that outro again," Rodney suggested after we'd laid down the main parts. "But this time, I want y'all to really go at each other. Like you're fighting over this dude for real."

We stood at opposite microphones, headphones pressed to our ears, and locked eyes across the small space. When we reached the final "not yours, but mine" section, something electric happened. We started off singing in unison a few times, then naturally shifted into a call-and-response pattern:

"Not yours . . ." I began, my voice soft but firm.

"But mine . . ." Monica countered, adding a gritty inflection that sent chills down my spine.

"Not yours . . ." I repeated, raising an eyebrow playfully.

"But—" she started, then broke character, laughing. "Girl, I know he's mine, cut it out." She handed me a steaming cup of tea with lemon and honey that she'd prepared for both of us during our last break.

We really had an incredible time creating together. Hearing our voices blend on the playback confirmed what my gut had been telling me—this was special. Where the original version was contemplative and understated, Rodney had dialed up the tempo to build dramatic tension in our back-and-forth. Our voices now worked toward a climax that was almost operatic in its emotional build. Everyone in the room felt the magic happening—the kind of session that reminds you why you fell in love with music in the first place.

And then we returned to LA and learned that Monica wanted to recut her vocal with her own producer.

Dallas Austin was her primary collaborator, the architect of her sound, and she wanted him to handle her vocal production. I was crushed. We had nailed it in Atlanta. We had done it together, and that had felt special—not just for the song but for the relationship we were building. The original session had been so pure, so free of industry politics.

But as artists, we all have our creative processes and trusted collaborators. I understood her desire to work with Dallas, even as disappointment settled in my chest. She redid her vocals without compromising any of the original feeling of the record. If anything, her performance was even more powerful, more assertive—the perfect counterbalance to my more measured delivery.

Duets between women were relatively rare in R&B at that time. Even without the backdrop of our supposed rivalry, the song would have generated significant interest simply because two young, ascending artists were joining forces. We had more similarities than differences—both Black teenage girls with church backgrounds, both inspired by Whitney, both navigating the treacherous intersection of music and television careers. These parallels likely contributed to the perception that we were in competition.

Now we had a song that played into the rivalry narrative while simultaneously subverting it. We had managed to harness the manufactured drama and transform it into something commercially viable and artistically significant.

But label politics proved harder to navigate than our personal dynamics. I was signed to Atlantic Records, while Monica was under Clive Davis's leadership at Arista. Clive was legendary in the industry—a virtuoso at developing and breaking talent. His track record spoke for itself: he had revitalized Dionne Warwick's and Aretha Franklin's careers before launching Whitney Houston into the stratosphere. He possessed the charisma of a master salesman, the strategic mind of a chess player, and the assertiveness of a Wall Street shark. His greatest talent was his ear—an almost supernatural ability to identify hit potential. They didn't call him "The Man with the Golden Ears" for nothing.

Not that it required any special insight to recognize what we had with "The Boy Is Mine." You could feel the anticipation building around us like electricity before a storm. The single dropped and exploded on radio. You couldn't go anywhere without hearing our voices spilling from car windows, department store speakers, restaurant sound systems. We couldn't have imagined a more perfect launch for both of our sophomore albums.

Without warning, Clive announced he was renaming Monica's album *The Boy Is Mine.*

"We wanted to reflect that it was a duet, not just a song on Brandy's album featuring Monica," he told the press with practiced smoothness. I was taken aback. The song was being positioned on both of our albums—which were scheduled for release just weeks apart. This was meant to be a career-defining moment for both of us, not a marketing ploy to prioritize one over the other.

The title change felt like a calculated move to claim ownership of the song—the very thing the lyrics protested against. Clive was a brilliant businessman who saw an opportunity to create additional buzz for his artist, but the decision poured kerosene on the flames of our supposed feud. I blamed Monica before I knew the full story. Neither of us truly wielded much power in those days. We were teenagers in a world where men twice our age made decisions about our careers, our images, our narratives.

Our albums being released so close together only heightened the drama. When *The Tonight Show with Jay Leno* invited us to perform "The Boy Is Mine," Monica had a scheduling conflict and couldn't appear. *Never Say Never* was due for release a month after our single dropped, and I desperately needed to maximize every promotional opportunity. I convinced myself I couldn't afford to pass on national television exposure, so I performed our duet alone, singing both parts.

My intention wasn't to slight Monica, but the optics were problematic at best. The media pounced on the solo performance as evidence of a deepening rift between us. Headlines screamed about snubs and betrayal. What began as a creative collaboration designed to challenge the rivalry narrative had instead become its most compelling evidence.

By the time we were booked for the VMAs, I doubt either of us was particularly thrilled about sharing a stage. The nonexistent rivalry had boiled over into genuine tension. The song that was supposed to flip the script had instead become a self-fulfilling prophecy, driving a wedge between us that would take years to remove.

When the lights snapped on, the stage became a battlefield. We stood atop opposing spiral staircases as fog swirled dramatically below us. Monica was statuesque in a crimson gown that looked as if it had been carved from molten lava. I was encased in a sleek leather mini with a crystal-embellished bodice that caught every light. We both had dramatic trains sweeping behind us like the capes of opposing royalty.

Our voices collided—sharp, urgent, unyielding. There was bad energy vibrating in the air, no use pretending otherwise. The lyrics took on a new dimension, loaded with a subtext neither of us had intended when we first recorded the song.

But here's the thing about chemistry—it transcends personal differences. That inexplicable magic that happens when two complementary forces come together cannot be suppressed by hurt feelings or professional rivalries. Beneath the friction was an undeniable current—raw and electric—that neither of us could resist.

As we descended our respective staircases, moving toward the center of the stage for the climactic ending, the tension loosened. Our eyes locked, and for a brief second, I remembered the girls who had screamed together on roller coasters, who had shared fluffy cotton candy and inside jokes. The girls who had created something special while the world told us how to feel about each other.

Monica's expression softened imperceptibly. I felt the corner of my mouth twitch toward a smile. That was when everything clicked into place. Without a word being exchanged, we reached an understanding. Even in a space where we'd been pitted against each other—where we'd allowed ourselves to become adversaries—we couldn't help but recognize our shared experience, our parallel journeys, our combined power.

Five months later, Monica and I showed up to the Grammy Awards hand in hand, draped in complementary cream ensembles that symbolized a fresh start.

We were nominated for Best R&B Performance by a Duo or Group with Vocals, and I was anxious and fidgety. By the time our category was announced, I was shaking so badly I got out of my seat and knelt down. Monica reached for my hand.

"Breathe. Win or lose, we got this," she said.

Faith Hill walked out to present the category. She wore a stunning lilac gown, and it looked as if she was gliding across the stage.

Watching the nominated videos cycle through, I felt my nerves racing. Monica's grip got tighter, as did mine.

"And the Grammy goes to . . . Br—"

The *r* was barely off the tip of Faith's tongue when I leaped up and ran full speed to the stage, the train of my cream overcoat whipping the air behind me.

Meanwhile, Monica was graceful, slinking toward the stage like a model. I was jumping up and down like I'd just won the lottery.

"I know this is totally out of my image, but this is a Grammy, man!" I yelled.

Monica reached for my hand, which brought me back to gravity, and we accepted the Grammy—our first—together.

The lesson wasn't lost on either of us. The industry would always try to create narratives that served its purposes, especially for young Black women. But we had the power to write our own stories, to define our own relationships, to control our own legacies.

THE GIRL IN THE PLASTIC BUBBLE

IN THE SEASON FOUR premiere of *Moesha*, she comes face-to-face with Brandy, the pop star. It's a classic sitcom stunt. The celebrity popping up to "play" themselves. A little wink to the audience. But for me, it was more than a gag. It was a rupture.

Up until then, the existence of Brandy in Moesha's world had been a way of keeping the character separate from my music career. It gave me breathing room, a way to keep Brandy, the artist, distinct from the character people invited into their homes each week.

That boundary worked—until it didn't.

As both my career and the show exploded into the stratosphere, the space between the two Brandys narrowed to a whisper. Moesha became more confident with each episode, her shoulders squared, her voice certain. So did I. Moesha got bolder in her choices and in the way she navigated the world. I did, too. The two personas began to intertwine into a tapestry of expectations until I could no longer tell who was borrowing from whom—the character from the artist or the artist from the character—and I got lost in the dizzying performance of two women who were both me and not me at all.

The episode "Moesha Meets Brandy" was supposed to be lighthearted, a playful nod to the absurdity of fame. Moesha forgets to buy tickets to a Brandy concert (already meta), and her friends—with that sitcom logic that only exists in thirty-minute blocks—convince her to use her uncanny resemblance to the singer to sneak them into the show.

"I should have never let y'all talk me into this, can we leave?" Moesha protests from a crowded line of fans waiting to get into the venue.

"Nooo, not until *after* your performance, Brandy," Kim insisted, her voice rising with the exaggerated inflection that made Countess Vaughn's character so lovable.

". . . Not that lookalike madness again," I'd responded as Moesha, shaking my head with practiced exasperation.

Through a little on-screen trickery, I got to play both roles—Moesha and Brandy—a split-screen dance with myself that had me changing outfits at lightning speed between takes. This was an "event" episode, a ratings grab that allowed us to acknowledge how big Brandy, the star, had gotten. *Never Say Never* had debuted at No. 3 on the Billboard 200 when it was released in June of 1998. With the fourth season premiering that October, the episode would be used as a launching pad for "Have You Ever?"—a song that still catches in my throat when I hear it, a time capsule of who I was then.

But stepping into Brandy's shoes—my own shoes—while the cameras rolled made me dizzy with a vertigo that had nothing to do with the bright lights or the breakneck pace of the shoot. It forced me to see myself from the outside, through the kaleidoscopic lens of public perception.

And the truth was, I didn't recognize her—this glossy, perfect creature with her immaculate micro-braids and megawatt smile that never quite reached her eyes.

I did know how to be Moesha. I knew her mind, her humor, her insecurities like the geography of my childhood home. I knew how she walked into a room—the slight hesitation before she committed, the way her hand sometimes found the doorframe for support. I knew how her voice lifted when she was nervous, how she paused for just a beat too long when she was hurt, buying time to swallow the emotion. I was attuned to her inner thoughts, how she moved through life, her emotions, her fears, her dreams—all carefully crafted by writers but embodied by me until they became as familiar as my own heartbeat.

But Brandy? Who she was without the show and the music and the fame . . . was a mystery hidden beneath platinum records and magazine covers. A question mark dressed in designer clothes.

Out of all the phases of my life and career, I've been asked the most about this particular time, and I understand it. The world was witnessing me become Brandy, the superstar, in real time—a transformation as public as it was disorienting.

Getting a Barbie doll with my face, my skin tone—little Black girls finally seeing themselves reflected in plastic perfection.

Transitioning into film, stepping onto sets where nobody knew me as Moesha, where I had to prove myself all over again.

Doing *Cinderella* with Whitney, the weight of being the first Black princess sitting heavy on my shoulders.

Landing a Cover Girl campaign, my face on billboards and in magazines, selling beauty to a world that had only recently begun to acknowledge that Black was, in fact, beautiful.

Modeling clothes I could never have dreamed of wearing growing up, fabrics so fine they felt like water against my skin.

My first world tour—the roar of the crowd a physical force that pushed against my chest each night, the hotel rooms blending into one another until I couldn't remember what city I was in when I woke up.

I was exhausted, bone-deep tired in a way that sleep couldn't touch, but I loved the opportunities that were coming my way like waves, one after another, lifting me higher, even as they threatened to pull me under. But it all came at a cost that I wasn't prepared to pay. I had become a brand—a product to be packaged and sold. And the pressure to maintain that image—that flawless, bubbly, wholesome image—was suffocating me from the inside out.

In the '90s, before music journalism collapsed into itself like a dying star, there were publications dedicated solely to covering young Black stars. All of us wanted a *VIBE* cover. That was the epitome of cool. In those days, a journalist would spend an extensive amount of time with you, immersed in your day-to-day world, taking note of everything you did and said, looking for the cracks in your armor, the glimpses of authenticity that slipped through when you were too tired to keep up the pretense.

I'd always wanted the experience of the big, splashy *VIBE* cover, and when my time came, I was heart-racing, palm-sweating excited. Even more so when the magazine sent a young Black woman to spend time with me for the profile. I felt seen in a way I rarely did with journalists, who often approached me as a curiosity, a phenomenon to be studied rather than a person to be understood.

I brought her to the *Moesha* set, where the familiar rhythms of filming provided some comfort. And to a photo shoot for *Never Say Never,* where I posed for hours, my body contorted into positions that looked effortless on film but left my muscles screaming. She came by the house to hang with my mom, who had grown weary of the press by then, her smile tight around the edges as she offered sweet tea and deflected questions she deemed too personal.

"They're not your friends, baby," my mother would remind me in private, her voice low even though we were alone. "Remember that. They're doing a job."

I had grown weary, too. The constant scrutiny, the expectations, the way every word was picked apart for hidden meanings. The need to be perfect in a world that was waiting for me to fail.

Whitney once said to me, her voice like velvet over gravel, "Never let anyone else tell you who you are." Her eyes had locked onto mine with an intensity that made me feel both seen and transparent. "The minute you give them that power, it's over." I tried to hold on to those words like a talisman, but once I lost myself in these two personas—the real Brandy buried somewhere beneath them both—it became easy for me to be influenced by the world's opinion of me, to start seeing myself through their eyes instead of my own.

Though I'd mostly stopped reading anything about myself—a hard-won lesson—when my *VIBE* cover came out, I had it sent straight to set. I loved the cover. It's glamorous with a playful twist that captured the duality I was living. I'm wearing a burnt-orange deep V-neck and white high-waisted pants. My top is twisted into a knot at the center, creating a cinched silhouette that accentuates my waist and collarbones, making me look older, sophisticated, a woman rather than the girl America had come to know.

The sultriness of my look juxtaposed with the bubbles floating around me toyed with that tension of the innocence of girlhood colliding with the realities of adulthood—a threshold I was crossing in the public eye, every growing pain magnified. In the beginning, there had been so much made of my styling—specifically my mother's refusal to allow me to show my belly button in photos. No midriff shots. Ever. Because that would make me appear "fast." Those early images of me are undeniably girlish. Braids in bunches, my midriff covered by a strategically placed backpack (a compromise, of course, after hours of negotiation).

"I'm trying to protect you," my mother would say, her voice firm but her eyes soft with worry. "This industry . . . they'll take a young Black girl and turn her into something she's not. Something she'll regret."

She wasn't wrong. But when I was ready to embrace a new direction, that Goody Two-shoes image turned out to be impossible to shake, a gilded cage of my own making. I was now seen as inauthentic and trying too hard to be something I wasn't—as if growing up, evolving, was an act of betrayal rather than the most natural thing in the world.

Now, here's a meta image that could only happen in the surreal circus of celebrity: reading a cover story on yourself while waiting to shoot a scene as your fictional character meeting your real self. The layers of identity were so tangled I could barely breathe beneath their weight.

The opening of the profile was . . . intense, a sucker punch disguised in elegant prose:

> "The only things you really know about Brandy are the things she wants you to know: that she likes McDonald's hamburgers, that Whitney Houston is her favorite artist, and . . . by this time, you don't care."

I remember how the words seemed to smudge on the page, how the air in my trailer suddenly felt too thin. The piece continued, relentless:

> "Brandy seems to be a very good girl who does very good things. . . . Brandy has suffered for this good reputation."

Brandy has suffered for this good reputation . . . It's a tough line to read, the kind that reverberates in your chest long after you've put the magazine down. Some people didn't like what I represented—this image of perfection that felt unattainable, unrealistic.

And the truth is, I didn't always like it much, either. I was preserved in a fleeting glimpse of innocence that no longer reflected who I was becoming. Unallowed to make mistakes, to get it wrong and learn from those experiences. I wanted to be liked. I also wanted the career that I had. If I'd stumbled, or fucked up—even once—would my career have ascended to what it had? Would TV executives have wanted to greenlight a family sitcom with me at the center? Would Disney have made me their first Black princess? Would the dolls or endorsement deals or sponsorships have happened?

These questions circled in my mind like vultures as I sat in front of the vanity, watching in the mirror as my braids were being pulled into a high, messy bun—Brandy's signature look for the concert scene. The stylist's fingers moved with practiced precision, but I barely felt them. I was too busy thinking about how much harder it had gotten to flip between these two personas, these two versions of myself that were simultaneously everything and nothing like the real me.

A production assistant poked his head into the trailer.

"They want me to show you the stand-in mark for the Brandy scene," he said, a brief show of confusion crossing his face. "Um, I mean where we need you to look when you're playing Brandy. I mean, yourself."

I smiled, the expression not quite reaching my eyes. "I know what you mean."

But did I? I could slip into either like a costume and be what the world expected—Moesha with her relatable struggles and earnest heart, or Brandy the untouchable star with her perfect life and wholesome image.

But once the cameras stopped rolling, I was back to that old feeling—the hollow ache of standing at a crossroads with no map, no guide, just the echo of applause ringing in my ears and the weight of expectations pressing down on my shoulders.

Who was I when no one was watching? When the lights dimmed and the music faded and the scripts were set aside?

That was the question I couldn't answer, the one that kept me awake at night, staring at hotel ceilings in cities whose names I'd forget by morning.

That was the real performance—pretending I knew.

GHOST IN THE MACHINE

IT WAS A rare Tuesday off from *Moesha*. No 5 a.m. alarm. No script pages to memorize over lunch. No twelve-hour day on set. I'd fantasized about this free day for weeks—a lazy afternoon at the Beverly Center sounded like heaven, just wandering from store to store without a schedule or a handler or a photographer trailing me. I slipped downstairs in my favorite silk pajamas, the baby blue ones with clouds that Ray had gotten me for Christmas, hair piled messily on top of my head. I was looking for my mom. Maybe she'd want to grab lunch or get our nails done. A mommy-daughter day like we used to have.

I found her in her office, the converted sunroom that now housed three phones, a fax machine, and stacks of papers that seemed to multiply every week. Her glasses were perched on the tip of her nose, her voice low and stern on the phone—that business tone that meant somebody was about to get set straight. She was scribbling furiously on a yellow legal pad, nodding even though the person on the other end couldn't see her.

"No, no, that's not what we agreed to," she was saying, underlining something for emphasis. "The call time needs to be adjusted. She's coming straight from another commitment and—"

I slipped into the room like a ghost, curling up in the plush leather chair across from her desk. I didn't even think she'd noticed me, but her eyes flicked up briefly before returning to her notes.

"We need to revisit this section of the contract," she continued, tapping her pen against a document. "Listen, I appreciate that, but this is nonnegotiable. My daughter's well-being isn't something I'm flexible on."

I picked up a magazine from her side table—my face stared back at me from the cover, all glossed lips and straightened hair.

She hung up the phone with a sigh and immediately started dialing another number before seeming to remember I was there. She set the receiver back down, removed her glasses, and rubbed the bridge of her nose where two deep lines had formed.

"I was hoping you'd pop in," she said, somehow sounding both exhausted and energized. "I had a call earlier—"

I plopped both feet up on her desk dramatically, making sure she saw the contrast: me in my pajamas, looking like the teenager I was, while she sat there in a pressed blouse at 11 a.m., already juggling the world on her shoulders.

"Can't I have one day off without talking about work?" The whine in my voice surprised even me.

She lowered her glasses, rubbed the sides of her head, and let out a sigh that seemed to come from the depths of her soul. She was used to this battle, this push-pull between mother and manager, between nurturing me and building my career.

"Bran . . . just because you have the day off from shooting doesn't mean the phone stops ringing. And trust me, it's been ringing all morning like there's a fire on the other end. *You're* off today. *I'm* not," she said.

Of course, she was right. She always was. But that didn't stop the feeling that my mother had been replaced by my manager years ago, and I didn't know how to get her back.

I stood to go call one of my homegirls to see if they wanted to hit the mall instead. But a curiosity gnawed at me, as it always did. The business side of me—the part of me that was undeniably my mother's daughter—couldn't help itself.

"What was the call about?" I asked, half pouting, half intrigued.

She looked up again, her face softening just enough that I could see my mom peeking through the veneer.

"It was Neil Meron and Craig Zadan," she said, a smile playing at the corners of her mouth. "They want you for a film. With Diana Ross."

I sat back down so quickly I nearly missed the chair. "Wait—*Diana Ross*?"

She nodded, lips curling into the tiniest smile, but her eyes were dancing now. "*The* Diana Ross."

Suddenly, I was wide-awake, pajamas forgotten, the mall a distant memory. "Tell me *everything*."

I could feel the quiet kind of chaos that lived beneath my skin. A tension between ambition that burned like a fever and exhaustion that weighed on my bones like wet cement. I wanted to be everywhere. I wanted it all. Wanted it with a hunger that kept me restless.

But I didn't know how to say no. I didn't know I was *allowed*.

So, I said yes.

Yes to every project that landed in my lap.

Yes to every endorsement deal that promised to put my face in another household.

Yes to every collaboration that might stretch my wings a little further.

Yes to every opportunity that knocked, tapped, or merely whispered at my door.

My yes was currency. Proof that I was worthy of the spotlight widening around me. That I wanted this life with everything in me. That I deserved this chance when so many others didn't get theirs.

But beneath the relentless drive was a girl slowly unraveling at the seams. Thread by delicate thread.

And the person who bore the brunt of that unraveling? My mother.

She walked into rooms full of executives with their Italian leather shoes and Harvard degrees, men who looked at her like she was speaking in tongues when she talked about my potential. And because she was our mother, because she wouldn't back down when they pushed, because she knew our worth to the penny, they labeled her difficult. Pushy. A stage mom.

They didn't see the strategist with her calculator and contracts spread across our dining room table at 2 a.m. The visionary who could see ten steps ahead on a chessboard most people didn't even know they were playing on. The heart that would break in private so it could be steel in public.

But I did. I saw it all. And still . . . I resented it. Resented her. And worse, I was terrified that if I ever said those thorny truths out loud, to her face, that she'd think I was ungrateful. Or weak. That I'd wasted everything she sacrificed to give me.

In the spring of 1998, while on hiatus from *Moesha*, I had filmed *I Still Know What You Did Last Summer.* It was going to be my big-screen debut, my first real taste of Hollywood beyond the squeaky-clean sitcom world, and everything about the experience felt deliciously rebellious—cussing on camera, shooting a love scene, fighting and running and screaming for my life through jungle sets. Playing someone wilder, freer, more dangerous than the sweet girl next door America had come to expect.

I even had it written into my contract that my character wouldn't die in the film. There was a long-standing joke—the kind that isn't actually funny—that Black girls were always the first to die in horror films. We were disposable, just bodies to build the body count. And I wasn't about to be another Black girl who didn't make it to the credits. I wanted to be a final girl. A survivor with blood on her shirt and fire in her eyes, standing strong.

But my God was that shoot brutal. We were in Mexico at the peak of spring, filming in a coastal resort where the air was so thick with humidity you could practically drink it. The place was gorgeous on postcards—sugar-white beaches kissing turquoise waters, swaying palms, margaritas with salt-crusted rims.

The reality was less transcendent. The place was crawling with prehistoric-looking beetles and mosquitoes so aggressive their attacks seemed personal. I was a TV girl, used to air-conditioned soundstages with trailers and craft services and wardrobe people who steamed your outfit between takes—not sweating through tank tops amid creepy crawlers.

Still, I loved it. Loved stretching my wings beyond the nest I'd built. Loved showing people I could be more than a sitcom lead with a pop record and a pretty smile. I could be gritty. I could be raw. I could make you believe I was fighting for my life.

And now this new opportunity. A drama. With a legendary Supreme. *Double Platinum* was a mother-daughter story that hit closer to home than I was ready to admit—an interrogation of family versus career, of sacrifice and resentment and redemption. In the film, Diana Ross plays an aspiring singer who leaves her infant daughter and unsupportive husband behind to pursue what turns out to be a wildly successful pop career. Eighteen years later, she is reunited with her daughter, played by me, and repents by becoming her professional mentor.

This was the kind of story that would require me to mine the emotional ore I'd been carefully burying. To really tap into something tender and bruised to bring this character to life. I looked at my own mother and wondered what dreams she'd set aside to nurture mine.

Of course, I said yes. The word left my lips before I'd even read the full script.

ABC fast-tracked *Double Platinum* and moved mountains to make the project happen. Nothing about the shoot was going to be easy. Miss Ross had one request, but it was a big one that sent producers scrambling and network executives reaching for antacids. The film needed to be shot in New York City. Not Los Angeles, where the majority of us were stationed. Not Toronto, which usually doubled as New York in movies, since it was far cheaper to shoot there. We needed to shoot in the actual city so that she could go home to Connecticut to be with her youngest kids every night. Diana had missed Thanksgiving to tour Japan and made it known that missing Christmas wasn't an option, which left us with a short window in December that worked for everyone.

The shoot was going to be tight. Extraordinarily, anxiety-inducingly tight. Typically, you need twenty days for a TV movie shoot. We had seventeen. Our schedules only overlapped for fourteen of those days, but 90 percent of the film was scenes between the two of us, so that meant we had to shoot all of it in those fourteen days—including half a dozen elaborate musical numbers with choreography that made my knees weak just thinking about.

Miss Ross was grace incarnate. From the time she glided onto set—and I mean glided, like her feet barely touched the ground—everything changed. The crew moved differently around her. They whispered instead of shouted. They straightened their backs. Friends of the crew would mysteriously materialize on set, as if summoned by the promise of breathing the same air as music royalty. They would pop up with their children, their friends' children, their second cousin's neighbor's children. Everybody wanted to meet Miss Ross and get a photo with her.

But they also wanted to meet me. That was the surreal part.

Perhaps it was the energy of the big city with its relentless pulse, and the constant electric buzz of the set, but this was one of those rare breaks in the timeline when I could actually feel, in my body, how famous I was becoming. There were days when fifty to sixty people were just hanging around the set, watching us shoot a scene, whispering behind their hands when Diana threw her head back and laughed at something I said. When she adjusted my posture with a gentle touch to my spine. When she showed me how to hold a note with my diaphragm instead of my throat.

There was no time to waste on this breakneck schedule, but there were stolen seconds. Little pockets of stillness between takes when I'd sit next to Miss Ross in her chair, our names embroidered on canvas backs, and just bask in her presence. In the knowledge that I was sitting shoulder to shoulder with the woman who'd shattered ceilings before I was born.

Diana was just fifteen when she started with the Supremes. Fifteen. The same age I was when *Moesha* began. Barely out of childhood, baby fat still clinging to her cheeks, yet already being shaped and molded into a star. The Supremes would go on to be Motown's most successful act, not by accident or divine intervention, but because Diana was a force of nature. The voice that could pierce your heart. The hair that defied gravity. The poise that seemed impossible for someone so young. That unmistakable presence that turned heads when she entered rooms. She just had *it*. That indefinable quality people spend lifetimes chasing.

And when she stepped away to launch her solo career, she didn't just walk—she soared even higher. By 1993, Guinness crowned her the most successful female artist in music history. That title wasn't just about numbers on a page or plaques on a wall—it was about legacy. Impact. Mythmaking.

But legends aren't made without costs. Diana made untold sacrifices to etch her name in pop history. Blowing the door open the way she did for women—Black women especially—meant swallowing things that would break most people. It meant smiling through indignities and injustices that would have crushed a lesser spirit. If there were no Diana, there could be no Whitney. And if there were no Whitney, I wouldn't have had a model to look toward when I started dreaming bigger than my bedroom mirror.

Diana was the door. She didn't just walk through it—she built it, painted it, hung it, and held it open for the rest of us.

And yet, watching her on set—not just the performer with her megawatt smile, but the woman underneath it all—I learned a sharper, subtler lesson. One I didn't expect in the slightest.

She had boundaries.

Firm, clear, nonnegotiable boundaries.

She'd toured the world over, crossing oceans and continents. Headlined stages from Vegas to Tokyo, commanding audiences of thousands with a flick of her wrist. And still, she chose home. She carved out space to be a mother. When we finished *Double Platinum*, she would be going back to her home to celebrate the holidays with her family. It was the first time I'd seen a woman at that level of power and fame have a firm boundary around work. And she did it without guilt or apology.

One of our tougher shooting days was at this creaky 1840s clapboard lake house on Long Island Sound filled with hand-carved decoys and antique horse tack. It was cold enough to see your breath, the sky a sheet of hammered steel, the wind coming off the water as sharp as a slap across the face.

The scene was emotional quicksand. My character was confronting Diana's for leaving. A daughter aching to be seen and a mother begging for forgiveness. There was nothing in this world more challenging than having to be angry at Diana Ross on-screen. That was truly the hardest thing about shooting *Double Platinum*. Not the breakneck pace or the bitter cold or the pressure of being in her shadow.

Between takes, while the crew reset the lighting to capture the fading winter sun, Miss Ross retreated to a corner, off to the side, wrapped in a cashmere blanket the color of cinnamon. I approached her slowly, nervously, like I was interrupting something sacred. Like I might break the spell if I spoke too loudly.

"Miss Ross," I said, sitting beside her on a wooden bench weathered by salt air, "can I ask you something?"

She nodded, her eyes never leaving the slate-gray waves in the distance, hypnotic in their rhythm.

"How do you . . ." I searched for the right words, wanting to sound mature, thoughtful. "How do you balance it all? Being a mom. Recording. Touring. Being . . . well, *being Diana Ross.*" The name felt starlit in my mouth, like speaking an incantation.

She turned to me then, her gaze gentle but penetrating, measured in a way that told me she wasn't giving a rehearsed answer.

"I hate giving advice," she said, running her fingers through big buoyant hair, those defiant curls that had become as iconic as her voice. "Even with my own girls, I don't try to teach them lessons they haven't asked for. I just try to be an example. That's all I can really do."

She looked straight into me then. And I swear, she saw everything—the weight I was carrying like stones in my pockets, the exhaustion that had made a home in the hollows beneath my eyes.

"Honey, you're nineteen," she said with the tenderness of a mother. "You have a good head on your shoulders. Two incredible parents who would walk through fire for you. That's really all you need. Anything else, you can figure it out as you go."

She reached over, took my hands into hers, and smiled. "Now, because I do think you're going to be around for a *very* long time, young lady . . . I will tell you three things I learned back in my Motown days."

I nodded, eager as a student before a master.

"No chewing gum while talking—it's distracting and unprofessional." She tapped my jaw lightly. "Sit up straight—posture is presence." She placed a finger between my shoulder blades, encouraging me to straighten my spine. "And keep your knees together—because the cameras are *always* watching, even when you think they aren't."

She tapped my knees, which I'd unconsciously spread apart in a casual stance. I laughed, blushing at being so gently corrected, and sat up straighter, spine lengthening. I spit my gum into the napkin she handed me and got back to my mark, ready for the next take. Ready to give her everything I had as an actress, because Diana Ross deserved nothing less than the best.

Double Platinum was a reckoning I didn't see coming. Playing this girl wounded by a mother who chose career over daughter, who grew up with a Diana Ross–shaped hole in her heart, forced me to sit with a truth I'd been running from at a full sprint.

And the truth was I resented my mom.

I resented this precarious balancing act that had been our life since the second I signed my record deal at fourteen.

I resented how often I got her strategist's mind when I *wanted* her heart.

I resented that she couldn't just be my mom. That our late-night talks were more about call times and contract negotiations than the messy, complicated chaos of being a teenage girl.

I wanted her to hold me, not schedule me. To see me, not manage me. To comfort me, not handle me.

I didn't know how to say: I'm lost and feeling like I'm disappearing beneath the weight of being "Brandy."

But she didn't have the luxury of always being soft with me. Not in an industry that would chew me up and spit me out if she showed weakness. Not when there were always people waiting for us to slip, to fail, to confirm their belief that we didn't belong at these tables.

I was nineteen now. We had achieved the very thing we'd set out to do. But we hadn't thought to save a piece of our essence, just for the two of us.

I admired Diana—not just for her success, her voice, her legacy, but for her audacity to draw a line in the sand. That was the kind of woman I wanted to be. Needed to be, if I was going to survive this journey with my soul intact. Only I could draw the boundaries that would keep me whole. Only I could learn the power of saying no, so that my yes would mean something again.

COVER GIRL

1.

You're not drop-dead gorgeous.

Four words. Simple. Devastating. A poisonous seed planted by a woman who thought she was doing me a favor, tempering a young girl's Hollywood dreams with what she called "reality." Those words burrowed deep, finding fertile soil in my teenage insecurities, taking root alongside every magazine cover I'd ever studied. Fair, porcelain skin that wasn't mine. Elegant, slender noses that weren't mine. Symmetrical eyes that weren't mine. Chiseled jawlines and flowing, silky hair that would never be mine. The mirror became both companion and enemy, reflecting back features that the world had not deemed worthy of being described as true beauty.

2.

"She's sweet-looking." "Exotic." "Interesting."

Never beautiful. Never gorgeous. Never sexy. Words like stones, each one carrying the weight of a thousand unspoken judgments. They transported me back to Ambler Elementary, where bullies circled like vultures, poking at my undeveloped body, their laughter as sharp as knives. Back to the high school hallways, where mean girls dissected my appearance with surgical precision, their whispers forming an inescapable chorus.

I hung my worth on the threads of other people's opinions, believing what I heard about myself because it was easier than fighting. The distance between my eyes felt vast like the Pacific. The shade of my brown skin was too pale, not golden or warm enough to be celebrated. The hair that fell from my scalp was not long enough, not straight enough. My cheekbones were too high, too prominent, too . . . different.

Mom would cup my face in her hands, her eyes reflecting mine. "Baby girl, these features are your crown. You come from queens," she'd whisper. Dad would smile that smile that crinkled the corners of his eyes. "You're the most beautiful girl in the world, princess."

But the world didn't echo their sentiments. What was once a seed had bloomed into irrefutable fact in my mind, branches of doubt spreading through every thought about myself.

3.

There was a time I thought beauty lived in numbers, hiding in the cold precision of mathematics. The sacred digits: 24 inches around my waist. Size 2 jeans. 115 on the scale. I'd memorized them all, worshipped at their altar, sacrificed at their temple.

The girl in the mirror watched me with condemning eyes. She knew all my secrets, all my flaws. Her voice was quieter than the screaming tabloids and industry executives, but somehow crueler, more intimate with its knowledge of my deepest fears.

Just lose three more pounds. Maybe then they'd call you beautiful.

4.

I wanted to disappear, to become as small as possible, to take up less space in a world that seemed to grant beauty only to those who could vanish into their clothes.

Each morning unfolded with ritualistic precision. I'd stand naked before the full-length mirror, my reflection a stranger I was determined to transform. My fingers would pinch at my sides, searching for evidence of failure, my brow furrowed in disgust at what I found. All I saw was someone unrecognizable—a girl pretending, an impostor waiting to be exposed.

"Who are you?" I'd whisper to her. She never answered.

I had never been what anyone would call heavy, but under the relentless glare of the camera, every ounce felt like evidence of inadequacy. The other girls on BET and MTV seemed carved from divine material—their bodies sculpted with effortless perfection.

Some nights, alone in hotel bathrooms across the country, I'd press my forehead against the cool mirror and wonder if someday I'd see someone deserving of the blessings showered upon her, someone worthy of love.

Life has a cruel sense of humor, and I was in on the joke.

5.

I believed salvation would come through discipline. The gospel of control promised redemption through sacrifice.

Working out. Constantly. Before dawn in hotel gyms. After midnight in empty studios. Between takes on set, sneaking in squats and lunges while the crew reset lighting.

Counting calories became my private mathematics, a silent calculation running behind every conversation, every interview, every performance. Foods that once brought comfort—pasta, pizza, cake, McDonald's apple pie (specifically overseas, where the golden fried ones are easier to find)—transformed into enemies lurking in wait, threatening to undo all my hard work.

But discipline is a seductive master that soon demands obsession as tribute. Before I recognized the shift, I had become a prisoner to numbers, routines, and that merciless voice that chanted its mantra: *Just a little less food. Just a little more exercise. Just a little less of you.*

6.

The numbers bled together in an endless loop—1200 calories per day, 500 calories burned, 110 pounds on the scale. Each number a verdict, each meal a negotiation, each bite cataloged and judged. Dread became my constant companion, clinging to me like designer perfume.

My changing body as womanhood claimed territory previously occupied by girlhood led to whispers and gossip, first as gentle murmurs, then growing bolder.

"Is she pregnant?" "She's definitely gained weight." "Her face looks different." "Maybe she's just . . . eating better."

That last one always followed with knowing laughter, and I pretended to not hear.

7.

I gripped the cold porcelain, knuckles white with determination, stomach churning with disgust—not at what I'd eaten, but at what I'd become. The ritual turned into habit: the silent closing of the door, the water running to mask any sounds, the head bowed in both shame and purpose.

I pushed my fingers down my throat, feeling my body resist. My muscles clenched tightly as I gagged. The room held its breath. Then came the release—a bitter wave crashing up and out, purging everything I'd consumed along with pieces of my dignity, my health, my spirit.

I believed I was purging more than food. I was expelling the weight of disappointment, washing away the residue of other people's expectations, cleansing myself of perceived failure. But the emptiness that followed was always temporary, a fleeting relief quickly replaced by crushing guilt and bone-deep shame.

"This is the last time," I'd promise myself, sitting on the bathroom floor, tears mixing with water as I splashed my face. "No more after today." A promise I knew was as substantial as morning mist, destined to evaporate once that voice started again: *Just a little less, just a little more.*

8.

There's a point in purging—a strange, unmissable turning point—where your body sends up flares of resistance. Where something deeper than conscious thought begs you to stop. I imagine it's the same divine spark that makes flowers turn toward sunlight, that pulls the tide to the shore, that whispers *live* when everything else says *die.*

But the need was stronger. A brutal, urgent emptiness that demanded to be fed by making me hollow. I would lean into it, pushing my body past that breaking point, past the fear and shame that threatened to drown me, trying desperately to escape the prison of my own making.

My throat burned raw from stomach acid. My eyes stung with broken capillaries and spent tears. My head swam with dizziness.

For a few blessed seconds after, I felt lighter. Thinner. Prettier. Worthy. The sensation never lasted, but I chased it like an addict.

9.

When I took the pill, the world shifted on its axis. Hunger—that constant, nagging companion—disappeared like smoke. In its place: clarity, energy, power. For the first time in what felt like forever, I didn't feel weak or lacking or desperate. I felt in control.

This tiny white tablet became the one thing in my chaotic life I could depend on. One pill in the morning with black coffee, sunlight streaming through my kitchen window as I prepared for another day of being "on." Another pill before arriving at the studio, swallowed dry in the back of the town car, my driver's eyes carefully averted in the rearview mirror.

Food became an afterthought, a prop in the performance of normalcy. A bowl of dry cereal pushed around until milk would have made it inedible. A muffin broken into pieces during afternoon meetings, creating the illusion of consumption while actually eating nothing. I skipped meals with practiced excuses.

"I had a big breakfast." "I'm saving room for dinner." "My stomach's been upset."

I lied to everyone—my team, my family, my castmates. And I lied to myself.

At first, it seemed like magic—the numbers on the scale dropping with satisfying consistency. My clothes hung loosely from my frame. Because I was thin—finally, gloriously thin—everyone told me how amazing I looked.

"You're absolutely stunning!" "Girl, what's your secret?" "The camera loves you even more now!"

It didn't matter that my insides were a wasteland, that my hands trembled when I tried to sign autographs, that sleep had become a distant memory. My outward appearance had finally aligned with the girls I'd envied on magazine covers. The gaze of a studio audience no longer made me want to disappear; the unblinking eye of the camera became a lover rather than an enemy.

Feeling confident about my appearance helped ease the darkness inside, creating flash points of genuine happiness that broke through like sunlight between storm clouds.

The elaborate architecture of lies necessary to keep the machine churning forward was taking its toll. But I was thin. And in that world, at that time, nothing else mattered.

10.

The pills—once my salvation—became my chains, binding me to a reality increasingly disconnected from the world around me. I knew it somewhere in the recesses of my mind, could feel the warning signs my body was sending: the heart palpitations that woke me at night, the days when sounds seemed too sharp and colors too bright, the moments when time seemed to stutter and skip.

But I couldn't stop. Not when the numbers were getting lower, each milestone a perverse victory. 125 . . . 120 . . . 115 . . . 110 . . . 105.

"Just five more pounds," I'd whisper to myself, moving the finish line farther back each time I approached it, the horizon of "enough" constantly receding before me.

11.

I stood before a massive white backdrop, surrounded by the controlled chaos of a photo shoot. Lights as bright as miniature suns illuminated every pore, every eyelash, every doubt I carried. A small army of stylists buzzed around me—adjusting my braids, smoothing the silky fabric of my dress with reverent hands, giving quick instructions with each click of the camera.

"Turn slightly left." "Chin down just a touch." "Eyes to the camera." "Perfect, hold that!"

I would be making history as the first Black singer to be a Cover Girl model, my face soon to grace magazines and billboards across America.

It was a barrier-breaking achievement that should have filled me with nothing but pride.

But beneath the smile, tension coiled tight as a spring. That voice in my head—the one I couldn't escape even with pills or purging or punishing workouts—started to whisper.

You're not drop-dead gorgeous.

Those four words always threatened to surface at times when I should have felt most powerful.

The photographer approached, reviewing images on his digital screen.

"These are magic," he said, turning the screen toward me. "Absolutely stunning. They're going to love these in New York."

I nodded and smiled, wondering if he could see the lie in my eyes.

12.

When my first ad debuted, plastered across a Times Square billboard and in glossy magazines nationwide, I almost couldn't bear to look.

The makeup, the perfect lighting, the masterful photography—they had sculpted me into someone who embodied the glamour I'd spent years dreaming about. My skin appeared luminous, sun-kissed perfection. My face, artfully contoured, showcased cheekbones that suddenly seemed made for cameras. My hair fell in elegant waves, catching light that seemed to emanate from within. The girl in the image was undeniably gorgeous. And she was undeniably thin.

I traced my finger across the page, across this beautiful stranger's face, and whispered the question that echoed through the empty hotel suite: "Is this really me?"

The answer came back hollow: it was . . . and it wasn't. It was the me they wanted. The me I had nearly killed myself becoming. But somewhere beneath the powder and promise, beneath the starvation and struggle, another girl was waiting—one I hadn't yet found the courage to meet.

CAMOUFLAGE

IN THE SPRING of 1999, I would be hitting the road for my first world tour as a headliner. There was just one big caveat. The tour could only happen during the three months I had off from *Moesha*, which would limit the scope. Five years of living my life around a television production schedule while trying to nurture a music career had stretched me thin. I was starting to resent the show, especially when it required me to sacrifice other creative opportunities.

Still, the Never Say Never World Tour was going to be the biggest production I'd ever had. A spectacle of lights, sound, and choreography. But I was most excited about getting a backing band together and working out the arrangements for the show. Everything else was an added bonus.

Now, I've never been the most comfortable with choreography. My body sometimes betrays my brain's intentions, and I joke that I have two left feet. Being surrounded by dancers onstage was intimidating. Their perfect synchronicity made me self-conscious about how much harder I had to work to keep up, but The Dreamer always put me at ease. He was one of my background dancers, and by then, we'd worked together for years. He moved with such smooth fluidity and charisma that you couldn't keep your eyes off him—all grace and controlled power.

The Dreamer was so talented it made my heart ache to watch him. He had all these ambitious visions for his future, but his head floated in the clouds. He was so far disconnected from the realities of an industry I knew all too well. What he wanted, what he craved with an intensity that sometimes alarmed me, was fame. He couldn't understand why his star hadn't risen the way he'd hoped.

"You have this light," he told me once. "It's like you were born with it. Some people chase it their whole lives and never catch it."

I could see the hunger in his eyes. The fire. I connected to that drive. That passion.

The Dreamer was sweet. Charming. Wonderful. He had a gentle charisma, the kind that draws people in without effort. He made me laugh—really laugh. And he was fine. The energy between us morphed into flirtation—subtle at first, a private joke, a lingering touch. He made me feel . . . comfortable. Like I could take a breath around him. He didn't treat me like Brandy. He teased me. Challenged me. Flattered me in ways that weren't overt, but intentional.

"You're thinking too much again," he said after I stumbled over a move.

"Easy for you to say." I laughed, trying to mask my frustration as I fumbled through the eight-count again. "Your body actually listens to your brain."

He stepped behind me, close enough that I could feel the heat radiating from his chest, smell the clean scent of his skin mingled with sandalwood cologne. His hands—those hands that could tell stories without words—gently gripped my shoulders.

"Close your eyes," he murmured, his voice like warm cognac against my ear, smooth and intoxicating.

"Stop trying to dance perfectly. Just feel it and dance *true*."

"I don't know what that means," I whispered, but my eyelids fluttered closed anyway.

His hand slid down the small of my back, leaving a trail of goose bumps in their wake. "You're *Brandy*. Your voice, your music. That's why people are coming to see you. So just—" his hands settled at my waist, his touch featherlight but magnetic "—feel it."

That one line stuck with me. *Just feel it.*

So, when he asked me out a couple of weeks into rehearsals, I didn't hesitate. Not even for a heartbeat. I said yes. He felt safe enough to get lost in.

We fell into each other with the urgency of two people who'd been searching too long, colliding with the force of inevitability. Afterward, tangled in sheets that smelled of us, I felt anchored.

We hit the gas. Hard. I had just moved into my first apartment, a chic little space that overlooked the Verdugo Mountains. He was waking up next to me and making breakfast for us in the morning before rehearsals. The speed of it should have alarmed me. But when you're running from one commitment to another, from set to studio to rehearsal, having someone constant feels like stability.

Like home.

I didn't even question it. I wanted him there, and so I welcomed him in—all the way into my life.

The tour kicked off on May 23, 1999, at the Dôme de Paris. Europe was a fugue state. Seven shows across France, Germany, England, and the Netherlands before flying to Japan for a handful of shows in Tokyo, Yokohama, and Osaka. This is when I really felt like a huge star. Seeing thousands of fans screaming for you night after night—it validates you in ways little else can.

But I'd quickly learn it would come at a cost. Tokyo brought jet lag that made my bones ache and my mind fog. After a sixteen-hour day of press interviews, photo shoots, sound check, a show, and meet and greets left me drained, I curled into a ball on our hotel bed and broke. The sobs came from somewhere deep. This wasn't just exhaustion. It was more than that. The years of juggling careers and the weight of the scrutiny I felt had taken a toll.

The Dreamer didn't ask questions. Didn't try to fix it. He just wrapped his body around mine like a human shield, his chest against my back, the rhythm of his heartbeat against my spine, grounding me. I was living my dream. It was hard as hell. And getting harder by the day. But I was living my dream. And I had this man who held me up and was loving me fiercely. It felt like the kind of ride-or-die love that the songs promised and the movies romanticized. But the speed of it all—the intimacy, the entanglement, the hazy boundaries—wasn't rooted in stability. It was rooted in need. In a kind of mutual ache we mistook for love. I couldn't see it because I was too caught up in the fantasy.

When the tour ended and we returned to Los Angeles, to routine and reality, things changed. The playfulness that had drawn me to him began to curdle at the edges. His teasing took on a sharper edge. His charm would vanish without warning, leaving behind something cold and brittle that made me tread carefully, choosing my words with the precision of a bomb technician.

"You coming to set with me today?" I asked one morning, my voice deliberately light as I got dressed. He was lounging in bed, watching me with those eyes that used to make me feel adored but now made me feel . . . assessed.

"Why? So I can sit around for ten hours explaining why Brandy's background dancer is hanging out on the set of *Moesha*?" The acid in his tone made me flinch.

"I just thought—"

"You don't think. That's your problem." He got out of bed and stormed out of the room. Only to come back two seconds later. "You don't think about how it feels for me to stand in the shadows while everyone fawns over you."

"That's not fair," I said.

"Fair?" His laugh was cold, nothing like the warm sound that could make my heart skip. "You want to talk about fair?

You have the world, and you constantly complain about how hard life is."

The words hit like physical blows, stealing my breath. But instead of fighting back, instead of throwing him out, I found myself saying, "I'm sorry."

Sorry for what, I didn't know, but I'd already begun to believe him. That voice in my head—the one that had always whispered I wasn't enough, wasn't worthy—found an ally in his criticisms.

My mother saw through him immediately. We were in her kitchen, the familiar scent of her perfectly spiced chicken sizzling in oil hung in the air. He had come with me to visit, hovering just close enough to feel protective, but with a subtle possessiveness I hadn't yet learned to name. She watched him the way mothers do—silently, thoroughly, with that unspoken language of intuition that sees through performance. Seriously, she had one eye on the deep fryer, the other on him—and didn't drop focus from either. If it weren't for the heat coming off the stove, you'd think we were near the Arctic Circle, given the chill that hung in the room. His phone rang, and even I was relieved that he had an excuse to duck out of the kitchen.

"Brandy Rayana Norwood," my mother said, using my full name like a spiritual invocation, "that boy is *not* the one."

She hadn't even waited to see if he was out of earshot.

I sucked my teeth. "Mom . . . you don't like anybody I date."

"I like people who see your worth," she said simply. "Who add to your light instead of trying to dim it."

I looked away first, focusing on the pattern of the counter tile. "He supports me. He understands the pressure I'm under."

She made a sound—part sigh, part hum—that spoke volumes. Her look said the rest: *You don't see it yet, but you will.*

"He's sweet," I insisted. "He's different."

She didn't push. She just nodded slowly, almost sadly, and went back to flipping chicken.

My mother knew best, but I was infatuated and unable to

see past the high of being wanted. I'd traded one performance for another, stepping offstage only to enter a different kind of spotlight at home.

At twenty, I didn't entirely know my worth. I wanted affection. I wanted to feel desired. I wanted to be chosen. But I believed love meant giving every fragment of my being. I couldn't see that his love was laced with thorns, each barb hidden in a smile I taught myself to believe was sincere.

Little slights floated between us. I brushed them off as nothing at first. *He's just having a bad day*, I would tell myself.

But bad days turned into bad weeks.

If a man so much as looked in my direction at an event, The Dreamer's jaw would tighten, a muscle jumping beneath his skin like a warning. "Did you see how you were looking at him?" he'd ask later. If I dared look back at someone, acknowledged their existence with a smile or a nod, he'd twist it into a story, a script he'd written in his head that painted me as the villain and him as the wounded lover.

One night, we were out at dinner and ran into a rapper-producer I'd been hoping to work with on my next project. I stopped to chat for ten minutes, and the entire time I could feel his eyes burning into me as he watched from across the room. The second we got home, he spun out.

"You embarrassed me tonight," he said, his voice low and solemn. "Everyone could see what was happening. Everyone was watching you flirt with him right in front of me."

"Come on, I wasn't flirting," I said, unable to mask my exasperation. "You know how badly I want him on this next album."

"Album," he scoffed, the word twisted into something ugly. "You know without the music and shit, nobody would give a fuck about you."

The verbal jabs became sharper. He called me selfish, the word hissing between his teeth like a curse. He called me ungrateful, as if my success was something I'd stolen rather than worked my ass off for. He would say I owed him for standing by my side, for the sacrifices he was making to dance in my shadow.

And I began to believe him, his words waking up insecurities his attention and affection once washed away.

"I gave up opportunities for you," he told me once. "I could have went out with Janet or TLC, but I chose to be here. And what do I get for it? Nothing but disrespect."

He'd apologize afterward, and I'd allow guilt to cloud my judgment, convince myself that his intensity was just passion, his jealousy just devotion. It became this dance we did, and when you're caught in that dance, you don't notice that you're just going around in circles.

The poison of his perception seeped into my bloodstream drop by drop, until I couldn't distinguish his voice from my own thoughts. Instead of recognizing his scorn for what it truly was—jealousy wrapped in insecurity, festering beneath his beautiful exterior—I started believing him. Maybe he was right. Maybe I didn't deserve any of this. Maybe my voice was merely a marketable commodity, packaged and sold by executives who could have chosen anyone.

These thoughts circled my mind like vultures, patient and persistent, waiting for my self-worth to die completely.

And so, like water seeking the path of least resistance, I tried to make it right. I learned the art of contraction—of making myself smaller, dimmer, less threatening to his ego. I declined invitations to industry parties, and when I did go, I transformed myself into his personal publicist, introducing him to everyone with effusive praise that made my throat ache with its inauthenticity. "This is my boyfriend—he's the most incredible dancer you've ever seen. He choreographed half my tour. He's brilliant. He's everything."

I became an expert at deflecting compliments toward him, at redirecting spotlights so they wouldn't leave him in shadow. I dimmed my own glow, thinking it would help him shine brighter.

But diminishing my light never increased his.

I can't say I remember what the catalyst was. It was something so minor it's been lost to time. What I do remember is that he once called me a bitch thirteen times in the space of twenty minutes.

I counted each one.

"You selfish bitch." One. "Ungrateful little bitch." Two. "Fame-hungry bitch." Three.

And so on, each one spat from the same lips that once pressed against mine in reverence. The same mouth that used to whisper "I love you, baby" while his fingers gently brushed my braids back from my forehead.

The most devastating part wasn't the venom in his voice or the contortion of his face into something unrecognizable. It was my response.

I didn't unleash the righteous fury I'd been raised to wield when disrespected. I didn't throw him out of the apartment I paid for. I didn't raise my voice to match his. I just . . . left. Silently gathered my purse, my keys, my dignity.

He apologized later, of course. Showed up to set with roses, tears, and promises. And I accepted it all, the way I always did. How could I not? That was our routine, as choreographed as an eight-count.

And so, slowly, deliberately, I began to withdraw further.

By the time we reached season five of *Moesha*, I hated the character.

I hated the way she always had the right answer. The way she judged everyone around her. The way the writers made her a mirror of how folks believed teenage Black girls should behave—smart, sassy, righteous, respectable. I didn't recognize myself in her anymore. Looking at her on the page was like staring into a funhouse mirror.

All the while, I was quietly abusing my body to stay thin

and going home to a man who showed me less kindness as time went on. There were days I'd show up to set despondent, but I always managed to smile and hit my mark. I thought I was convincing, but one of the producers called my mom . . . who then called me the second I was back in my trailer packing up after wrapping for the day.

She got straight to the point. "Baby, what's going on with you and that boy?" she asked, her voice gentle but insistent.

"Nothing, Mom. We're good," I said, the lie sour on my tongue.

I put my cell on speaker while I washed Moesha's face off mine.

"Mmm-hmm. Okay," she hummed, unconvinced. "And when that boy gets tired of being reminded that he works *for* his girlfriend? How does that 'nothing' look?"

I could envision my mom pacing the kitchen, hand on her hip. This was not something I was going to be able to brush off.

"Sometimes he says things," I said gently. ". . . When he's stressed."

"What kind of things?" The sharpness in her voice could have cut glass.

"Just . . . you know. About my weight. About the show. About how other men look at me."

"Sometimes?" she asked, her voice vibrating with barely contained fury.

I hesitated. The truth stuck in my throat like a fish bone. "More than sometimes," I finally admitted, the words barely audible, as if speaking them at full volume would make them too real to bear.

A chorus of murmured curses, tuts, and sighs echoed through the phone before she spoke again. "I'm coming to see you."

"No, Mom, you don't need to—"

"Bran."

"Mom. You don't need to come," I insisted.

The next morning, I woke to the sound of the doorbell. The Dreamer was gone—early meeting, his note on the counter said. Lucky timing.

When I opened the door, it wasn't my mother—or anybody—standing there. On my doorstep was one of those thick bubble mailers. I could tell from the handwriting on the front, elegant and soft, that it was from my mom.

Inside was a thick paperback book. "*The Verbally Abusive Relationship*" was printed in bold letters across the cover. A Post-it note was attached: "Bran, read this . . . and then we're gonna sit down and talk."

Shame flooded my body, hot and suffocating, like a summer heat wave. My mother's love—persistent, uncompromising—terrified me more than The Dreamer's criticism ever could. Because her love demanded honesty. It required me to face what was happening in the shadows of my perfect life.

My phone rang ten minutes later.

"Did you get it?" my mom asked, not bothering with hello.

"Yes," I whispered.

"Good. Start reading."

I shoved it into my nightstand drawer, as if hiding the book could hide the truth it contained.

But truth has a way of demanding to be acknowledged, and mine chose a chilly October night. We were at a party. Some industry event where the champagne flowed freely and everybody wanted my attention. Those were the only places where I really felt worthy. In those rooms, I was Brandy, this huge pop star with the hit sitcom. The attention fed my ego like sugar, sweet and addictive.

The Dreamer saw the attention I was receiving and felt threatened. Some guy complimented my performance on a recent awards show, his words kind and professional. That was it. A handshake. A warm, harmless gesture exchanged between peers in the parade of industry friends and entourages. The

Dreamer's smile disappeared the instant the guy walked away, replaced by a coldness that made me shiver despite being in the middle of an overcrowded, overheated room. He was standoffish the rest of the party. It was exhausting trying—and failing—to manage his feelings, to balance enjoying being out with monitoring his mood shifts.

After the party, in the darkened quiet of the car, he started lashing out at me. I pressed myself against the passenger door and stared out the window, trying to create distance between us in the confined space.

"You embarrass me every time we go out," he yelled. "You act like you're so much better than me. Like I'm nothing."

"That's not true," I whispered. "I was just being polite. It's part of my job to—"

"Your job?" His laugh was bitter and cynical. "Your job is more important than respecting me? Than how I feel?"

His words were meant to wound rather than communicate. He said things that burned deep into my chest, leaving marks no one would see but I would feel for days afterward.

"Can you just take me home, please?" I said, still turned toward the window.

"Look at me . . . If I ever catch someone holding your hand like that again . . ." Without breaking my gaze, he clamped his hand down on mine with a force that shook me. He must've seen my pupils widening in panic as he bent my fingers back, stretching them to agony—his breath hot and fast against my face. "If I ever see it again, we're done. You understand me? Done."

Pain shot through my hand like fire, radiating up my arm.

I whimpered, "You're hurting me," the words barely audible.

Something flickered in his eyes—recognition, maybe, or shame—and he released my hand. I wept the rest of the ride home as he apologized, his mood swinging from rage to remorse. "Baby, I'm sorry," he kept saying, reaching for me as

I pressed myself against the door. "You know I'd never really hurt you, right? Please tell me you know that."

When we reached my apartment, I fled to the bedroom and locked the door.

"Baby, I'm sorry," he called, his voice cracking with what sounded like genuine remorse. "You know I'd never really hurt you, right? Please, B. Tell me you know that."

I didn't answer. Instead, I reached for my nightstand drawer, my fingers still throbbing where he'd gripped them. The book my mother had sent stared back at me, no longer an accusation but a lifeline.

Opening to a random page, I found a checklist titled "Signs You May Be in an Abusive Relationship."

He seems irritated or angry with you several times a week, although you hadn't meant to upset him.

Every day. Sometimes every hour.

You find yourself apologizing for things that aren't your fault.

Constantly. Reflexively. Like breathing.

You sometimes think, "What's wrong with me? I shouldn't feel so bad."

Every time I looked in the mirror. Every time I tried to understand why I couldn't make him happy, why I wasn't enough.

I began reading from the beginning, tears streaming down my face as I recognized myself on page after page, as if the author had been witness to my slow unraveling.

In the hallway, his apologies had turned to silence. I heard the front door open and close, the sound of his departure like the period at the end of a painful sentence.

The air shifted—slightly, but enough. I picked up the phone.

"Mom?" My voice was small.

She knew. Instantly. "You read the book."

"I did," I admitted, each word weighted with the truth I'd been avoiding. "And . . ."

"And?" she prompted gently.

"Mom," I whispered, the dam finally breaking, "I think I'm being abused."

We cried together, miles apart but connected by the invisible thread that had always run between us, stronger than distance, stronger than my stubbornness, stronger than my pride.

When our tears subsided, her voice came through the receiver with the clarity and authority that had guided me since birth.

"Grab a bag," she said. "Come home."

BORDERLINE

THE RUPTURE COMES like an avalanche, sudden and violent. My heart thunders against my rib cage like it's trying to escape, each beat threatening to crack my sternum. An uncontrollable tremble takes hold of my body—not the quiver of stage fright I'd grown accustomed to since childhood, but an intense anxiety that starts in my core and radiates outward until even my fingertips vibrate with panic.

My throat constricts like an invisible hand is crushing my windpipe. I can't breathe. I can't think. I can't speak. The world around me—my trailer with its too-bright lights and that damn script sitting open on the vanity—turns to vapor. It feels like the lifeblood is draining from me, replaced by liquid fear that freezes my veins from the inside out.

Outside these thin walls, an entire soundstage teems with crew members, makeup artists, and production assistants. All of them are waiting for me to emerge as Moesha Mitchell, and I'm definitely not in any shape to go out on set.

I can't recall what we were shooting that day, but every word of Moesha's sanctimonious lecture in the script felt like a splinter working its way under my fingernail. After years of living in her world, something inside me snapped like an overstretched rubber band.

"This character has got to go," I whispered as I flipped through my sides for the day.

A soft knock on my trailer. "Five minutes, Brandy," called a production assistant, his voice muffled through the metal.

I couldn't do it. Not today. Not ever again.

I'd never walked off set before. The good girl in me wouldn't have dared. But today, she was dead.

With movements that felt mechanical, like my body was operating on its own emergency protocol, I collected my things. As my fingers fumbled with my purse zipper, I caught a glimpse of myself in the mirror—eyes too wide, skin ashen beneath my makeup—and quickly looked away. I didn't recognize the reflection staring back at me.

I pushed open the trailer door, the California sunlight assaulting my vision. The production lot swam before me—golf carts zipping by, crew members calling to each other, the endless maze of cables snaking across the asphalt. I made no eye contact with anyone. I spoke to no one. I just left.

Each step toward my car felt like wading through cement. Somewhere behind me, I could hear my name being called with increasing urgency, but the sound was distant, as though filtering through water.

I don't want to be on the world's time. I want to be on my own, I thought as I pulled out of Sunset Gower Studios with no destination in mind. I reached for the digital clock on my dashboard and pressed the power button until it shut off. Then I picked up the phone and dialed his number. "Can you meet me? Please?"

I don't know why I called The Dreamer, but I did. I hadn't seen him since I left and went to my parents'. And I wasn't returning his calls. But he answered on the second ring, his voice a mixture of surprise and relief.

"Where are you?" he asked, concern etched in every syllable.

I glanced around the studio parking lot as if seeing it for the first time. "Somewhere I don't want to be."

"The café off Ventura," he said without hesitation. "The one with those cinnamon rolls you like. I'll be there in fifteen."

He pulled me into his arms the second I got there, enveloping me in the familiar scent of his cologne—sandalwood and something uniquely him. This was what I needed, I thought as I melted against his chest. This feeling of being held together when everything inside me was falling apart.

"You're shaking," he whispered into my ear, his hands running up and down my back as if trying to generate heat. "What happened?"

I couldn't answer. Couldn't find words for the void that had opened inside me. We moved to a secluded corner table, the waitress taking one look at my face and discreetly placing a glass of water before me without asking for my order. Recognition flickered in her eyes, but mercifully, she said nothing.

He didn't press about why I'd left work, and I didn't tell him. We just sat in silence as I traced patterns in the condensation of my water glass—until his cell phone beeped with an insistent rhythm that matched the throbbing behind my eyes.

"Hey, I have a dance audition," he said. "I should go."

Panic rose in my chest like floodwater. The thought of being alone with this chaos in my mind was more terrifying than anything I'd ever faced.

"Take me with you," I pleaded. "I can't be alone right now. Please."

He studied my face, and whatever he saw in my eyes made him nod slowly.

"Okay, come on. We can get your car later."

I slid down in his passenger seat until the world outside disappeared from view.

"I don't want to see cars or anything the world has to offer," I said, my eyes fixed on the strip of sky visible through the windshield. "I just want to see sky and trees."

He didn't respond, just turned up the air-conditioning and pulled out of the parking lot with careful movements, as if afraid sudden motion might shatter me completely.

The blue above me seemed to pulse and expand with each breath I took. The edges of my vision began to haze, colors bleeding into one another like watercolors on wet paper. Something in me surrendered and I drifted off into nothingness.

Sunlight stabbed through my eyelids as voices filtered into my consciousness. My mother's worried tone, someone else murmuring responses. I was in my apartment, though I had no recollection of how—or when—I'd gotten there. The cream-colored walls of my living room swam into focus, then faded again as my eyes struggled to adjust.

When I came to more fully, I found myself sitting cross-legged in my favorite chair—a wide, overstuffed thing upholstered in buttery-soft leather—watching dust motes dance in the sunbeams that streamed through half-drawn curtains. Each tiny speck became suddenly, inexplicably fascinating, their random ballet in the golden light both mesmerizing and profoundly hilarious. A giggle bubbled up from some long-dormant place inside my chest, growing into a wave I couldn't contain.

My mother appeared before me, eyes wide with a fear I'd never seen there before.

"Brandy, snap out of it!" She gripped my shoulders, but I felt only a distant pressure, as if her touch had to travel through layers of cotton to reach me.

I just smiled in response. Everything was so beautifully interconnected, so perfect in its imperfection. The dust, the light, her fear, my laughter—all of it part of a divine tapestry I could suddenly perceive like it was etched in light.

Couldn't she see? Everything was divine. The chair beneath me, the air in my lungs, the worry in her eyes—all of it was God's doing. God was in everything, and everything was in God, and I had finally, finally broken through the veil of illusion to witness this cosmic truth.

"I'm here, Mom," I said, my voice dreamy and distant even to my own ears. "I'm more here than I've ever been."

Later, I'd learn that my mother had received a frantic call from our housekeeper, Rosa, a woman who'd been with us since before *Moesha*. Rosa, who'd seen me through countless early-morning call times and late-night recording sessions. Rosa, who knew the difference between Brandy-tired and something more sinister.

"She's acting strange," Rosa had told my mother. "Like she's here but not here. You need to come right away."

When my parents arrived—my father breaking every speed limit between their house and my apartment—they found The Dreamer standing outside, leaning against the hallway wall with exhaustion etched into every line of his face. The bags under his eyes suggested he'd been there all night, watching me spiral into whatever this was.

"What's going on with her?" my mother demanded, not bothering with pleasantries.

He shrugged, the gesture so casual it would later infuriate me when I heard about it. "I don't know, but I'm tired of going through these changes," he said, as if he'd been inconvenienced by my breakdown. As if my unraveling was a deliberate act designed to disrupt his dance audition.

I floated in a bubble of my own making, everything distant and amusing. Time stretched and contracted in unpredictable patterns. Seconds felt like hours; hours compressed into heartbeats. My mother tried every tactic to break through—anger, pleading, even threats—but I remained unreachable, protected in a strange serenity that nothing could penetrate.

It was my dad who finally said what no one in the room wanted to acknowledge: "She needs help. Professional help."

I remember fragments of what followed: the back seat of my parents' car, the cool leather against my feverish skin, The Dreamer's hand in mine despite my mother's glare of disapproval. The world outside rushing by in technicolor streaks as we sped toward help.

"This is great!" I announced, beaming at the back of my parents' heads. "They *finally* like you!"

They exchanged worried glances in the rearview mirror, a silent communication honed through decades of marriage, as my father pressed harder on the gas pedal. My mother reached back to make sure the child locks were engaged on the doors—a precaution that would have offended me in any other state of mind but now struck me as adorably unnecessary. Where would I go? The universe was everywhere.

The car sped down the freeway, carrying me toward help, while I drifted in and out of awareness.

It would be years before I could look back at this day and recognize it for what it was: the breaking point when the carefully constructed edifice of my public persona finally collapsed under the weight of everything I'd been carrying.

The pressure to be whatever everyone needed me to be—daughter, sister, role model, star—while sacrificing whoever it was I might have become if left to grow wildly and freely like a child should.

When we got to Cedars-Sinai Medical Center, my mom, ever protective, *and* ever aware of the public relations nightmare unfolding in real time, pushed for an older nurse—someone who might not have recognized me from TV, someone too old or too white to have heard of *Moesha* or "The Boy Is Mine." Really, someone who wouldn't be tempted to call the tabloids as soon as our backs were turned.

"My daughter is dehydrated," she told the triage nurse. "She's been working too hard. She needs rest and fluids."

The doctors agreed, putting me on fluids to replenish my dehydrated body. I hadn't been eating or drinking properly for days without realizing it. For forty-eight hours, they monitored me around the clock. The doctor who examined me had kind eyes, eyes that saw beyond the chart in his hands to the broken girl on the hospital bed.

"The body can only take so much before it forces a shutdown," he told my parents in hushed tones he thought I couldn't hear. "Think of it as a circuit breaker flipping to prevent a total electrical fire."

Moesha went on a short hiatus, and I went home to my parents' house.

The comfort of my parents and Ray being near nourished me far more than sleeping in.

My parents put me under strict orders: rest and relax. And that was what I did. I moved slow and tried not to think about anything at all—not the show, not the music, not the public waiting for my return, not the executives tallying lost dollars with every day I remained hidden away.

I started going on morning walks with my mom—gentle strolls through the neighborhood before the sun climbed high enough to bring out the paparazzi who had gotten wind of my "exhaustion." For as close as we were—mother-daughter, manager-talent, confidante–secret keeper—there was this unspoken thing between us when it came to work.

"Did I do this? Did I drive you to this?" she asked, her voice cracking with emotion, the question she'd clearly been holding back since the hospital finally breaking free. "Was I pushing too hard? Demanding too much?"

The question dangled in the air, as fragile as porcelain.

"No, Mom," I said, reaching for her hand. "I should have spoken up."

"And why didn't you?" Her fingers tightened around mine. "Why didn't you tell me you were drowning?"

I looked past her to the roses—blood-red and perfect—and tried to find words for something I barely understood myself.

"I don't know," I finally whispered. "I guess I was afraid of disappointing everyone. Disappointing you."

My mom stood directly in front of me then, her hands rising to cup my face, searching my eyes with hers—those same brown eyes I'd inherited, now looking back at me with fierce love and fiercer determination.

"I think it's time we figure that out."

We told the world I was simply overworked and needed a brief respite from the relentless schedule of *Moesha*—sixteen-hour days, press junkets, photo shoots, all while trying to maintain a recording career. What really happened was that I'd splintered into a thousand glittering pieces, each shard reflecting a different facet of my pain.

A nervous breakdown. That's what they call it when your mind can no longer carry the weight and stress your smile pretends doesn't exist. When the persona you've crafted with such care finally collapses like a house built on sand, leaving you exposed to elements you've been running from since childhood.

My dad was right. I needed more than just fluids and bed rest. I started therapy, and that was where the true work began—the excavation of buried traumas, the examination of patterns, the slow, painful process of meeting myself for the very first time.

"Tell me about the first time you felt your body was wrong," my therapist asked during one session, her voice gentle but unflinching.

There were days I'd sit across from her and sob for the entire hour, tears falling so hard and fast they soaked the collar of my shirt. Other days, I'd just stare out the window, silent but unraveling, watching hummingbirds dart between flowers in her garden and wondering how something so small could still find the strength to beat its wings a thousand times a minute.

Therapy wasn't some magical remedy. It was excavation work—dirty, exhausting. Sometimes it felt like I was clawing through concrete with bloodied fingernails just to uncover one small truth about myself. But slowly, painfully, I unearthed tools buried deep within. Tools to quiet the toxic chorus that had become the soundtrack of my days. Tools to rebuild what had been broken.

I had to relearn how to look in mirrors without flinching, how to eat without calculating the caloric cost of every bite, how to breathe without apologizing for the space I occupied in the world. I had to understand, truly understand, that my worth wasn't hanging from some digital scale or trapped inside a magazine spread or frozen in a frame of a music video.

When I finally went back to my apartment after weeks of healing under my parents' watchful eyes, the place felt foreign—as if some stranger had selected the furniture, hung the art, arranged the accessories that were meant to say something about who I was. The clarity hit me hard and soft simultaneously, like a velvet-covered hammer.

The Dreamer emerged from the bedroom as I stood in the living room, taking inventory of this life that no longer felt like mine. And he, too, seemed unfamiliar to me—beautiful still, yes, with those eyes that had once made my knees weak, but like a character from a film I'd watched long ago rather than the man who'd shared my bed and my secrets.

I knew, right then, that my journey forward no longer included him. I wasn't angry or sad. Just done. The realization settled over me with the quiet finality of the last autumn leaf touching ground.

I don't see a reflection of myself in him anymore, I thought as he embraced me, his familiar cologne now cloying.

"We need to talk about what happened," I said when he released me, my voice steady and certain in a way it hadn't been in months.

"Nothing happened," he replied. "You had a bad day. A breakdown. It's over. Move on."

I studied his face—the face I'd once traced with fingertips in the darkness, the face I'd once believed knew me better than anyone else.

"You're right. I did have a breakdown, and I am moving on," I said, the double meaning clear in my tone if not in my words.

I didn't care to hear whatever smooth charm he might have had left in him. I just walked to the door, held it open, and told him I'd have his things sent to him. No drama. No tears. Just the quiet dignity of choosing myself for perhaps the first time in my life.

He looked at me for a long beat, confusion giving way to understanding and then to something like relief. Maybe he'd been looking for an exit strategy, too.

"Take care of yourself, B," he said as he walked out, and I couldn't tell if it was genuine concern or just something people say when they have nothing else to offer.

"I'm learning how," I replied, and closed the door behind him.

The apartment I had once cherished now felt haunted. I needed a new beginning, and I found it nestled in a quiet corner of Calabasas—a newly built home I could transform into a sanctuary.

A blank slate was exactly what I needed. I decorated the house top to bottom in earth tones—soft browns, gentle beiges, creamy taupes. No bright chaos, just warmth radiating from every room.

Stillness.

Peace.

The crown jewel was the cathedral-sized artificial waterfall I had installed in the main hallway—an extravagance that raised eyebrows but settled my soul. From anywhere in the house, you could hear its gentle lullaby, water cascading over stone in rhythmic meditation. Sometimes, in those early days of healing, I would sit cross-legged on the floor beside it, closing my eyes and letting the sound wash over me, baptizing me in tranquility.

Before returning to the set of *Moesha*—a return both financially necessary and psychologically daunting—my mother suggested dinner. Just us two. We'd been deliberately avoiding discussing work while I'd been resting, but it was time to get back to it. I had made a commitment. And there were hundreds of people who were depending on me to show up to set and work—crew members with families to feed, writers with stories to tell, co-stars with scenes to share.

At a quiet table in the back of our favorite restaurant in the valley—a place that had known me since before I had a driver's license—my mother reached for my hands across crisp white linen.

"Two things are clear to me now," she said. "You need to pull back from work, truly pull back, and I—" Her voice caught for just a second, a rare glimpse of vulnerability from the woman who'd navigated the sharky waters of Hollywood on my behalf for years. "I need to step back from being your manager."

"Mom—" I started, but she shook her head, silver earrings catching the light.

"Listen to me, baby. Nothing, and I mean nothing, is more important to me than being your mother. Don't ever forget that." Her fingers tightened around mine. "We lost sight of that somewhere along the way, didn't we?"

I nodded, unable to speak past the knot in my throat, understanding that this was her own form of healing, her own recognition of what mattered most. She was, in the end, simply my mother—a woman who loved me beyond measure, who would set fire to empires if it meant keeping me safe.

"I just want you back," she whispered, and I knew she didn't mean back on set or back in the studio. She meant back to myself—the self that existed before fame rewrote my story.

"I'm working on it," I promised her, and for the first time in longer than I could remember, it felt like the absolute truth.

Before the breakdown, I was yearning for answers. I was looking for a way to connect with my higher self. I questioned everything in my life. Who was I really, and what was my purpose?

When I was in the hospital, I took the opportunity to ask God, "Do You exist?"

I was raised within the Church of Christ. Early on, my eyes saw things that didn't align with the scriptures. I noticed the way love was preached from pulpits but rarely practiced in pews. The way righteousness seemed reserved for those who looked the part, dressed the part, spoke the part.

Over time, those quiet contradictions became louder until they drowned out the hymns, and I started searching for God and enlightenment everywhere and anywhere I could—in other faiths, in ancient texts, in the words of modern prophets and philosophers, in the silence of meditation and the chaos of ecstatic dance.

I welcomed unfamiliar spaces and teachings. Once, at a friend's house, a speech from Minister Farrakhan flickered across the television. His words were potent, filled with a power that pulled me through the screen. When he spoke of God, he spoke of God as both male and female, and the conviction in his voice captured my attention. I had never heard God described like that; it felt both foreign and oddly familiar, as if a truth I had always known was being named for the first time. The Nation of Islam called to me. I learned the teachings and rituals of the Nation, the discipline. How to eat. How to live. How to connect to myself.

A meeting with Minister Farrakhan was arranged—a privilege extended to me because of my platform, not because of my devotion—but I wanted to do more research first. My reading led me to the autobiography of Malcolm X, to his evolution from hustler to holy man, and to his own questioning of the Nation in his later years after his pilgrimage to Mecca.

The more I read, the more discomfort emerged—subtle at first, then widening like a crack in foundation. Some beliefs upheld by the Nation clashed fundamentally with how I viewed humanity, with the love I believed should be extended to all people regardless of race or background. The meeting never happened.

My awareness of the Church of Scientology was largely informed by judgment, but I was in a space where I had curiosity and wanted to find out for myself.

A friend was undergoing something called the Purification Rundown. The idea fascinated me—cleansing body and spirit simultaneously, sweating out impurities that had accumulated over years of silent suffering, of prioritizing "the dream" over my own well-being. I felt toxic, poisoned by expectation and performance and the corrosive acid of self-hatred. Purification sounded like salvation. That was my introduction to Scientology.

I started reading Dianetics and Scientology books, sprawling tomes as heavy as my doubts. They spoke of immortal spirits who had forgotten their true nature—and wasn't that exactly how I felt? Like I'd forgotten who I truly was beneath the layers of performance? Scientology promised knowing *how* to know, and I was desperate for certainty, hungry for anything that might bring me closer to understanding.

I explored the process of auditing, tracing painful memories to their source, examining trauma that had settled into my bones. The precision of it appealed to me—the idea that healing could be systematic, that freedom could be achieved through careful procedure.

"Locate a painful incident you can comfortably face," I was instructed during an auditing session, the E-meter's needle jumping with my pulse.

I closed my eyes and traveled back, overwhelmed by how many scenes quickly appeared in my mind.

For a while, I believed this was the path—the structure I needed, the answers I craved. But something kept me from full surrender, some quiet voice of caution that whispered beneath the promises of clarity and freedom. Ultimately, it was not the path for me, either.

I found gurus and prophets in unexpected places—some legitimate teachers of ancient wisdom, others charismatic peddlers of feel-good platitudes. I sat at their feet, absorbing their enlightened tongues, learning about surrender and simplicity. I devoured holy texts, like the Quran and the Torah, until the words trailed off before my tired eyes. I learned to sit in meditation, crossing my legs and straightening my spine, closing my eyes and waiting for divine movement within.

"Focus on your breath," a shaman instructed during a weekend retreat in Sedona that cost more than most people's monthly rent. "Let thoughts come and go like clouds across the sky of your awareness."

But my thoughts weren't clouds; they were hurricanes, and no amount of breathing seemed to calm their devastating winds.

I chased peace through Buddhist teachings, finding momentary refuge in the saffron-robed simplicity that asked nothing of me except presence. The meditative chants soothed my weary soul like a gentle spring breeze after a lifetime of storms. The silence was both a blessing and a curse—freedom from external pressures but also a void that confused my performance-oriented mind.

I loved the communion of voices raised in chant, the vibration of sound in my chest like a second heartbeat. But questions still plagued me: What was I chanting for? And to whom were these prayers directed? The practice remained foreign, beautiful but distant, like admiring a masterpiece through museum glass. I could see its beauty but never truly touch its essence.

I sought wisdom from every tradition I could find, desperate to piece together a spiritual practice that made sense for the fractured woman I had become. I thought spiritual fulfillment required disappearance, that to connect with the divine meant erasing myself entirely. I let go, again and again and again, until I was stretched as thin as cellophane, transparent and fragile, on the verge of tearing completely. I gave away possessions that once defined me—designer clothes, shoes, jewelry. I tried to strip away every trace of ego, every desire, every remnant of the girl I had been.

One morning as the sun rose over my backyard, painting my new safe haven in hues of gold and promise, it hit me with the gentle force of revelation. In my journey to find myself and my relationship to faith, I had forgotten the most essential truth: God wasn't something to be found through elaborate rituals or teachings authored by men who had never known what it was to live in my skin.

God was already present—in the resilience that kept me breathing through my darkest nights, in the love that surrounded me even when I couldn't feel it, in the voice that had whispered "enough" when self-destruction seemed the only path.

God was in the tears that cleansed me during therapy sessions. God was in my mother's hands, offering unconditional love when I felt most unlovable. God was in the water that sang through my house, reminding me of renewal's constant possibility.

God was in the care I poured into rebuilding family connections, in the laughter I shared with friends who loved me at my worst, in the kindness shown to me by strangers who had no idea who I was, in the passion that still flickered inside my soul—the passion that made me want to keep trying, keep giving, keep loving, keep singing, keep living.

Meditation has become my compass, not as escape but as return—a silent conversation with my inner self that guides me through fog and illuminates what matters most. I no longer sit cross-legged expecting transcendence; I sit in gratitude for the gift of my next breath, for the miracle of continued existence after coming so close to its end.

This facade I had created—perfect child star, flawless performer, disciplined professional—had isolated me from the very essence of my being. And what I knew more than anything, sitting in the golden morning light with birdsong as my only company, was that I needed more time to just be. Away from the cameras, away from public view, away from the spotlight that had both illuminated and burned me. I needed shadow and silence in which to grow something authentic, something that couldn't be packaged or marketed or sold, something that belonged only to me.

NEW MOON

THE SIXTH SEASON of *Moesha* would be its last. The end came into view as our ratings slipped. We were the highest-rated comedy on the lowest-rated network—or, as the *New York Times* once put it, "the nonwhite hit nobody knows." We had leaned into more provocative, mature storylines, trying to grow the show up with the times. But in the process, we lost our way and strayed too far from what drew viewers to *Moesha* in the first place.

Fans were heartbroken. They deserved a proper goodbye. Closure. We all did. But here's the thing about unfinished stories—they live forever in possibility. I tried not to dwell on what could have been, or what we should have done differently, but of course I've imagined where Moesha might've gone next. By now, knowing her, she was probably running her own media empire.

I had mixed feelings about our cancellation. Our incredible cast and crew were now out of work. The family we built on set was disbanded, which gutted me. But for the first time in years, I was free.

No call times.

No interviews to prep for.

No studio sessions.

No album deadlines.

No rehearsals.

Time belonged to me. Just *me.*

It terrified the hell out of me. And I needed that. I needed the time to find myself. To ask, for real this time: *Who am I without all of this?* Not the character, not the voice, not the brand. Just me.

Alongside my deepening spiritual journey, I turned to the books that had been collecting dust in my study waiting for "someday." That someday had finally arrived.

Toni Morrison's *Paradise* transported me into a world where Black women's power and vulnerability intertwined like vines. I underlined passages until the pages resembled encrypted messages, blue ink mapping my journey through her masterpiece.

Jill Nelson's *Straight, No Chaser* put a name to so many of the feelings I was unpacking in therapy, and *Everyday Immortality* by Deepak Chopra opened doors within my spirit I hadn't known existed.

But it was Neale Donald Walsch's *Conversations with God* that split me open entirely. I didn't just read it once—I devoured it seven times, each reading revealing new layers, like examining a diamond under different light. It was like someone had reached into my soul and turned on lights in rooms that had been dark for years. What I desperately wanted to hear was nestled in those pages, patiently waiting for me to be ready to receive it.

My body, too, began to remember its own wisdom. Tennis racket in hand, I'd watch the neon ball soar across the court and feel something primal awaken in my muscles. The satisfying thwack when I made contact sent vibrations up my arm—solid, certain, real. Each morning, I unrolled my yoga mat as the sun streaked pink and gold across my bedroom floor. Downward dog. Warrior pose. Child's pose. Names that became prayers, movements that became meditation.

Every day, I could feel myself strengthening from the inside out. My body remembering its own power. My mind clearing like the sky after a storm.

The absence of a packed schedule gave me the space to take a step back and actually enjoy the things I'd accomplished. I reconnected with my music, not as product but as pieces of my soul I'd offered to the world.

Late nights found me cross-legged on my bedroom floor, surrounded by journals dating back to my teenage years. My fingers traced lyrics I'd scribbled in hotel rooms across continents, in tour buses rumbling through sleeping cities, in recording studios when inspiration struck like lightning at 3 a.m. Reading them now was like having a conversation with an earlier version of myself. That Brandy, I could tell now, had been naive, wounded, and searching.

"Wow," I whispered to no one, reading aloud from a journal entry written when I was just seventeen:

I'm afraid people only love the me they see on-screen. Would they love the real me? The messy me? The silent me?

I was getting inspired and wanted to create.

Still, I wasn't in a rush to jump back into the spotlight. When the offer came for *Osmosis Jones*—a weird but funny live-action animated buddy cop movie with Bill Murray, Chris Rock, and Laurence Fishburne—I said yes almost immediately. Voice work felt like the perfect transition—creative without requiring me to surrender my newfound freedom. I could show up in sweatpants, no makeup, hair twisted under a cap, and nobody would care. Just me and the microphone, creating magic in the sound booth.

I knew with unshakable certainty that I would eventually reconnect with Rodney and the Darkchild camp, but for now, I was exploring new waters with producer Mike City. Our collaboration felt like a gentle courtship—no pressure, no deadlines, just two artists playing in the sandbox of sound. We cut demos that might never see daylight, and that was perfectly fine. The joy was in the creating, not the releasing.

One of those songs—a lush, midtempo ballad called "Open"—

sounded like a love letter to the woman I was becoming. The melody curved and dipped like my own emotional landscape, the lyrics raw with honesty. When it eventually landed on the *Osmosis Jones* soundtrack, I felt a quiet pride. It remains one of my favorite deep cuts—a secret handshake between me and the fans who truly see me.

One afternoon, my phone lit up with Mike's name.

"I need you to come to the Record Plant," he said, words tumbling over each other. "There's something you have to hear."

"What is it?" I asked, already reaching for my car keys.

"Can't explain it. It's . . . different. From anything you've done. From anything *anyone's* doing right now." He paused. "Just trust me."

That feeling—when someone believes they've struck magic—is spine-tingling. I rushed right to the studio.

When I arrived, Mike was perched on the edge of his seat, fingers drumming against the console.

"I've been wanting to do an up-tempo with you. Something feel-good, but not bubbly, you know? Something with substance," he said.

He hit Play, and what came out of those speakers? Man. It was a lulling piano melody dancing with this heavy bass line, horns that seemed to drop from the heavens, and just the faintest bell underneath the piano—it was so subtle you almost missed it. It was sweet and celestial like a lullaby, but also brooding and sensual. I started humming along, mimicking as if playing the piano with my voice.

The hook came so clearly, like it wrote itself on the spot.

I ain't even gonna front, I ain't even gonna lie
Since you walked up in the club, I've been giving you the eye

I looked right at him. "Yo, let me get in the booth."

He was already reaching for the controls.

We spent the next two weeks building that record piece by piece, like master craftsmen. We shaped verses, sculpted the bridge. That record became "Full Moon," and I knew from the first playback that it was going to be the heart of whatever my next album would be.

In the summer of 2001, I flew down to Miami to reconnect with Rodney Jerkins and the Darkchild camp.

They had set up at the Hit Factory, a legendary studio whose walls had absorbed the sounds of music's greatest innovators. Reuniting with Rodney, Freddie, and LaShawn felt like coming home after a long journey. Our chemistry was still electric, still effortless.

By then, Darkchild was easily one of the most in-demand producing camps in pop music. After the success of *Never Say Never,* Rodney and his crew worked with Jennifer Lopez, Destiny's Child, Toni Braxton, the Spice Girls, Britney Spears, and Whitney Houston.

There were some new faces in the camp, too: singer-songwriter Nora Payne, who could translate emotions into lyrics like some kind of alchemist; vocal producer Kenisha Pratt, whose ear for harmonies was superhuman; and Rodney and Freddie's cousin Robert, whose quiet intensity pulled me in likc gravity.

When I arrived at the Hit Factory, I felt an aura. It's difficult to describe. Like you could feel this light, this glow, in the air.

"Guess who's next door," Rodney said, grinning like he'd just won the lottery.

"Who?" I asked, settling into a chair, curious but clueless.

Rodney leaned in close, like he was telling me a secret. "Michael."

My heart skipped a beat. Dead serious.

"Michael *who*?"

Rodney just stared at me.

My jaw dropped. "Michael? . . . As in Jackson?"

He nodded.

"Oh my GOD!" I screamed.

He held his finger up and motioned toward the door.

"Wait," I whispered, leaning in closer to Rodney. "Like he's literally on the other side of that wall right now?"

"He's in there *right now,*" Rodney whispered slowly, clearly enjoying my freak-out. "I'm gonna be going back and forth between you two."

Imagine being a tennis player and finding out Serena Williams is practicing on the next court. Or being a chef and learning Gordon Ramsay is cooking in the kitchen next to yours. It immediately put a battery in my back and inspired me to go hard.

My voice had changed *again*—deeper now, warmer, with this textured lower register and a much stronger falsetto. My instrument had new edges, and I was eager to explore my voice with a team who knew me so intimately.

"How far can we push this?" I asked the room. "I want this album to sound like nothing anyone's ever heard before."

One day, Rodney walked in with this beat. It was aggressive—chopping rhythms with these snarky sound effects lurking in the back. The bass lines were like something from a sci-fi movie, weaving around glitchy keyboard loops. It sounded like what I imagined the inside of a computer would sound like if it could make music.

"Oh my God, Rodney, *this is it,*" I said, practically jumping out of my skin.

"It's different, right?" His eyes searched mine for confirmation.

"This is exactly what the industry needs right now. We could change the whole GAME with this," I said.

"Yeah, this is what I'm going for. This is what we gotta

do," he agreed, nodding the way he did when he knew he had something special.

Kenisha and Nora quickly became my confessional booth. I told them everything about The Dreamer—the gaslighting that had me questioning my own memories, the rage I felt when he belittled me, how deeply he'd betrayed my trust, the broken promises.

All of the bullshit he put me through became "What About Us?"—a record dripping with attitude and raw emotion. We had so much fun doing that record. It was so outside the box. I wanted to sound angry on the song, so I sang like I was delivering the lines like throwing jabs, almost shouting at points. Rodney then distorted my voice into these jagged digital fragments, transforming my usual smooth tone into something with grit.

R&B had evolved dramatically since *Never Say Never.* It was brasher, bouncier, and sharper after years of rap's widening influence. We wanted to play with that and also draw from club sounds pulsating across Europe—garage, glitch, electro. I was keen on playing up the Y2K era—we'd survived the millennium bug, and technology was evolving at warp speed. So, I thought, what would my voice sound like if it was from the future?

I never wanted to be anybody's clone. My mission was always to carve my own lane, hoping that by being authentically me, I might inspire others to be authentically them. Everyone in our circle shared this vision. We all wanted to take the music somewhere new. We let our instincts drive the car.

Having Michael next door was inspiring . . . and torturous. Rodney tried to keep me focused, but how could my heart not do backflips knowing Michael Jackson was just through that wall? And not only was he on the other side of that wall, he was also giving Rodney notes on *my* music.

Rodney came into one session with this serious look on his face.

"Listen," he said, settling into the chair beside me. "Do you want to be the greatest?"

I was caught off guard and unsure how to answer. Of course I wanted to be great. But Rodney's question invited pressure. And that wasn't a feeling I felt ready to invite back into my life.

"The greatest? That's . . . a lot to put on anybody," I said.

"Well, do you want to be the greatest version of *you*?" he clarified, eyes locked on mine.

I've never cared about competing with other artists, but I've always been obsessed with outdoing myself, with climbing higher than my last peak. We were creating freely, but of course everybody was thinking about how to top *Never Say Never*—even if none of us were saying it outright.

"Of course," I said simply.

"Well, here's how you do it," he said, leaning in like he was about to share the secret to eternal life.

Then Rodney broke down Michael's approach to recording vocals—similar to what I'd been doing with layering, but taken to an almost obsessive level. Michael built mountains with his voice, stacking layer upon layer upon layer. More. More. Always more. It reminded me of what Quincy Jones had told me years earlier about creating a wall of sound using nothing but the human voice.

We'd played with this technique on *Never Say Never*, but now we were pushing it to the extreme. Sometimes we'd stack sixteen separate takes of me singing the exact same note for just a tiny section of a song. I attacked every single note like I was scaling Mount Everest, pushing past where comfort ended—then pushing even further.

Rodney knew exactly how badly I wanted to meet Michael. I wasn't even trying to be subtle about it, dropping hints left and right like breadcrumbs. One night, we were in our usual groove—LaShawn and I in one room working on lyrics, Rodney in another room cooking up sounds that seemed beamed in from another dimension. Ray had come down to Miami to hang out with me and vibe out in the studio. He even got in the booth and laid down some incredible background vocals on a couple of tracks, his voice blending with mine in that special harmony only siblings can create.

Rodney walked in and sat down, way too casual for what he was about to say.

"Would you like to come and meet him?" he asked, examining his fingernails as if we were discussing something as mundane as lunch options.

I tried to play dumb, my heart already racing. "Meet *who*?"

"Bran . . . come on . . ." Rodney gave me that look—part amusement, part exasperation. "Who do you think?"

"Are you serious?" All pretense vanished instantly. "Of course I want to meet Michael Jackson!"

"Okay, come on, then," he said, rising from his chair with the nonchalance of someone who wasn't about to fundamentally alter my existence.

My heart nearly exploded, beating so hard I could feel it in my fingertips, in my temples, behind my eyes. "You mean NOW?"

"Yes, *now*!" Rodney said, already heading for the door.

I reached for Ray's hand as if I needed an anchor to keep me from floating away. Rodney led us from our room to Michael's, each step bringing us closer to a moment I'd dreamed about since I was old enough to understand what music was.

"Oh my God. It's actually happening," I whispered to Ray, my voice quivering somewhere between excitement and terror, my palm sweaty against his.

Ray is much better at this than me—always has been. I know he was over-the-moon excited, too, but he was playing it cool, his face a mask of casual interest that didn't fool me for a second. I could feel his pulse racing in his wrist, betraying his own excitement.

When we first entered Michael's studio, it was dimly lit—almost dark, like a lair from a fairy tale. We could barely make out a figure sitting in the far corner, silhouetted against a faint blue glow from a mixing board. Ray and I exchanged this look like, *Is this for real, or are we being pranked?*

"Hey, Mike," Rodney called into the shadows.

The figure turned in his chair, and it was like he rotated directly into a golden spotlight. It was actually Michael Jackson. Not an image. Not a video. The real Michael, in the flesh. He was wearing a blue satin outfit that seemed to catch what little light there was. He looked exactly like you'd expect a legend to look—otherworldly.

"Hi," he said, his voice fluttering up in the air like a butterfly released from cupped hands.

And that was when my body betrayed me. I actually blacked out. Legs turned to Jell-O. Down I went.

"B, get up! You're embarrassing us! Get up *right now*!" Ray yelled. "This is Michael Jackson, and you are on the floor! GET UP!"

"It's okay. It's okay. This has happened before," Michael assured everyone, one hand partially covering his face as he tried not to laugh, the other gesturing gracefully toward me. "Are you okay, Brandy?"

The fact that he said my name snapped me back to reality faster than smelling salts. "Oh my God, he knows my name," I mumbled, still dazed, allowing Ray to help me to my feet.

"Of course I do, silly," Michael replied, warmth in his voice, eyes crinkling at the corners with amusement.

He waited until I was standing and had somewhat composed myself—which, let's be honest, was a relative term—before bursting into a fit of giggles that sounded like music itself. His laughter made us all laugh, the tension dissolving into genuine joy.

Rodney's simultaneous work on both *Invincible* and *Full Moon* created a beautiful synergy—that's Michael's heavenly vocals elevating "It's Not Worth It" to another dimension, his voice intertwining with mine like complementary strands of DNA. And that's me in the background of his "Unbreakable," pushing my voice higher than should be legally allowed because I was determined to keep up with the King, even if it meant straining toward notes that lived in the stratosphere.

Our creative energy was through the roof in Miami. Kenisha, Nora, and I developed a bond that deepened the more we worked—they understood exactly what was in my head and heart, translating my jumbled thoughts into perfect lyrics. When I couldn't find the words, they somehow extracted them from my silence, like they had access to a language only we shared.

With Robert, there was a different kind of energy.

Like all of us, Robert found music in church, playing piano and drums while his siblings sang in the choir, Sunday mornings filled with harmonies that reached toward heaven. After Rodney brought him in for an Enrique Iglesias project, he moved to Los Angeles and joined the Darkchild family, another planet pulled into Rodney's orbit. He had barely unpacked in LA when our paths first crossed, fate disguised as coincidence.

Robert radiated warm, gentle energy, but his intense focus reminded me of a laser beam. I felt connected to him instantly on a soul level—he became my best friend, sharing late-night conversations that stretched until dawn. That friendship grew into something deeper while we created the album, evolving naturally like a seed becoming a flower.

Early on, he told me he didn't want a public relationship, that fame wasn't his thing—he was a behind-the-scenes person by nature, content to create magic without needing applause. I treasured that boundary. After living most of my life under flashbulbs, I was ready to experience love without an audience.

Before Robert, I thought love was about protection and

possession—building walls to keep the world out and the loved one in. With him, I felt like I was the guiding light—helping someone navigate their path through darkness toward something beautiful. Our connection felt pure, untainted by the complexities that had haunted my previous relationships. His heart captured mine completely. And there was this kindness in him—genuine and pure.

One afternoon, I wandered into his workspace and found him tinkering with a keyboard, fingers dancing over the keys like water flowing over smooth stones.

"What are you working on?" I asked.

Without a word, he pressed Play, and the room filled with a romantic arrangement that felt like silk brushing against bare skin—soft, soulful, sensual notes cascading like a gentle waterfall. I immediately knew I wanted to create something sexy and passionate with it, something that captured the electricity between us.

Once again, Kenisha and Nora translated what was overflowing from my heart into perfect lyrics. I wanted to capture the sensation of finally finding safe harbor after weathering too many storms.

Tonight's the night
For loving you right
You know what I wanna do
I wanna give in to you

By the time we wrapped the album, exhausted but exhilarated, I knew for certain: this was the best version of me as an artist. Every note, every lyric, every melody felt authentic—music that could only have come from my particular journey, my specific voice.

There had been another seismic shift, too, one even more miraculous than the album we'd just created.

I was pregnant.

STARLIGHT

I WAS IN the back seat of my parents' car, drifting through Beverly Hills as if suspended in amber. The sun spilled through the sunroof. My dad was at the wheel, focused, humming along to something faint on the radio. My mom, in the passenger seat, was deep in conversation—head tilted, fingers twirling the car phone's cord like she was conducting the words.

I placed both hands on the swell of my belly—this beautiful, moonlike curve that had become the center of my universe—and drew in the kind of breath performers save for those impossible high notes. The kind that not just fills your lungs but claims space in a room, announcing itself before a single note is sung.

Inhaaaale. The air filled me completely, pushing against my diaphragm.

Exhaaaaaale. I released it dramatically, letting it whistle through my teeth.

Inhaaaale. Deeper this time, my chest expanding fully.

Exhaaaaaale. A long, theatrical sigh that would've made Mr. Bialik proud.

"Whewwww," I moaned, infusing my voice with *just* enough tremor to convey distress.

My mom's head whipped around so fast I swear I heard the wind crack—the business call forgotten instantly, her eyes widened with maternal alarm, zeroing in on my face with laser precision.

"What's wrong, Bran?"

I cradled my belly with exaggerated tenderness, eyes downcast, channeling every bit of Moesha Denise Mitchell at her most dramatic.

"I think I'm going into labor."

The transformation of her face was instantaneous. The color drained from her cheeks, her eyes ballooned with panic, and her mouth formed a perfect O of horror. For a split second, I glimpsed something rare: Sonja Norwood—manager extraordinaire, negotiator supreme—completely unscripted.

I couldn't hold it in. The laughter bubbled up from my core, spilling out in a cascade of giggles that filled the car.

"I'm just playing, Ma!" I managed between gasps of laughter.

Her hand flew to her chest. "Don't *scare* me like that! Shoot. You nearly gave me a heart attack, girl! I was about to tell your dad to turn this car around and head straight to Cedars-Sinai!"

In the rearview mirror, my dad's eyes caught mine—those same eyes I'd inherited—crinkled at the corners with silent amusement. He'd always been my quiet accomplice, the still waters to mom's crashing waves.

"Willie, don't encourage her," my mom scolded, catching his expression. But there was no real heat behind it. Just the familiar dance of our family dynamics, steps we'd been perfecting since before I could harmonize.

As our laughter settled into comfortable silence, my hand still resting on my belly where my little one was performing her own private choreography against my ribs, a question blossomed in my mind—one of those vulnerable thoughts that only family could handle.

"Mom," I asked, my voice softening, genuine this time, "the labor. Are you afraid? To see me in that much pain?"

She turned fully in her seat now.

"Bran, of course I am." She reached back to place her warm

hand over mine. "I'm afraid to see you hurting, knowing I won't be able to take some of it myself." Her voice cracked slightly.

Then, just as the moment threatened to overwhelm us both, a mischievous spark lit her eyes.

"But on the other hand," she continued, her voice lifting, "I think you're deserving of the pain."

She let out the most glorious cackle and slapped my knee, absolutely tickled with her own joke. "That's what you get for scaring me half to death!"

"Touché, Mom." I laughed, squeezing her hand. "Touché."

I was now six months pregnant, and we were getting ready to release "What About Us?" as the lead single from *Full Moon*. I was worried about how the masses would receive the evolution of my sound. But people went absolutely crazy for the record. It exploded across continents, pulsing through clubs from Tokyo to London. Dave Myers directed a video that finally torched that good-girl image I'd been trying to shed, replacing it with something futuristic, something untamed and gloriously, unapologetically sexy. I felt so badass in those leather dominatrix outfits.

More than anything, I was ecstatic to be able to reintroduce myself as the grown woman I was. After vanishing from the spotlight for what felt like a lifetime, being welcomed back with such excitement was incredible.

A connection that already felt heaven-sent only deepened once life was growing inside me. Robert and I really blossomed in the studio. The hours stretched like caramel as we carved out more time there together—just us. No Darkchild. No entourage. No managers hovering. We were simply two friends in love, creating together.

Robert was spreading his wings as a producer in his own right, stepping out from under Rodney's shadow with a gentle but determined confidence. And I was finally embracing my voice as a songwriter, no longer content to simply interpret others' visions. Working with Kenisha Pratt and Nora Payne on *Full Moon* had unlocked something in me—a belief that my words, my stories, deserved to be heard.

We cut records, playing with sounds and styles, imagining where my artistry might venture after *Full Moon*. Some of those demos eventually found homes with other artists. Few people realize I've penned tracks for Jennifer Lopez ("Ryde or Die"), Kelly Rowland ("Love/Hate"), and Toni Braxton ("Selfish," "Always")—that's the beauty of this industry. Demos get passed around and eventually find their rightful vocalist, and I loved having a small bit in the process.

When word of my pregnancy spread, every congratulatory call inevitably curved toward the same question: "So when's the big day?"

Robert and I shared a love as profound as any vow could capture. But neither of us felt ready for marriage. We had pledged ourselves to one another—emotionally, physically, spiritually. We made promises to one another that meant more to us than any certificate.

That was enough for us. But the pressure only got louder, more insistent.

I understood it. The "good girl" narrative that had been stitched into my public persona demanded a specific sequence: marriage first, then motherhood. Having a baby out of wedlock threatened to tarnish the all-American image that had been meticulously crafted around me, despite the fact that I was now a twenty-three-year-old woman making my own choices.

Our commitment was unshakable, beyond question. So I suggested a simple solution to Robert one night as we lay in bed, my swollen feet in his lap receiving the nightly massage that had become our ritual.

"Let's just tell people we're married if they ask."

The words hung in the air between us. One little white lie. It seemed so harmless, like a small pebble tossed into a vast ocean.

I couldn't have known that this single deception would eventually alter the trajectory of my life in ways I couldn't possibly imagine—that the tiny ripples would return as waves powerful enough to reshape the very shoreline of my existence.

Nothing compared to the miracle expanding within me.

Being pregnant was magic, pure and simple. I loved how I felt in my skin. I had never felt more present, more embodied. And I had never felt so confident. So beautiful. So sexy. So *powerful.* Like all the scattered pieces of myself had finally aligned into perfect harmony.

God had blessed me with this angel to protect and nurture inside my own flesh. The transformation was instantaneous and absolute. The Brandy before pregnancy and the Brandy after were different beings entirely—as if I'd undergone a spiritual metamorphosis more profound than any religious conversion.

I was grateful for an easy pregnancy. No morning sickness. No swollen ankles until the very end. Just a radiant glow that makeup artists commented on during photo shoots, asking what highlighter I was using when I knew the luminescence came from somewhere much deeper than any cosmetic could reach.

Robert and I created a bubble—just high vibrations, quiet joy, and our love. We filled our home with soft music and softer lighting. We read books aloud to my belly, Robert's deep voice rumbling against the curve of my stomach as he narrated Dr. Seuss with the same reverence others might reserve for Shakespeare.

My two biggest cravings emerged with such specificity that they became jokes among my family and friends. The garlic noodles from Crustacean in Beverly Hills became an obsession—silky strands of rich, buttery, garlicky goodness that lingered on your fingertips no matter how many times you washed your hands. Robert would drive across town at midnight sometimes, just to satisfy the intense yearning that would hit me without warning.

"These noodles," I'd moan, eyes closed in ecstasy, "are better than sex."

He'd raise an eyebrow, amused. "I'm going to pretend I didn't hear that."

And then there was the veggie burger from the New York Palace Hotel—a seemingly simple creation that somehow contained the perfect balance of textures and flavors. Crisp on the outside, tender within. The right amount of salt. The ideal ratio of condiments.

It was the first thing on my mind when I flew to New York to start promoting *Full Moon*. Robert was already in the city working, so when I landed, I went straight to the hotel, gave him a huge hug before making a beeline for the phone. I didn't need a menu—the order was etched into my brain:

"The Palace veggie burger with no cheese, fresh onion—not grilled—crisp lettuce, and juicy tomato," I said to room service, practically salivating at the thought.

The woman on the other end chuckled. "Let me guess—you're eating for two?"

"Is it that obvious?" I laughed, one hand cradling my belly.

"Honey, we get all kinds of specific orders, but there's something about the way pregnant women order food—like it's a matter of life and death."

"Because it *is*," I insisted, only half joking.

As I hung up the phone, I heard the faintest beeping.

Beep. Beep. Beep.

At first, I thought I was imagining it—some auditory hallucination born of hunger—but the sound grew louder, more insistent.

Eventually the pungent scent of smoke crawling under the door like an unwelcome guest made its way to my nostrils.

Beep. Beep. Beep.

"You smell that smoke?" Robert yelled from the bedroom, alarm threading through his voice.

It was just months after 9/11, and we were all still very much on edge. The slightest hint of danger in New York City carried an added weight. My heart started racing as I lunged for the television remote, flipping frantically to the local news.

The anchor's perfectly coiffed composure seemed obscene as she calmly reported on a fire that had broken out at the Palace Hotel.

The Palace Hotel.

The hotel we were currently standing in.

On the fifty-third floor.

"We gotta go," Robert said, his voice steady but urgent as he grabbed my hand, already reaching for the door.

We rushed into the hallway, joining the exodus of panicked guests. Six months pregnant, I descended fifty-three flights of stairs in hotel slippers, one hand protectively cradling my belly, the other clutching the railing as my knees threatened to buckle beneath me.

"You good, baby?" Robert would ask every few flights, his hand firm against the small of my back.

"Keep going," I'd manage between labored breaths, the smoke thickening as we descended.

And yet, ridiculously, tragically, one thought kept circling through my mind like a shark that refused to abandon its prey: *What about my veggie burger?*

We finally emerged onto the street—a circus of chaos. Fire trucks lined the block, their sirens howling like wounded animals. Hotel guests scrambled in every direction, some clutching hastily packed belongings, others in various stages of undress.

A firefighter approached us, his face smudged with soot.

"Ma'am, you should sit down," he said, eyeing my pregnant belly with concern.

I nodded, suddenly aware of how badly my legs were shaking. Robert guided me to a nearby bench, his arm never leaving my waist.

Turned out, it was a kitchen fire. Contained. No injuries. Just a scare.

Thank God.

But once we were cleared to go back to our room, I had only one question for the concierge—a question that made Robert laugh so hard he had to lean against the wall for support:

"So . . . is room service still up and running?"

The concierge blinked, then smiled. "For you, Ms. Norwood? We'll make it happen."

(They did. And that burger was divine intervention in the form of a perfectly toasted bun.)

When Robert and I got back to LA, we hired a midwife named Grace to help us put together a birth plan.

She was, in every sense of the word, grace embodied. Soft-spoken but steady. Eyes that held wisdom from a thousand births before mine. Hands that seemed to know exactly where to press to ease the aches that had finally started to visit my lower back.

"Your body knows what to do," she'd assure me during our sessions. "It's been preparing for this since before you were born."

I hated hospitals with a visceral intensity that surprised even me—the antiseptic smell that couldn't quite mask the undercurrent of suffering, the overexposed lighting, the cold metal instruments gleaming with sterile menace. A home birth seemed the preferable option.

"Just a tour," Grace suggested. "To familiarize yourself with the space. To remove some of the unknown."

I reluctantly agreed to tour Encino-Tarzana Regional Medical Center. The second I stepped through the automatic doors,

I felt like I couldn't breathe. The air itself seemed thinner, processed. Machines beeped their Morse code of distress. Doctors in white coats glided by like ghosts—all wearing that smile that's meant to be reassuring but somehow never quite reaches that critical threshold of sincerity.

"This is where family can wait during delivery," the guide announced cheerfully, gesturing toward a room with vinyl chairs in various shades of institutional despair.

"Wait?" I echoed, my voice small. "My family won't be with me?"

"And this is the high-risk unit where we'd monitor you before delivery," she continued, while gesturing toward a room filled with blinking machines that looked like props from a sci-fi movie.

"Monitor?" I blinked, the word tasting metallic in my mouth.

"That's only if there are problems," my mom said, squeezing my hand, trying to keep me calm.

But I couldn't hear anything beyond the rushing in my ears. I was catching every third word, the rest disappearing into the white noise of my mounting panic.

My eyes darted to a glass nursery, where tiny newborns lay tucked in incubators, separated from their mothers by walls both literal and symbolic.

"That little thing," a nurse said, pointing to a silver contraption hovering above one of the cribs, "detects warmth and adjusts the heating lamp to keep the baby cozy."

A machine deciding what's warm enough for my baby?

It was too much.

"Bran, baby, what's wrong?" my mom asked, pulling me into her arms.

"I don't want to deliver my baby here," I sobbed into her shoulder. "It feels wrong. It feels cold. It feels—"

The doctor touched my arm gently. "This just makes it feel real, doesn't it? Many first-time mothers have this reaction."

Robert led me outside for air. We sat on the curb, both of us shaken.

"I'm trying to compromise," I said, wiping my face with the back of my hand. "But everything about this place makes me feel scared instead of safe."

Grace squatted in front of me and took my hand.

"Remember," she said softly, her voice a balm to my raw nerves, "this is still *your* birth. It's not about a room. You bring the love. You bring the energy. You create the space you need, even within these walls. Wherever you are, your baby will feel that. And this is the safest place to deliver."

Her voice felt like a prayer for protection, a spell cast around us.

"Okay," I said, breathing deeper, drawing strength from some ancestral well within. "I'll deliver here."

She smiled, helping me to my feet. "And I'll be with you every step of the way."

Everything accelerated from that point, the world shifting into a rush of motion and sound. As Robert drove me to the hospital, I focused on my breath, on staying anchored to the present.

Nurses in blue scrubs led us through a labyrinth of corridors, their voices a chorus of instructions that flowed around me like water. Questions and paperwork came at me so fast I could barely focus on steadying myself against the first waves of what would soon become a tsunami of sensation.

"Name?"

"Brandy Norwood."

"Date of birth?"

"February 11, 1979."

"Any allergies?"

"Just fear," I whispered, but no one heard except Robert, who squeezed my hand in silent understanding.

They settled me into a bed that felt nothing like the one I'd imagined laboring in. But Grace was there, as promised, her presence immediately transforming the sterile room into something more sacred.

"Remember your affirmations," she encouraged, helping me into a more comfortable position.

A hush of calm. Stillness. The eye of the hurricane.

Robert rubbed my back with one hand and with the other he found the remote and clicked on the US Open. The monotonous golf commentary was oddly soothing—white noise that filled the spaces between my thoughts.

With each deep breath, something loosened, and the first real contraction came.

Like a thunderclap—sharp and loud and impossible to ignore. Pain radiated through me in waves, each one more intense than the last. Robert was my rock, whispering encouragements in my ear as I gripped his hand with strength I didn't know I possessed.

"You're doing amazing, baby. Just breathe through it."

I noticed his eyes flickering to the television, where Tiger Woods was lining up a putt.

"I'm having a contraction and you're worrying about golf?" I snapped between gritted teeth, sweat beading along my hairline.

He had the decency to look sheepish. "Sorry, sorry. I'm here. All eyes on you."

Barely three hours had passed since we arrived at the hospital, and I was ready—beyond ready—for my baby to make her grand entrance into the world.

"Are we gonna have a baby tonight?" Robert asked the nurse as she checked my vitals.

The nurse—an older woman whose hands moved with practiced efficiency—shook her head. "She may not arrive until midafternoon tomorrow—"

"Ma'am," I interrupted, panic rising in my throat, "that's a lot of labor."

"Normal first-time labors last about twelve to eighteen hours," she said merrily, as if announcing the running time of a feature film rather than a marathon of pain I was expected to endure.

Robert and I locked eyes—half panicked, half exhilarated.

The contractions grew sharper.

"I don't think I can take any more of this," I whispered during a brief reprieve, tears mingling with sweat.

"Just breathe. You got this," Robert soothed, dabbing my forehead with a cool cloth. "Remember what Grace said about visualizing each contraction as a wave you're riding to your baby."

The next contraction hit before I could respond, stealing my breath and my resolve in one fell swoop.

Fifteen seconds later, I was done being Zen.

"Give me the fucking medicine!" I shouted, all thoughts of natural childbirth evaporating like morning mist under a brutal sun.

The anesthesiologist appeared as if summoned by my desperation, a guardian angel in scrubs. The relief of the epidural was immediate and profound—not a complete absence of pain, but a dulling of its sharpest edges. It allowed me to reclaim some sense of control.

I didn't care about candles or soft lighting or gentle mantras anymore. I wanted for this little human to be out of me and in my arms where I could see her, touch her, count her fingers and toes.

It took just five pushes. At 6:48 p.m. on June 16, 2002, our baby girl entered the world with a cry that sounded to my ears like the highest, purest note ever sung.

She was perfect.

Tiny. Warm. Radiant. A constellation of possibilities in human form.

There was so much love in that room it hung in the air, delicate like spun sugar, making each breath sweeter than the last.

My mom, dad, and Ray J stood around us, eyes glazed with joy and wonder.

Reality warped and re-formed around me, and I understood with sharp-edged clarity: nothing I did before, or would do after, would ever be as important as the purpose bestowed on me in this single breath. Every note I'd ever sung, every award I'd ever won, every film I'd ever made—all paled in comparison to this tiny being now cradled against my chest.

My father held his granddaughter for the first time, his strong hands suddenly so gentle they seemed transformed. He looked at me, shaking his head in wonder, tears tracking unashamedly down his cheeks.

"Oh, Brandy . . . you are just incredible," he said, his voice thick with emotion. "My little girl just had her own little girl."

I looked at her, really looked at her, as she curled into me like a prayer answered. Her tiny fingers wrapped around mine with surprising strength, and her eyes—though unfocused—seemed to look directly into my soul.

"It hasn't even hit me yet," I whispered as he gently placed her back on my chest, her heartbeat a perfect counterpoint to my own, "but she looks just like me."

We named her Sy'Rai—a name that means "princess." And that's what she was. A divine peace. A new moon in my sky. The beginning of a chapter more beautiful and challenging than any I could have written for myself.

TALK ABOUT OUR LOVE

"LOOK AT WHAT we made," Robert whispered our first night home with Sy'Rai, his eyes glistening as he gazed at our daughter sleeping in my arms. The wonder in his voice matched the miracle between us.

We eased into parenthood with a grace that surprised even me. Between his family's gentle warmth and my parents' unflinching support, we were cocooned in love. Robert and I moved like well-trained dancers—anticipating needs, sharing midnight feedings, finding laughter in the chaos of new parenthood.

"You're a natural," my mother said one evening, watching me rock Sy'Rai to sleep. "You were born for this."

I believed we were invincible. But the universe had other plans. Robert and I were friends long before we became lovers, our foundation built on trust and shared secrets. So, when the romantic love between us began to fade, I truly believed we could transition back into friendship without scars. I was naive.

The speed with which our relationship evolved sparked a wildfire of speculation. Critics and fans alike seemed to forget there was music to discuss. Instead, interviews became interrogations—not about the songs I'd poured my soul into, but about why I'd kept my relationship so close to my chest.

"The last time I looked, you were Cinderella," a morning show host said, leaning forward with barely concealed judgment, "and now we're expecting a baby." His tone dripped with incredulity, as if the woman sitting before him—no longer the wide-eyed teenager America had fallen in love with—was some impostor who'd committed a cardinal sin by growing up.

Almost every interview followed this script. Carson Daly's boyish smile did nothing to soften the inquisition on *TRL*. Teens in the background held signs with my name while he dissected my personal life.

"We're playing a little rumor mill game," he said, too casual, too scripted. "When did you actually get married? Why were you so secretive?" The studio audience leaned forward, hungry for gossip. I smiled through clenched teeth, feeling the foundation of my privacy crumbling brick by brick.

The speculation metastasized after Robert and I separated. The questions grew more pointed, more personal.

"Why didn't you work out?" "What happened to your fairy tale?" "Was there someone else?"

The prodding only intensified with each deflection. Everywhere I went. Every microphone thrust in my face. Every camera lens that followed me from car to venue. I felt the veil lifting, felt control slipping like sand through my fingers.

"I wasn't ready for commitment," I said in an interview, the words tumbling out before I could catch them. I wanted to appear forthcoming while still guarding my truth. The reality was complicated—I did not love him romantically anymore. He had become my protector, my confidant, my best friend in the trenches of new parenthood. But our passion had withered on the vine, leaving behind something different, something I couldn't explain to an interviewer who wanted sound bites, not nuance.

I should never have offered even that morsel to the public. Some truths don't need to be shared with the world. I hadn't planned on keeping our situation secret forever, but I wanted to reveal things on my terms, with my daughter's well-being secured.

I was collapsed in a hotel bed somewhere in Manhattan when I heard Wendy Williams announce with barely contained glee that she had scored an exclusive interview with "Brandy's ex." The words sliced through my exhaustion like a cold blade. My brain pinballed between panic and disbelief.

He wouldn't.

He couldn't.

Why would he speak to anyone—let alone the self-proclaimed Queen of Gossip—about us? About me? About the mother of his child?

The promotional tour for *Afrodisiac*, my fourth album, had already drained every last reserve. Hotel rooms blurred together in a haze of beige walls and minibars, each city indistinguishable from the last. I had been running on adrenaline and prayer, anxious about the album's reception, missing my baby girl with an ache that physical distance only amplified.

A chasm opened in my stomach when his voice filtered through the radio. There he was, casual as Sunday morning, gossiping with Wendy as if discussing the weather.

"It wasn't your ordinary situation," he said of our relationship, his voice unnervingly calm.

I could just see Wendy leaning in her studio chair, ready to swoop in for the kill.

"She got pregnant and you decided to marry, or was there pressure to marry?" she asked, her voice honeyed with false sympathy.

A pause. My breath suspended.

"There was never a marriage."

He proceeded to tell Wendy—and by extension, the entire world—that we had fabricated our marriage to protect my pristine image. That I had been the "other woman." That he had reconnected with his girlfriend, who was now carrying his child. And most devastating of all, that the entire charade had been orchestrated by my mother.

I was stunned. The fragile peace I'd constructed—the narrative I clung to that we were still a family, just reconfigured—shattered into a million pieces.

My phone vibrated against the nightstand, jolting me back to reality. My publicist's name flashed across the screen, a visual alarm that the crisis had only begun.

We had crafted a lie about being legally married. And now I realized I had built myself on a foundation of calculated moves—a house of cards that now collapsed in spectacular, public fashion. And the betrayal cut deep. Before our daughter entered the world, we'd made a commitment to protect one another no matter what. If I could have dissolved into the hotel carpet, vanished into thin air, I would have. But reality anchored me: I had Sy'Rai waiting at home. Music to promote. A career still worth salvaging. I was still standing, still breathing, still here—a mantra I repeated silently as reporters began circling like vultures, eager to pick apart the carcass of my credibility.

My dishonesty had sprouted from terror, pure and simple. I'd known nothing but the suffocating pressure to maintain the spotless image of America's teenage sweetheart. Even as I crossed the threshold into my twenties, I carried the weight of that crown. I was paralyzed by the potential judgment I might face having a child outside of marriage.

But by lying, I had only made things worse. When I finally confessed, the professional consequences were swift and merciless. Cover Girl, whose fresh-faced campaigns had featured my smile for years, severed ties without ceremony. Other endorsements followed, dominoes falling in quick succession. I tried to insulate myself from the noise, focusing instead on the perfect curve of my daughter's cheek, the miracle of her tiny fingernails, the way she smelled after a bath—talcum powder and infinite possibility.

"They don't matter," my mother said fiercely one night as I

sobbed in her kitchen, away from Sy'Rai's innocent eyes. "You and that baby—that's what matters. The rest is just noise."

But even as I nodded through tears, I could feel the weight of it. I was a new mother, navigating the greatest love and responsibility I'd ever known, while simultaneously watching my career implode. And that reality filled me with a sadness so profound it bordered on spiritual.

I have paid incalculable costs for that single decision. The judgment I fled from found me anyway, raising questions that haunt me still: What if I had embraced honesty from the beginning? How much of the backlash stemmed from my pregnancy outside marriage, and how much from the deception itself?

After years crafting an immaculate public image, I'm certain the reaction would have been severe had I told the truth initially, and my child would have suffered in the cross fire of public opinion. Yet ultimately, I met the same fate anyway. Perhaps the lie amplified the fallout, but before the truth emerged, I believed with a mother's fierce conviction that I was protecting what mattered most—my baby.

My daughter, Sy'Rai, has blossomed into a magnificent woman—messy, complicated, and gloriously imperfect. She possesses the strength and clarity I wish I'd found in my twenties instead of searching for it in others' approval. On nights when doubt creeps in, I watch her sleeping—grown now, but still with that same peaceful expression from infancy—and know with bone-deep certainty that she remains the greatest gift I have ever known.

When I discovered I was pregnant, something primal and protective awoke in me. My baby belonged to me, not to the public eye that had consumed so much of my youth. They wanted my life to be flawless—a template for their daughters to follow—so I fabricated a facade of textbook happiness, performing the prescribed steps of respectable adulthood in the correct order. But no one can exist indefinitely within a bubble of perfection, and when mine finally burst, I lost everything I thought defined me.

Yet in the aftermath, I found freedom. In the sting of disapproval, a strange new power emerged. No longer the perfect polished role model, I could finally exist in the world exactly as I was—perfectly human.

ECLIPSE

EVEN NOW, IT'S difficult to think about my collaborations with Rodney without feeling the ache of what could have been.

I believed I was Rodney's muse, that our musical connection transcended the physical realm and touched something spiritual. I thought what I had with Rodney and Darkchild would stretch into decades—building the kind of lifelong artistic bond you witness once in a generation. Like what Janet Jackson had with Jimmy Jam and Terry Lewis, what Toni Braxton had with Babyface, or what Aaliyah had with Timbaland, their avant-garde vision reshaping R&B's very foundation.

On August 25, 2001, a Cessna carrying Aaliyah and eight others crashed leaving the Bahamas. She had been there to shoot the music video for her single "Rock the Boat." Her death cut to the bone. She wasn't just a peer and a friend—she was a kindred spirit. We came up together. After navigating the same rocky waters of fame as teenagers, we had *just* really started coming into ourselves as women. Adding to the pain, our mutual friend and makeup artist, Chris Maldonado, had died with her.

I was tight with Timbaland, so I'd check in on him regularly after we lost Baby Girl. We'd share memories that made us both laugh through tears, stories that kept her spirit pulsing between us like a heartbeat.

One night, we were in his studio. Tim had recently launched his own label, Beat Club Records, and brought me in to do vocal production for one of his artists, this sweet young lady named Kiley Dean. She grew up in a small town in western Arkansas and had a gorgeous voice molded by a childhood spent in church. While I had the experience of writing and producing demos that landed with different artists, I hadn't had the opportunity to help a new artist find her sound. I loved writing for Kiley and collaborating with her in the studio.

Tim's fingers danced across a keyboard as he spoke.

"You know . . . 'Liyah asked me not to work with you," he told me.

My chest hollowed in an instant. "What? Why?"

"Nothing to do with you," he added quickly, hearing the hurt in my voice. "She just felt like the sound we made was so singular, so uniquely *hers*, that she wanted to own it." He finally looked up. "She also knew the second I worked with another female artist, there would be endless comparisons, and she hated when people did that to her."

I understood exactly what she'd meant.

When I first linked with Rodney and Darkchild, I wanted to bottle that cosmic connection. But everybody—and I mean *everybody*—wanted a Rodney Jerkins song. How could they not? He is a brilliant producer. A musical wizard with the Midas touch. Him working with other artists wasn't an issue for me. I was exceptionally proud of what Rodney built with Darkchild; I celebrated every one of his victories as though they were my own.

But the pride got harder to hold when I started hearing our sound—*my* sound—echoing from the mouths of other women. The same intricate vocal arrangements with stacked harmonies that had become my signature. The same song structures, the same approach we'd innovated on *Never Say Never* and *Full Moon*. At first, I brushed it off. Told myself I was being sensitive. Petty, even. "This is the business," I'd whisper to myself. "No one owns sound."

One night in the studio, Rodney played me a track just to get my read on it.

It was called "If I Gave Love."

I closed my eyes as it played, swaying as the demo swirled around. It was bubbly and upbeat and sounded like an edgier take on the up-tempos we cut for *Never Say Never.* I could already hear my voice floating over the record. I could feel the melody in my head as if it had been written for me.

"I'm feeling this," I said, eyes still closed, lost in the possibility of what we could create together. "A lot. Let me take a pass at it." I opened my eyes, already mentally arranging harmonies, planning ad-libs, hearing the finished product in my mind.

He shook his head. "Nah."

The single syllable hung between us like a wall suddenly erected. "Rodney, come on. Are you serious?" I leaned forward in my seat, hands gripping the armrests. "This track is *me.*"

"I can't, B. This is for Chanté Moore."

I forced a mask of indifference even as disappointment shot through my veins like ice water.

"Okay. Well, the song is really dope. She'll sound amazing on it."

The song indeed went to Chanté. It hurt more than I admitted, even to myself. And then Rodney basically made a carbon copy of the record, called "If You Had My Love," that launched Jennifer Lopez's music career.

There were so many songs he played for me—songs I begged to sing on—that he'd already earmarked for someone else. Beyoncé. Whitney. Toni. I wasn't mad he was working with them; I was hurt that I kept getting the leftovers. The album cuts. The deep tracks. The ones fans adore but never hear on the radio. He gave me foundations. But not fireworks.

I thought of saying something to him. Sometimes I'd even rehearse a speech in my mind. *Rodney, do you see what you're doing? You're giving away our sound like it's nothing.* But I shied away from the conversation. Who was I to tell Rodney or LaShawn how they worked outside of what we did together? Of course they were getting calls from Whitney and J.Lo and Destiny's Child and Toni Braxton. They were hot, proven hitmakers. But I kept hearing our sound—*my* sound—replicated by other artists. A record like "He Wasn't Man Enough" could've seamlessly fit into *Never Say Never.* It just kept happening and all I could think was *It's not right, but it's okay.*

Eventually, though, I started to wonder if he was holding back the hits on purpose. If maybe he was saving the best beats, the most radio-ready melodies, for artists with bigger names, larger platforms, fresher energy, less baggage when it came to their public image.

That suspicion hardened into certainty one day in the studio. We were midclash—what about, I don't even remember—but we were going at it like usual, the way siblings do when they know exactly which buttons to push. Only this time, he looked me dead in the eye and said, "Go do what you're gonna do, while I go sell five million records with Beyoncé."

The words landed like a gut punch. I stormed out of the studio. Humiliation burned through me like a wildfire. Left behind in the ashes was a sadder realization—it was time for me to move on.

For years, I dreamed of working with Timbaland.

What Tim did with Aaliyah on *One in a Million* immediately made him one of my favorite producers. He was a visionary who heard tomorrow's music today. We finally got the chance to work together for my fourth album, *Afrodisiac.* I told Tim I didn't want to concentrate on being so technical and perfect this time around. I just wanted to sing my heart out and let people into my head. I wanted to sing about codependency, anxiety, grief, career insecurity—all the complex emotions swimming inside my spirit as I approached twenty-five and everything around me was changing.

Timbaland wasn't just a producer I'd been wanting to collaborate with. We'd been friends for years, our bond forged through mutual respect and late-night conversations about everything from sampling techniques to spirituality. Before *Afrodisiac*, we'd worked on a few things outside of Kiley's project, including a record for *Under Construction, Part II*, the last project he put out with his partner, Magoo. But this—this was different. This was about us building a world together, brick by sonic brick.

But the powers that be at the label had their own ideas. My focus has always been on making the best art possible—pouring my soul into melodies that might touch someone else's in the dark. Not that I don't care about the business side of things, but it isn't where my spirit lives. The reality of being a major label recording artist is that you deliver hits.

Today *Full Moon* is revered as a seminal album. It's regarded as the blueprint of modern R&B, and I have profound gratitude for that recognition. Back then, however, the story read differently. The album wasn't a multi-platinum sensation like my first two albums. Because of that, the label executives didn't mince words about needing to come back swinging—with guaranteed hits, not artistic evolution.

One evening, my phone lit up with a call from a high-level executive at the label. One I trusted implicitly.

"Hey, so we were thinking." His voice oozed false casualness. "What if you did a few records with Kanye West?"

"Kanye?" I hesitated, the name feeling foreign in the context of my project. "I don't know—"

"He's blowing up right now," he continued, not waiting for me to finish my thought. "The work he did with Alicia Keys was incredible. 'You Don't Know My Name'? Come on."

I sighed. "I know he's hot. But this is my project with Timbaland. I don't want to break that flow."

"Brandy . . . we need a slam dunk out the gate. Kanye is a guaranteed slam dunk."

There it was. Not a suggestion. A decree wrapped in the thin disguise of collaborative decision-making.

This is the thing people don't understand about being an artist—regardless of how many hits, accolades, or awards you've accumulated, working with a major label sometimes means wrestling with opposing visions. The artist may want one thing and the executives another, and that tug-of-war doesn't always end in the artist's favor, given how much power the label wields. It was heartbreaking to find myself in that space at this point in my career—feeling like a newcomer again after years of building my legacy.

Looking back, I should have stood my ground. Said no. Suffered whatever consequences might have come. My two biggest champions at Atlantic, Sylvia Rhone and Darryl Williams, were no longer at the label. Gee Roberson and Benny Medina had come on to manage me after my mom pulled back from handling my career. Between the weight of *Full Moon* not matching the commercial success of *Never Say Never* and adjusting to a new team, I was knocked off my square a bit. And *I* wanted a win just as desperately as the label. Since Gee was already working with Kanye, agreeing felt as safe as it did strategic.

The dust had barely settled when I discovered the truth: the label was hoping to court Kanye to come to Atlantic. Without consulting me, they had offered Kanye two placements on my album, with the added condition that one of his records would be the lead single. They would also give him free rein to create the video treatment for that single.

We worked on two records—"Talk About Our Love," which ended up as the lead single, and "Where You Wanna Be."

Two versions of "Where You Wanna Be" were cut.

Kanye liked the first version.

I liked the second.

The album was otherwise complete, and I was still hot over having to compromise my creative vision by bringing in another producer at the eleventh hour. But I made the concession and played the team game. The records came out dope—no denying that. But our disagreement over which version of "Where You Wanna Be" would make the final cut became a power struggle. And I didn't understand why Kanye was fighting me on it. I just wanted a different mix of the vocals. We went back and forth for days, and I refused to make another concession. Especially not about how my voice was presented.

I'd gotten word that Kanye had a session booked at the Record Plant to work on his album, so I decided to pop by, in hopes of finding common ground. I followed a dimly lit hallway reverberating with bass. I took a deep breath before pushing open the door, preparing for another battle, but praying for peace.

The instant I walked in, the atmosphere shifted. The scowl on his face when he turned around and saw me spoke volumes.

"Kanye," I began, trying to keep my voice calm. "Can we please compromise? Just take the vocal from the new mix and put it on the old one. Best of both worlds."

He barely looked up from the soundboard. "Nah, I can't do that."

"You can't, or you won't?"

His eyes met mine, unflinching, a challenge in their depths. "I can't because I turned it in already."

The words hit like a brick. *I know he didn't just say what I thought he said.*

"What do you mean you turned it in already?"

He shrugged, turning back to his work as though this conversation was already over. "You'll be aight," he said with a smug grin that set my teeth on edge.

That may sound like a minor disagreement to someone on the outside looking in. But to me, it represented a stripping away of my agency, on a deeply personal project. But I couldn't afford to be upset or angry. I still had a video to shoot and a record to promote with Kanye. I'd also promised Gee that I would return the favor and do a record on Kanye's sophomore album, *Late Registration*. So, I swallowed my pride along with the lump in my throat, forced a smile that didn't reach my eyes, and nodded like this was all part of the process.

Kanye has undeniable magic when it comes to producing R&B records, and I remain proud of those songs. But it didn't change the fact that my vision had been dismantled by label politics and industry games.

By contrast, making music with Timbaland was the freest I'd ever felt. I walked into the studio and left my perfectionism at the door. I wasn't trying to impress anyone. I wasn't chasing a hit. I was just . . . creating from my heart and soul. Our chemistry was phenomenal. We played with genres, weaving together eccentric hip-hop breakbeats, indie rock samples, and ambient soundscapes to create a mellower sound.

I worried constantly that Timbaland would think I'd betrayed him. He'd produced the bulk of the album only for me to record a new lead single with a different producer at the last possible second. Worse, I looked like I didn't have a backbone or any creative leverage in the process—like a puppet whose strings were pulled by invisible hands. Tim understood the predicament I was in, and we've worked together a ton over the years and remain friends to this day.

In the end, the compromise was for naught. The Kanye record didn't turn out to be the guaranteed chart-topper the label had banked on. And none of the singles with Timbaland could gain traction after that. It was like watching a beautiful ship sink before it ever really left the harbor, the weight of expectations and miscalculations dragging it down to the ocean floor.

Released June 25, 2004, *Afrodisiac* became my most critically lauded album. But acclaim and commercial performance are two different currencies, and the label deemed it a flop. I had poured my whole self into creating something classic with a producer I deeply admired. We had crafted an innovative body of work filled with progressive, experimental R&B that pushed boundaries and broke new ground. But because it didn't move units in the expected numbers, none of that artistic achievement seemed to matter.

In the spirit of starting fresh, I made a decision that terrified me. Atlantic had been my label for eleven years—the only professional home my music had ever known—but it was time for me to move on. I asked to be released from my contract. It was one of the hardest things I've ever done. But it was necessary. Like leaving a house you've outgrown but still love deeply, every corner filled with memories both beautiful and painful.

I knew if I was going to continue in this industry without losing myself completely, it was time for a change. Time to find a new place where my voice—both literal and figurative—could truly be heard.

LUCID DREAMS

IT WAS JUST a drive, another day traveling the pale concrete veins of the 405. How many times had I coasted along this mundane stretch of freeway?

But all familiarity was shattered on a chilly December morning in 2006.

There had been no warning. No shiver down the spine. No flicker in the atmosphere hinting at what was to come. My eyes were steady. My mind was clear. I wasn't lost in thought or fumbling with the radio. I was focused. Present. Alert.

And still, I couldn't see the danger in time.

I didn't see the car ahead of me strike the vehicle in front, didn't register the sudden chain reaction until my world was being split into two halves: before and after.

The memory exists in fragments, blinding and visceral: the sickening crunch of metal folding into metal like some grotesque origami, the white-hot burst of light across my eyes as if someone had suddenly switched the world off and on again, the paralyzing scream that tore from somewhere deep inside me—a place I'd never accessed before—that I didn't even recognize as my own.

And then silence.

Deafening, impossible silence.

A man emerged at my window, his face tight with concern. The door creaked open.

"Are you okay, ma'am? Are you hurt?" His voice penetrated the high-pitched ringing in my ears, warm and steady like an anchor. Those two questions were the tether that pulled me back into my body, back into reality.

I felt the ground fall through my chest at the realization that I was still here, still inhabiting this shell of flesh and bone. My hands trembled against the steering wheel. My chest heaved with jagged breaths that couldn't seem to fill me. Hysteria swallowed me whole. My body turned cold with panic.

"This is my fault. This is my fault. This is my fault," I sobbed, the words spilling out of me like a burst dam, uncontrollable and relentless.

"Ma'am, it was an accident," the man said. Through the haze, I could see his hazard lights on behind me. He'd witnessed the whole thing, and his voice softened as he squeezed my shoulder, warmth seeping through my thin silk blouse. "You have to try to calm down. Can you breathe with me? In . . . and out . . ."

But his words couldn't calm the storm as I left the car and the scene hardened into focus around me. Twisted fragments of metal and glass littered the asphalt, the wreckage of several cars scattered like fallen dominoes. A sea of faces—some panicked and distraught, streaked with tears and confusion, others twisted in pain.

The cool December air seemed to evaporate as I watched the man race toward another vehicle. I prayed for someone to emerge. Like I had. My breath froze as emergency workers pulled a woman out of the wreck.

She was rushed to the hospital with sirens wailing into the distance. She passed away the next day.

That morning carved itself into my marrow. A life gone. A family forever altered.

Unimaginable grief spread its roots beneath my skin, growing deeper with each passing day. Guilt gripped my throat, squeezed harder and harder—until breathing became a conscious effort.

It was an accident—a tragic convergence of circumstance and human error.

But a woman had lost her life.

And I had lived.

I felt it in every interaction, a thin veil of politeness stretched over thick layers of disdain. The sideways glances in grocery stores. The whispers that haunted me like ghosts. Every day, it seemed, TMZ had a new headline about the accident. About what I was wearing that day, as if it somehow mattered. The comments section was ugly.

"Don't read those," my mother would plead, taking my phone from my trembling hands. "Baby girl, they don't know. They weren't there."

But I couldn't stop myself from scrolling.

I no longer felt I had the right to continue living my life, or even to experience fleeting glimmers of joy. The woman who had died would never again feel sunshine on her face or hold her children close. Who was I to smile? To sing? To exist in a world where she no longer could?

And so, I shut myself in the house. Days turned to weeks. Weeks turned to months. It was easier to hide than to face the world.

I tried to keep my sorrow hidden from Sy'Rai. But even at four years old, she possessed an emotional intelligence and a heart far beyond her age. She would drift into my bedroom during those hollowed-out hours when I thought she was occupied with her dolls or cartoons.

Without fail, she'd climb onto my bed and press her lips to my forehead, wrap her little arms around me—and say nothing, because sometimes there are no words. That little girl became my lifeline. I knew I owed it to her to keep going.

More than that, I wanted to make my life matter in the shadow of the one that had been lost.

I told myself I could be strong, that I could weather this storm and rebuild. But the universe had other plans. The headlines intensified. Her family sued. I understood their need for someone to blame, someone to punish. They needed resolution. Compensation. Some symbol of justice in a situation that offered none.

I wanted to tell her family I felt their anguish, that I prayed for their comfort and peace and forgiveness every single day. But words were such fragile things, so inadequate against the mountain of their loss. What could you possibly say to a husband whose wife was gone? To children who would never see their mother again? Nothing I could give or say would ever be enough. No amount of money or atonement could rewrite that December morning.

An investigation eventually concluded that this tragic alignment of circumstances wasn't the result of my negligence.

Claims were settled. No charges were filed against me.

But by then, the guilt had already calcified in my soul, hardening into something permanent and unmovable.

About a year after the accident, my mother, and my then publicist, Courtney, called a meeting. Although I'd stopped hiding completely, I rarely ventured beyond familiar walls. For months, they'd fielded calls for interview requests. And they believed it was time I sat down and talked about that morning.

"People haven't fully heard from you," Courtney said, his voice gentle but insistent.

"What is my purpose in doing that?" I asked.

"To clear the air," he said.

"Why? Because I want a career again?" My voice cracked around the edges. "This shouldn't be about me."

"If you fully share your story, you can move on. And one of the things you should address is how you were treated by the media during that time," he suggested, his tone careful, measuring each word as if it might break me.

"Like a murderer," I whispered, finally meeting his gaze.

"People are going to want to know exactly what happened," my mother interjected, her eyes holding mine. "Brandy, being the fourth or fifth car in the collision, doesn't really know herself what happened."

"And is the goal to tell the world that it wasn't my fault?" I asked, pulling my hand back and wrapping my arms around myself. "Because no matter who's to blame, a woman still lost her life."

"You deserve closure," Courtney added quickly, his PR instincts kicking in. "People want to hear your story, and your story is valid because people get into accidents like this every single day."

"But I'm not a victim in this situation. I still get to live. To go into 'it's not my fault' or—"

"But you were victimized in terms of reputation," Courtney interrupted, leaning closer. "That counts for something. The way they portrayed you—"

I held up my hand, stopping him midsentence. The conversation was sobering, and I appreciated the delicate way in which they handled me, but in my eyes, there was only one victim in this tragedy. A life had been lost. A family broken. I barely understood how to place one foot in front of the other most days. I couldn't imagine sitting beneath studio lights as I gave "my side" of a story that had only one true narrative—loss.

I promised them I would consider it. Which I did. But still . . .

"I can't do it," I told my mom later that night as I put away dishes, thankful for the mundane task.

"I know it's a delicate subject," my mom said softly. She circled around the kitchen island to stand before me, taking my hands in hers, her skin warm against my cold fingers.

This was one of those times when she needed to be both

mother and manager, to navigate the treacherous waters between protection and progress.

"Forget the interview for now," she said. "But at some point, you're going to need to talk about it a little bit. To someone. Anyone. Not for them. For you."

I knew she was right.

The stage, once a place where I found escape, became a torture chamber when I finally ventured back into the world. Applause that had lifted me up now felt brittle, insincere. I wondered who was in the audience to support me, and who had come to catch a glimpse of my suffering, to see if I looked remorseful, repentant, if guilt had left visible marks on my face like some modern scarlet letter.

When your existence is defined by how the world sees you, your own thoughts—your very sense of self—become clouded by the opinions of strangers. And I began to believe I was the awful, reckless monster the internet, and thus the world, believed me to be.

Sleep offered the only true escape. In my dreams, I floated free, unburdened by the tragedy that had swallowed my waking hours. I could drift away from the noise, the churning guilt, and the fragments of that morning that looped in cruel slow motion through my mind.

I sometimes fantasized about remaining in that twilight place forever.

If I could just slip away and escape. Just vanish like morning mist.

But there was always the sweetest sound to bring me back to earth. Sy'Rai's little voice would pierce the darkness, her small hands patting my cheeks. "Mommy, wake up."

And so, I would rise again. For her. Always for her.

I once had a therapist—a kind-eyed woman who never once looked at me with judgment—ask me what I believed closure looked like.

And the truth is there's no such thing as closure when someone's life has been lost. The word feels too neat, too final. I learned many years ago to stop reaching for it. What I found instead was a rhythm. A way to carry the weight and keep moving anyway.

"Have you forgiven yourself?" my therapist asked.

"I don't think I ever will," I said, my voice low and filled with the shame that still lived deep inside of me.

"But have you actually *tried*?" she prodded.

I hadn't tried. I didn't feel worthy of forgiveness. There were still mornings when I woke up and the memories flooded back, leaving me gasping for breath, the nightmare of metal and smoke still fresh in my lungs.

How could I ever forgive myself?

There was a night, not long after that session with my therapist, when I stood outside in my backyard, barefoot beneath the stars. The world was quiet. Sy'Rai was spending the weekend at her dad's house. My mind drifted to that morning, as it often did whenever I was alone with my thoughts. The kindness of that man holding my shoulders never left me. I wondered where life had taken him. If he thought of the woman as much as I did. If he thought of me. And I thought of the words he'd said to me in my moment of hysteria.

"It was an accident."

I let those words sit at the front of my mind. And then I whispered something I hadn't said aloud.

"I forgive you," I said.

It wasn't a release like in the movies, no swelling music or sudden rainbow. It was a beginning. A tiny seed planted in soil.

The grief never left. But it softened. It made room. I stopped asking it to go away.

SATURN RETURN

IT HAD BEEN four years since my last album, and after the accident, I didn't think I'd get the opportunity to make music again. And I wasn't sure if I should.

In spring 2008, I signed a deal with Epic Records. I asked my mother to come back and manage me. The truth is I felt the most confident, and the most protected, when she was in the fold. But we were committed to having a healthier work-life balance this time, so we brought on my younger cousin, Ryan, as a co-manager. Ryan had already been successfully managing Ray, and he knew me—and my career—inside and out.

On paper, it looked like a rebirth. But deep down it felt less like a relaunch and more like a crash landing.

The sound I had helped create with Rodney—the "Brandy sound"—was now everywhere. I didn't know where I fit anymore. And the questions started eating away at me: Was I ever really the magic? Or had I just been the vessel?

I started recording again—this time with new collaborators. James Fauntleroy. Lonny Breaux (who the world would soon know as Frank Ocean). Brian Kennedy. I was chasing something, but I wasn't sure what. A new sound? A new self? A way to feel worthy again?

I was feeling things out in the studio, and the label wasn't really loving anything I was doing.

One day, an executive called me into his office. No pleasantries, no small talk.

"You need to call Rodney," he said flatly, leaning back in his leather chair.

"Excuse me?" I asked, though I'd heard him perfectly well.

"We need hits. Rodney gives you hits." He looked at me, expression unchanged, as though he were telling me the time rather than discussing my artistic future.

They weren't subtle about it, at all. And on some level, I understood the cold business calculation. This was the pre-streaming era, when CD sales determined everything. After *Full Moon* and *Afrodisiac* hadn't performed to expectations, industry chatter about my commercial decline spread. And not just that I'd slipped, but that I could only properly make a comeback with one person: Rodney Jerkins.

At that point, I was so insecure and emotionally depleted that I absolutely believed it myself. And so, I picked up the phone and dialed his number. The silence between rings was thick with everything we'd left unsaid. When he answered, we made awkward small talk for a minute, circling each other hesitantly like boxers in the first round.

"So," I finally said, my voice catching slightly. "I was thinking maybe we could get the old team back together again."

There was a long pause. I could hear him breathing, could almost see him weighing his options. "Yeah," he finally said, the word landing softly between us. "I'd be down for that."

I was happy to be reunited with Rodney and LaShawn, but I was also hesitant about letting my guard down. In the studio, I was as fragile as a porcelain doll—especially when it came to feeling safe with Rodney. We'd have to work through the layers of hurt and misunderstanding before we could create anything authentic.

Those days, I was pretty much only truly happy when I was at home being mommy to my daughter. Her laughter was the only music that consistently brought me joy. In the studio, I felt lost—a stranger in my own skin. And I was still harboring deep sadness and anger toward Rodney that we weren't really confronting.

I had little focus during those sessions, and that lack of concentration inevitably spilled into the creative process. Songs that should have taken days to complete stretched into weeks. But I wanted it to work. I *needed* it to work.

We called the new album *Human* because that's what I was trying so hard to remember I was.

It was risky, to move away from the R&B core that defined me. The intention of chasing crossover success came across as desperate, which I hated. Yes, I was incredibly motivated by the reality of how this industry operates—big success requires big hits, which required pop radio. We hadn't yet reached the era we're in now, where songs can be viral sensations that break through the zeitgeist without ever once gracing the FM dial. On paper, I hadn't had a big hit since "What About Us?" in 2002—and I was constantly reminded of that.

Toward the end of recording *Human*, Rodney sent me a text.

I have your first single. It's hot. You're gonna love it, the message read.

I stared at the phone. I didn't feel excitement. I didn't feel magic. And I certainly didn't feel belief. So, I typed three letters and hit Send:

LOL

Then I got a phone call from my A&R manager, Brandon Creed.

"Hey, I need you to drop by the studio to hear this record from Rodney. I think this is the song you've been looking for," he said earnestly.

"Really?"

"Come hear it for yourself. I don't want to say too much."

Now I was intrigued.

An hour later, I pulled up to 2nd Floor Studios to find Rodney, LaShawn, and Brandon waiting for me at the soundboard.

"This song is so you—and what you've been wanting to say right *now*," Rodney said.

"It really is such a classic Brandy record—but different," LaShawn added.

That was all I needed to hear. Despite our pain points, one thing I never questioned was Rodney's or LaShawn's belief in a potential Brandy classic.

Rodney played the demo.

The first four lines left me speechless:

When you feel your heart's guarded
And you see the break started
And when the clouds have all departed
You'll be right here with me

The lyrics, about the importance of having someone by your side in your darkest hours, spoke to me. Despite my larger fears around the general public, I knew there were fans who still wanted to hear my voice. I saw this record as both an offering to them and a plea to the world to look into my heart.

Recording "Right Here (Departed)" was therapeutic, and it helped Rodney and me get some of our groove back in the studio. I wanted to make universal music, but when *Human* dropped in December 2008, it didn't land softly. It crashed with a deafening thud.

The critics were sharp. Some of the reviews stung in ways I hadn't prepared for, each word slicing through the thin armor I'd hastily constructed.

One called it "the most platitudinal release" of my career.

Another described me as "a fledgling, a personality still being formed, eagerly tagging along after her role models."

But the worst one didn't just critique the album—it came for me as a person.

"Brandy's strong suit has never been her thoughtfulness," it read. "Appropriately for someone with her Hollywood history, she's long been one of R&B's emptiest vessels, a gorgeous voice used by a series of gifted producers to communicate their own unique ideas."

Empty vessel? That one gutted me because it mirrored the fear I was too ashamed to say out loud: that maybe I had never really been an artist. Maybe I'd only ever been an instrument.

And the public? They echoed, with their silence, the same sentiment as the critics. The album didn't move. It came and went without so much as a ripple in the cultural conversation.

Seven months later, Epic terminated my contract.

A year or so after *Human* came and went, Rodney and I sat down at his studio and had a real conversation.

"Do you believe I wasn't focused on the project?" he asked me.

I took a deep breath, deciding that radical honesty was the only path forward. "Not as focused as you've been in the past."

Rodney nodded slowly, considering my words. "Were *you* as focused as you used to be? Because I didn't feel like you were."

His question caught me off guard, but I recognized its truth, harsh as it was. "Getting a second chance to put my music out there, my focus was probably all over the place," I admitted. "It was all about winning."

"The difference I saw, from my eyes, was Brandy wasn't there. I had a studio, but you'd go to *other* people. The Brandy I had on *Never Say Never* and *Full Moon* was down with Darkchild."

There it was. Finally named.

This wasn't just about music. It was about loyalty. When he came onto *Human*, I did have other producers in the mix. Rodney never wanted to be treated like a hired producer, which is what he felt he'd been—this entire time—simply because I hadn't signed to him.

"Rodney, that's not fair," I said.

"You didn't want that commitment to me, right?" His eyes searched mine for an answer I wasn't sure I had.

"Every time you've decided to work with me, I've dropped everybody else, and you know I have," I said, my words turning sharp. "But you've never done that for me. And you *never* will."

He looked at me, and for the first time in years, I could see it—the sadness behind his pride.

We didn't say it out loud, but we both felt it: the magic was gone.

Maybe it had been for a while.

I can appreciate *Human* now. I've heard from fans who said it helped them through depression, heartbreak, even suicidal thoughts. And that is reason enough for the album to exist.

Over the years, Rodney has reached out. His name on my phone screen always sends a jolt through my system—a complex cocktail of nostalgia, regret, and hesitation.

And I haven't picked up.

Not because I'm angry. But because I don't know what to say.

What we had was special. Anointed, even. Chemistry like that doesn't just disappear. But maybe it was never about his genius or my voice. Maybe the magic was in the lightning-strike timing that can't be replicated.

Sometimes I wonder what else we could've created together. In the quiet hours, when the house is still and the world is sleeping, I let myself imagine the albums that might have been.

Sometimes I grieve what was left unfinished.

But there's another part of me—quieter but stronger—that understood the lesson laid bare before me:

Sometimes the muse has to walk away to become the artist.

SUNNY DAY

"WE'RE GOING CAMPING. Pack a bag," my mom yelled from my foyer.

I ran out of my bedroom to find her at the bottom of the stairs. Sunglasses on. Hands on hip. Car keys in hand. I hadn't heard her let herself in . . . but more importantly, did I just hear the word *camping* come out of my mother's mouth?

"Like camping . . . with a tent?" I asked, unable to hide my disbelief.

"Yes, with a tent," she confirmed. "You said we need to do more stuff together that isn't about business. Let's go pack."

"Wait, you're like serious?" I asked, looking out the window to see her car in the driveway. An old family friend was outside unloading bags from my mom's SUV into an even bigger SUV.

She *was* serious.

I needed to see it for myself, so I walked out to the car. And yes, it was packed to the gills with supplies.

Marshmallows for s'mores. Snacks for days, organized in labeled containers. Tents. Sleeping bags. Folding chairs. A cooler. Sunscreen. Bug spray.

"Mom." I laughed, surveying the expedition-worthy pile. "Are we crossing the Sahara?"

"You don't know what we might need," she said while adjusting designer sunglasses that were entirely too glamorous for camping in the woods. "I've been watching videos online. Preparation is key."

"I don't even know what to pack!"

Right on cue, my mother whipped out a checklist of items to grab and shooed me toward the stairs.

We drove into the Ventura County mountains, the city gradually disappearing behind us as trees grew denser and the air sweetened with pine and earth. I pressed my face against the window, enthralled by the transformation of landscape. The winding mountain roads, however, proved challenging for my mother's equilibrium.

"I might have to throw up," she admitted as she pulled over to a narrow shoulder, the truck teetering precariously close to the edge of a steep drop. Cars whizzed by us and I bit back the urge to point out that if we'd gone to a spa or a resort, nausea wouldn't be on the itinerary.

My mother, who had navigated the shark-infested waters of the music industry without flinching, undone by a few hairpin turns? The absurdity of the sight made me love her even more.

Eventually, we reached our destination—without anyone losing their lunch.

Setting up camp was a comedy of errors, with instructions read backward, tent poles mismatched, and me muttering under my breath about insects and dirt. Meanwhile, ten feet away, my mom had set up the fire pit, unfolded the chairs, brought out the cooler, and pulled out stuff for s'mores.

In the firelight, with her guard down, she looked younger—more like the woman who used to dance with me in our living room before career and responsibility had complicated our relationship.

"I've been thinking a lot about what I want to say, and how to say it," she said. "We have pockets of problems, but when you feel like you're in trouble or need advice, we talk about it."

"Yes, but the issues we have aren't about that," I replied

softly, poking at the embers with a stick. "I come to you before anybody else."

I took a deep breath. We've tried to have different versions of *this* conversation over the years but have always been too stuck in our own heartbreak to hear each other. Our previous attempts had escalated into heated exchanges where neither of us truly heard the other, both of us speaking from places of old wounds rather than present understanding.

Somehow, the stillness of the mountain air, crisp and clean, filled me with the calm I needed to open my heart and say the thing that had been burning in my chest for the past fifteen years.

"I really wanted a mother-daughter relationship where it was just us spending time together," I said. "No business."

"I've longed for that, too," she said, her voice barely above a whisper, the admission cracking something open between us. "But because that wasn't my role, I couldn't do that. It was difficult being both mom and manager. If I had to do it all again, I probably wouldn't be a manager."

She poked at the fire with a stick, sending sparks dancing upward like fireflies reaching for the stars. "I know there have been times when you felt neglected," she continued. "It wasn't easy out there. People thought I'd be a failure, and that you'd fail with me. But no matter what, whenever you needed protection, I stood in front and didn't care about the arrows or what people said."

Her eyes reflected the dancing flames as she turned to me. "Still, I missed a few times, and I'm so, *so* sorry for that. But you can't keep holding it against me."

The dam broke then, tears streaming down my face as I collapsed into her arms like I was seven years old again, seeking comfort after the mean girls at school made me feel awful about myself. This was the conversation we'd needed for so long but had been too afraid, too hurt, too busy to come back to.

She cradled my face between her hands, her thumbs wiping

away tears as she'd done when I was small. The gesture transported me back to childhood injuries, to first heartbreaks, to life before fame complicated everything.

"I need you to hear something," she said, her voice steady despite her tears. "I'm always going to be there. Always. Not as your manager. Not as your career adviser. As your mother. That job doesn't end, baby. Not ever."

Raising Sy'Rai was like peering through time's looking glass, catching glimpses of my own toddler self—curious and teetering through the world, humming and singing tunes that seemed to come from somewhere ancestral and knowing. She'd wander around the house, her voice trailing behind her like ribbons of light.

I shouldn't have been surprised. I had serenaded her constantly while she nestled in my womb. When she was restless at night, I'd cradle her tiny body against my chest, her weight melting into me as I lulled her to sleep through song. During fevers, when her forehead burned hot against the back of my hand, I soothed her with my voice, the way my dad sang to calm me.

In those moments, I understood my mother's wide-eyed wonder when I first sang in church. I felt the full circle impact of generations of women watching their daughters discover their voices, and it was humbling and beautiful.

Now . . . did I ever tell my baby that singing was more than just *our* secret language—that it was how the world knew me? No, I never quite got around to doing that.

After *Human* failed to make a commercial impact, Epic Records dropped me, and music no longer felt like a safe space. Six years passed. I doubted I would ever do anything that came close to replicating the musical success of my teenage years.

It was one of those unseasonably sunny winter days in LA. We had family up from McComb, and I gathered everyone at my house. I felt like cooking. My mom's famous fried chicken was now *my* famous fried chicken after she'd taught me all her secrets while I was pregnant.

The oil popped and sizzled as I laid each piece of thigh and leg into the cast-iron skillet—a sound that still takes me back to those summers in McComb, racing home with Ray to find our mom, grandmother, and aunt whipping up Sunday dinner. Now the three of them were sitting at my kitchen counter, watching as I cooked for the family.

I didn't see who did it, but the chatter in the living room was interrupted by the sound of my sixteen-year-old self singing. Someone had popped in a DVD of my music videos—the retrospective collection that spanned my career from fresh-faced teenager to young woman.

The familiar opening notes of "Sittin' Up in My Room" floated into the kitchen, then came the patter of small feet from upstairs. Sy'Rai was running full sprint into the living room, drawn by a voice she'd known since before anything else. I hurriedly dipped a new batch of chicken into the sizzling oil, wiped my hands, and went out to join everybody.

By the time I got to the entryway of the living room, Sy'Rai was standing inches from the TV, mouth wide-open in disbelief, as she saw younger me on the screen.

Sy'Rai's head swiveled slowly from the screen to where I stood, then back to the television, recognition dawning across her face—first a flicker of confusion, then widening awareness, then, without warning, a collapse into tears.

"Why didn't anybody tell me?" she wailed, her voice breaking on the final word, the sound shattering something in my chest. The room fell silent except for her sobs and the continued soundtrack of my voice coming from the speakers—past and present colliding.

I ran over and knelt by her side as her tears turned to hiccups. I cupped her face with my hands.

"Baby, what's wrong?" I asked, though I knew the answer, had anticipated this rupture from the second I'd heard those opening notes from the kitchen.

"That's . . . YOU . . . Mommy. That's . . . YOU," she said, pointing accusingly at the frozen image, betrayal and wonder battling in her expression. "You're singing to everybody!"

A mixture of laughter and "awws" rippled through the room, but I barely heard them.

"Yes, baby," I said softly, wiping her tears with my thumbs. "That's me singing. Before you came along."

"But why . . ." She hiccupped again. "Why didn't you tell me? Mommy, are you famous?"

Famous. The word hung between us, loaded with implications she couldn't possibly understand yet. How could I explain to a small child the double-edged sword of this life I lived? Or the choice I'd made to shield her from parts of it? I did what felt right in my soul—I sat cross-legged on the floor, pulled her into my lap, and told her the truth.

"Mommy wanted to protect you for as long as possible," I explained gently, my chin resting on top of her head. "From a life you didn't get to choose. I wanted you to know me first as just your mommy—the one who kisses your boo-boos and reads you stories and makes you eat your vegetables . . . not as someone who belongs to everybody else, too."

Her eyes, mirrors of my own, searched my face. She reached up, placing her small palm against my cheek in a gesture so tender it nearly undid me.

"But I still get to keep you, right?" she asked, vulnerability making her voice small.

"Oh, baby girl," I whispered, pulling her close. "You get the best parts of me. The parts nobody else will ever see. Nobody knows me like you do—not even the people who've listened to my songs a thousand times."

What followed was nothing short of a revelation for her. She insisted on watching every music video I'd ever made. She ran over to the sofa and jumped up on her uncle Ray's lap.

"Show me more of Mommy."

She raced back and forth between the kitchen and the living room with questions.

"Do people know you *everywhere*, Mommy?" she asked, eyes wide as galaxies.

"Not everywhere," I answered carefully. "The world is very big, baby."

"Is that why sometimes people take pictures of you when we run errands?" Her perception had always been razor-sharp.

"Yes, sometimes people recognize me."

"MOMMY! YOU CAN FLY!" she screamed.

"No, Mommy can't fly. I was attached to big, long strings that swung me in the air, and the strings are edited out. It's called special effects," I said.

"MOMMMMMMMY! The lady in your video sounds like Ellie, but it doesn't look *like* her," she yelled.

"Ellie?" I asked, confused.

"From *Ice Age*," she said, hands on hips.

"Right! *Ice Age*," I said, pretending to know what she meant while googling on my phone.

"Oh, that's Queen Latifah, baby. She is the voice of Ellie," I said.

"And she raps, too?" Sy'Rai asked. The astonished look on her face was so pure and sweet.

"Yes, she was a rapper long *before* she was Ellie."

Her eyes widened and she ran back out to watch and discover more of me.

"Uncle Ray, that's you!" I heard her shout from the living room.

Over fried chicken, yams (with lots of cinnamon), buttery corn bread, and greens, everybody took turns telling Sy'Rai about her mommy, and then out came the old Barbies and

VHS tapes of *Moesha* and *Cinderella* and the CDs and cassettes and magazines I'd stuffed in boxes to give to her whenever the time came.

Sy'Rai, in her unique way, has been my greatest teacher. From the second the universe chose me to be her protector, my approach to motherhood followed one simple philosophy: I wanted my child to create her own story. I would be co-producer of that masterpiece—whatever it turned out to be—not its director.

From time to time, I'd catch her working through harmonies, massaging notes in that familiar way that only another vocalist would recognize. She'd repeat a phrase with subtle variations, searching for the perfect expression—I knew that process intimately. The meditation of it. The obsession. The way a melody can haunt you when it's not *quite* right, following you through your day, demanding resolution.

She had the bug—that beautiful, terrible, magnificent passion that had shaped my own existence.

One afternoon, I was folding laundry when familiar notes drifted down the hallway. That same lulling piano introduction that had once marked a turning point in my own journey now pulled me toward my daughter's bedroom like a magnetic force.

She was blasting "Full Moon," dancing with abandon, her small body twirling around her bedroom like she was in orbit. She hadn't heard me open the door, too lost in the music to notice. Her eyes were closed, arms stretched as she spun in circles, interpreting the rhythm in her own distinctive way.

Hot tears clouded my vision as I leaned against the doorframe. I was witnessing something profound—her communion with the very song that led me to her.

The chorus hit, and she sang along, her voice blending with my recorded one in a harmony that connected past to present.

"Mommy, did you always know you wanted to be a singer?" she asked one night as I braided her hair before bed. She was propped up on a pillow in between my legs, just as I had sat with my mother.

I turned her around so that we could be eye to eye.

"It was all I ever wanted to do, for as long as I can remember," I said.

As true as those words were, it pained me to say them. I was thirty and jaded toward the industry. I'd lost the passion I had for music.

"Even when you were my age?" she asked.

Uh-oh. Here we go. Deep breath.

"Yep, even when I was your age," I said carefully.

She was quiet for a long beat, considering. Then: "What if I wanted to sing?"

I tied off her final braid, then leaned down to kiss the top of her head. "If it's what you want to do, more than anything else in the whole wide world, then that's what you should do. But Mommy wants you to be a kid first."

"Did you get to be a kid?" she asked, her eyes searching mine. She had obviously watched enough videos of younger Mommy to piece it together.

"Not entirely. Mommy wanted to be a singer really badly, and I missed out on a lot of kid stuff to do it. *But*, I don't regret it. It's how I got to be your mommy, and that is my favorite thing to be," I said. "And I want you to do all the kid stuff you want. Whatever you want to be when you grow up will be there waiting for you. I promise."

There were so many times my mother had said, "You'll understand one day when you're a mother." The phrase had irritated me in my younger years, feeling like a conversation-ending cop-out when we disagreed about dating or wardrobe choices.

And of course, she was absolutely right.

TWILIGHT

THE REJECTION USUALLY came wrapped in platitudes.

"We love your voice, but . . ."

"Your sound is so influential, however . . ."

"The market is challenging right now . . ."

"*Full Moon* did a million, but *Afrodisiac* only did half of that . . . and *Human*?"

Translation: *You're past your prime. Too washed-up. Too much of a risk to invest in.*

The contract before me might as well have been written in blood. An ironclad NDA precludes me from being able to speak freely about the label or the deal. But what I will say is it felt like a crime to do this to an artist. On paper, my voice was owned for perpetuity, and I oscillated between feeling defeated and being optimistic.

"You don't have to do this," Ryan told me. He didn't like this deal. I saw it in his eyes. "We can walk."

"And go where?" I said.

Picking up that pen and signing that deal felt like lifting a thousand-pound weight. I was riddled with regret about how I had handled my career. I wished I hadn't prioritized *Moesha* over touring, or had my mother step back from management—because as much as I craved a boundary between our personal and professional relationship, I felt surer of myself when working with her.

But at least I had the music again, I thought.

The label wanted me to aim for a hip-hop sound with an R&B sense of melody on this new album. R&B artists were moving further into dance and electronic music, and after *Human*, I was eager to remind the world of my core. I decided to make the most of this opportunity and be fearless in the studio.

And that's what I did. I had fun, working with new energy—Rico Love, Sean Garrett, and Bangladesh gave me records that had more grit and edge than people were used to hearing in my voice. It was exciting. So was the chance to go back to the collaborations from *Human* that got shelved when we brought Rodney and Darkchild on board.

In the fall of 2010, I reconnected with Monica while I was working on my album. She was also recording new music, and we started talking about coming back together for a new duet.

Now, the *one* party to not miss during Grammy week is Clive Davis's annual pre-Grammy gala. Clive's gala wasn't just an event; it was the heartbeat of Grammy celebrations, and at one point it was the industry's most exclusive coronation ceremony—more so than the actual Grammys.

I heard Whitney was performing at the gala as part of a tribute to her cousin, the iconic Dionne Warwick. She hadn't been onstage in a few years, and there was no way I was missing her big night. I don't remember who texted whom first, but Monica and I made plans to go together and make a night out of it.

We were in such different places in our lives at this point. As artists. As thirtysomething women. We were both moms now, and since reconnecting a few months earlier, we had gotten more serious about collaborating on another record together.

Over champagne, we started batting ideas around.

"There's so much we could be doing. A joint tour. An album," I said excitedly as expensive bubbly danced across my tongue.

"Whatever we do, it's gotta feel right, you know. 'The Boy Is Mine' is *so* iconic," she said.

"Do you think we can top it? People have been asking us to do another record for years now."

"I don't want us competing with that," she said. "Whatever we end up doing should complement our past—not try to re-create it. And for damn sure we not gonna be fighting over no trifling-ass man!"

"Amen to that."

We laughed and clinked glasses.

Whitney emerged onstage to a standing ovation. She was radiant in a silver sequined floor-length gown, her auburn hair styled into soft curls that fell to her shoulder. I could see the joy in her eyes to be embraced like that.

She walked to the mic stand, the light catching the sequins and sending beams of light across the ballroom.

"Good evening, everyone. I am Dionne's cousin, Whitney," she said, as if *she* needed any introduction.

She flicked her hand to signal the band and tore into a jazzy medley of the Burt Bacharach and Hal David staples that had propelled Dionne Warwick to pop superstardom in the '60s. Watching Whitney relish the spotlight was glorious. She was so powerful standing there, arms stretched out wide, head tilted back. Tears flooded my eyes. Monica's, too. We were just two students proud of their teacher.

A year later, after Whitney's big return to the pre-Grammy gala, Monica and I were now preparing to perform at Clive's annual event. It was a Thursday afternoon in February of 2012. One of those days in Los Angeles where the sun drenched everything in the perfect amount of warmth, despite it being winter. The air vibrated with that unmistakable electricity that came with Grammy week, when the city opened its arms wide to make space for Music's Biggest Night.

Fourteen years had passed since "The Boy Is Mine," and

Monica and I had finally made good on our promise to record that duet we'd been plotting. The weight of expectations hung heavy in the air. Everyone—the label, the fans, the critics—silently demanded that "It All Belongs to Me" capture lightning in a bottle again, re-creating the record-breaking magic of our first collaboration. Adding to the pressure, we were launching the single with a performance at Clive's gala.

Because Clive was nothing if not a maestro of anticipation, he had invited international press to witness our rehearsal and get exclusive interviews with the three of us. The thought of rehearsing—still finding the delicate harmony between our voices and our histories—under the scrutinizing gaze of journalists made my insides fold like origami.

In the age of social media, I had grown more paranoid. And I was especially sensitive about my relationship with Monica. All I could think of was how they'd be staring at us, watching like vultures, hoping to catch just the slightest hint of tension. Anything we did or said onstage could be taken out of context and twisted into something that could go viral within hours.

I wanted this single to do well—which meant we couldn't afford any drama or mess distracting from the rollout.

"You ready for this?" Monica whispered backstage, her voice carrying that same Southern warmth I'd fallen in love with years ago.

"They're going to be watching us like hawks," I said, peeking out to the ballroom from behind a curtain. A few dozen reporters circled the room.

"You can't think about that. One thing we know, they gonna write and post whatever the hell they want to," she said.

We both had the scars to prove that was true.

"Hey you." A familiar voice from behind. I turned around and let out the biggest scream.

"RICKEY!!!!!!!!"

It always filled me with such joy to see Rickey Minor. Meeting him as an eleven-year-old with a dream had changed my life. Every time I saw him, I thought about that little girl who wanted nothing more than to meet her idol, Whitney, and get a record deal. I first worked with Rickey when I sang at the Grammys in 1997. It was the very definition of full circle. The *Waiting to Exhale* soundtrack had been up for eleven awards, including Album of the Year, and a medley performance was put together. Not only had I been tapped to perform "Sittin' Up in My Room," but I'd return for the finale to sing with Whitney Houston, CeCe Winans, Mary J. Blige, Chaka Khan, and Aretha Franklin. I had been terrified walking out onstage, but right there on the bass was Rickey. He'd shot me a reassuring wink. His way of saying, "Knock 'em dead, kid."

And now he was the musical director for this reunion performance with Monica.

Okay. I could breathe. We were in the best hands possible. Even with the discomfort of the press lingering, Rickey's presence took a heavy weight off my chest.

I just needed to stay focused on Monica, Rickey, and the band. Block out the rest.

"I know I tell you this every time I see you, but I am so, so proud of all you've done," Rickey whispered in my ear as he pulled me in for a long embrace. "Didn't I tell you that you were going to do everything you wanted?"

As Rickey introduced us to the band members, a cascade of gasps rippled through the press corps. I felt Monica gently squeeze my arm, and I looked up.

And there she was.

Whitney came bouncing—no, exploding—onto that stage like a chaotic meteor, trailing laughter, water, and the unmistakable scent of trouble. Her clothes clung to her damply, evidence of an impulsive swim, and she moved with the unpredictable rhythm of someone no longer tethered to the room.

"Baby girl!" she called out to me. "Baby girl!"

She hadn't known the press would be there. Or maybe she had and didn't care. Either way, she walked directly into the lion's den of industry eyes and media teeth, offering herself up like a lamb unaware of its own beauty or fragility. The air thickened. Some journalists smirked behind their lenses. Others reached for their phones with a giddy, feral instinct.

"Whitney," I managed, embracing her.

"I had to come see my babies! Y'all are gonna kill it," she said with genuine excitement. "Ain't that right, Rickey! Y'all gonna show them, right?"

"That's right," he said.

"Okay, now remember, you have three places to sing from," she said.

And like the good students we were, Monica and I both said in unison with Whitney, "Heart, mind, guts."

"Okay. Now lemme hear it," she said, bringing her hands to her hips and raising her eyebrow. "I didn't walk all the way up here from the pool to *not* hear my girls sing."

Whitney walked to a far corner offstage, out of view from the audience.

Monica and I did a quick run-through of "The Boy Is Mine." We hadn't sang it, together, since the MTV Video Music Awards in 1998. Hearing ourselves together, after all this time, sent a jolt of electricity through my veins. It was all the more special being able to look up and catch a glimpse of Whitney, in the wings, nodding with approval.

She shot us a thumbs-up and vanished just as quickly as she'd come.

About an hour or so later, Whitney returned to the ballroom—now with her daughter, Bobbi Kristina, by her side. They'd both had so much negative attention in the press over the past few years. I was afraid that this unexpected drop-in would warrant more of the same unkind treatment she'd endured for so long. Whitney appeared to be under the influence, and it was tough to be in a room crawling with strangers whispering and judging her. Whitney was becoming the story, and humiliation climbed up my spine like English ivy climbing a tree.

I smiled and retreated inward, my mind separating from my body, as reporter after reporter looked for clever ways to get us to open up about how we really felt about Whitney's surprise visit. I could see their eyes dart from me to Monica to Clive and then over to the door, where we could all hear Whitney asking about our whereabouts.

We were in between interviews when the double doors flung open and Whitney and Bobbi Kris walked in. Once the reporter finished, they came over to us. Out the corner of my eye, I noticed the cameraman with the last crew stopped breaking down his equipment—he was still rolling.

She guided Bobbi Kris over to embrace Clive, her daughter's eyes wide and watchful behind lowered sunglasses.

"This is for you," Whitney whispered, her breath warm against my ear. She pressed something into my palm. A small, crumpled note written on hotel stationery. Then she planted a kiss on my cheek so tender it nearly fractured the wall I put up to shield my emotions from the watching cameras.

When it comes to the note, I feel the world's longing to know what Whitney wrote to me. I know that people weave their own stories from my silence. But I hope you can understand—after giving so much of ourselves to the world, I want to keep some small piece of our bond untouched by the world. I've kept the paper folded away, a reminder that the bond we had was achingly, beautifully real.

The instant I got home, I called her, uncertainty pulsing through me about which version of Whitney would answer—the nurturing maternal figure who had guided me through *Cinderella* or the unpredictable force I'd glimpsed today.

"Hello?"

"Whitney? It's Brandy."

"Baby girl! I was hoping you'd call. You alone? We need to talk, just us."

It was no secret that Whitney had turbulent years. We'd had a few tearful discussions in the past about the things that haunted her. There was talk of her coming and staying with me, just to get out of Alpharetta and get a change in environment after her divorce from Bobby Brown was finalized. But she never did, and that made me sad.

For three precious hours, we talked. We reminisced. We laughed together. Cried together. Prayed together.

I broke down to Whitney, the tears coming in waves. I confessed the crushing pressure that was suffocating my career, the paralyzing fear that I would never recapture the magic of my earlier success, that I was becoming a relic. That I'd felt trapped in a deal and expected to become something—or somebody—else.

"It's just been loss after loss," I said. "And I don't know if I'll ever win again. I'm not sure I can take another disappointment."

Whitney listened as only someone who had walked the same treacherous path could—with complete understanding, without judgment. Her silence offered more comfort than any platitudes.

"Baby girl, what did I tell you all those years ago—when you were just a little girl begging to meet little ole me?" she asked.

I laughed. Of course, I remembered. I remember every single thing Whitney ever told me. "Never let anyone else tell you who you are," I said.

"That's right. And I know it's hard to remember that. Believe me," she finally said. "When you look up in ten years, twenty years, what do you hope people say about you? About your music? Is it gonna be about sales or what you did with that voice of yours?"

There were flashes of the old Whitney in that conversation—

glimpses of light breaking through. I heard it in her raspy laugh that erupted unexpectedly like sunshine after rain, in the way she scattered "baby" and "sweetie" throughout her sentences like musical notes, in how she returned every topic—no matter how dark—back to faith with the certainty of a compass finding true north. She spoke of getting back in the studio, of the redemption waiting just around the corner with *Sparkle*, the long-delayed remake of the 1976 film she'd put on the backburner after we lost Aaliyah, who she'd handpicked for the lead role.

"I'm gonna be better," she promised as our call wound down, and in that moment, I believed her with every fiber of my being. "You'll see. This is just a season, not the whole story."

I couldn't have known then that her words were both prophecy and farewell.

"I love you, Whitney," I said before hanging up.

"I love you more, baby girl," she replied. "Always have, always will. I can't wait to see y'all sing the house down on Saturday."

I woke up the next morning, February 11, 2012, with a hot, radiating itch in my throat. It was my birthday—I was turning thirty-three—and I was going to be celebrating it at Clive's gala. The performance with Monica was the talk of the town, and I wafted between exhilarated and terrified.

This feeling in my throat defied explanation. I didn't feel hoarse, nor was I raspier than usual. It was a strange sensation—like someone had taken a safety pin and slowly dragged it up my esophagus.

My phone vibrated. It was my mom.

"Happy birthday, Bran," she chirped. "Big day today!"

That fire in my throat left me gasping for air.

"Mom, something doesn't feel right," I confessed, unable to articulate the foreboding that had settled over me. "I have this burn in my throat. But I'm not hoarse, or losing my voice."

"Hmm. Preperformance jitters, maybe?" she asked.

"Yeah, maybe. I think I'm gonna run and get it checked out. I just want tonight to be perfect. We both need this."

"Well, call me if you need me. Actually, text me. Rest that voice," my mom said.

I texted Ryan and asked him to get me squeezed in at my vocal doctor's office.

An hour later, I got a diagnosis:

"There's nothing abnormal, Ms. Norwood," the doctor told me. "You haven't been onstage in some time. You're nervous. Maybe even a bit scared. But . . . you are *fine.* You have always taken remarkable care of your instrument. This is an intense weekend. You need to remember to take care of you, too."

"Yeah, just nerves," I said, trying my hardest to convince myself.

As the driver cruised down Wilshire Boulevard back to the Beverly Hilton, I tried to distract myself. I scrolled through the well-wishes that lit up my phone. I smiled as younger versions of myself stared back at me from the screen.

The air started to change as we got closer to the hotel. It got thicker, heavier. The clouds nudged the sun out of view, turning the afternoon sky into a vast expanse of darkening gray. It was eerie. I looked back down at my phone screen. 3:45 p.m.

That fire in my throat traveled down to the pit of my gut.

When we arrived at the Beverly Hilton, it was chaos. The entrance was gridlocked as a cavalcade of black cars streamed into the valet lane. A dozen or so news cameras lined the street. Our driver took a shortcut, and I prepared myself for the onslaught.

The hotel lobby, normally a symphony of elegant efficiency, had transformed into pandemonium—a discordant melody of urgent voices and hurried footsteps. A team of paramedics rushed through the gilded halls, their shoes clattering against the marble floor.

"Hurry up! Hurry up! She's not breathing!" one paramedic shouted into the remote speaker strapped to his chest.

As I approached the elevator bank, confusion clouding my mind, Nick Gordon spotted me. I had seen him in Whitney's orbit over the years. His face—normally composed into a mask of cool detachment—was contorted with panic, his eyes wild with an emotion I couldn't place.

"Brandy! Brandy! Come in the elevator! Come in the elevator!" he shouted, gesturing frantically toward an open car, where I glimpsed the edge of a stretcher and the clinical blue of paramedic uniforms.

I didn't connect the dots. My mind, perhaps protecting me from what it already suspected, refused to acknowledge what was happening. I mumbled something incoherent, stepped into a different elevator, and continued to my floor, my heart hammering against my rib cage.

My glam team were already inside my suite getting things ready for the night. My makeup artist got right to work. She was dusting powder across my cheekbones when my phone rang. The screen flashed my mother's name. That itch in the back of my throat now felt like a fire.

"Baby?" her voice broke on that single word, and I felt my world tilt on its axis.

"Mom?"

". . . Whitney's gone, baby. She's . . . gone."

"What are you saying to me right now?"

"Baby, I'm so sorry."

"No," I screamed. "No! No! No!"

I felt my body go limp, then I fell to the floor, convulsing with sobs. I could faintly make out the sound of my mom on the receiver trying her hardest to soothe me through the phone.

My heart didn't just break; it disintegrated.

The gala—obscenely, incomprehensibly—would proceed as planned.

After being told that Whitney's family had given Clive the blessing for the night to proceed, Monica thought we should still attend out of respect for Whitney, who had loved this damn gala so much. And the only thing she'd loved more than Clive's gala was Clive . . . so we decided to go together. For Whitney.

Monica and I clung to each other throughout that nightmarish evening, our shared grief forging a bond stronger than any hit record ever could. We made a tear-soaked promise to keep Whitney's memory alive, to honor her legacy through our own voices, to never let the world forget what real talent coupled with real pain looked like.

"I just talked to her yesterday," I whispered into Monica's shoulder. "She was going to be better. She promised."

The room swirled around me in a macabre carnival of industry faces—offering condolences with compassionate expressions one second, clinking champagne glasses and dancing to Pitbull the next.

It felt wrong.

Sitting here. In a gown. In makeup.

"You know you gained an angel today. Hold on to that. She's watching over you now," Monica whispered, her hand finding mine under the table.

I nodded, unable to form words through the stone of grief lodged in my throat, but somewhere deep inside, past the pain and disbelief, I felt the truth of her words take root. Whitney would always be with me—in every note I sang, in every challenge I faced, in every moment I chose courage over fear.

Two days after Whitney passed, Monica and I dragged ourselves to the video shoot for "It All Belongs to Me." We wanted to show a more elevated, fashion-forward version of ourselves. The last time people saw us together, we were teenagers blossoming into young women. But we were good and grown now. And we wanted our video to be super glamorous and over-the-top. We kept our word and didn't try to replicate or do a continuation of "The Boy Is Mine." Instead of being two girls beefing over a guy, we were two women—friends—supporting one another while we tossed a dude out of our life.

On set, we moved like sleepwalkers, our bodies present but our spirits still hovering in the Beverly Hilton, still searching for answers that would never come.

"Can we get a little more energy?" the director called after one take. "A little more attitude in the chorus?"

Monica and I exchanged glances—a silent understanding passing between us.

"We're giving you everything we have right now," Monica replied, her voice steady but edged with steel. *"Everything."*

Each take was an exercise in acting—pretending we weren't shattered into a thousand pieces, pretending the world hadn't just lost its most magnificent voice. Between takes, we huddled together, sharing memories of Whitney, occasionally dissolving into tears that the makeup team would hurriedly fix before the next shot.

"She would want us to shine," Monica said during one such moment, squeezing my hand tight enough to leave marks. "You know how she was. 'The show must go on, baby!'" Her impression of Whitney's distinctive cadence brought watery smiles to both our faces.

"I know," I whispered back. "We need to carry on her legacy. You know she was *so* happy we did another record together."

"It won't be the last time we work together. That much I know," Monica said, bringing me in for a hug.

"Promise?" I asked.

"I promise," she said.

Recording my next album, *Two Eleven*, was, in some ways, a lifeline through grief, each studio session a form of therapy.

The music helped me navigate back to my authentic voice, but I was still searching for a freedom that remained frustratingly elusive—a freedom from expectations, from comparison, from the suffocating pressure to recapture the success I'd found when I was barely more than a child.

I'm proud of the work that I did, but I hated chasing the ghost of my younger self, a version of me that only existed now in music videos and fan memories, enshrined in nostalgia but disconnected from present reality.

I had been so afraid of failure that I would have done anything to keep going forward. I stopped trusting my instincts and second-guessed myself because I wanted to please whatever label was giving me the opportunity to do music.

In therapy, I later learned I had been moving through life in a state called "learned helplessness," which happens after a person is repeatedly exposed to negative or stressful situations. My therapist explained it like this. Imagine a dog repeatedly getting shocked in a cage and not being able to escape. After trying over and over and getting shocked each time, it might stop trying to find a way out—even if the cage door suddenly opened.

Finding the courage to fight for myself, to advocate for my worth when I barely believed in it myself, required a strength I wasn't sure I possessed.

But I knew I didn't want to keep feeling like this.

I recognized with mirror-pure clarity that I wasn't in the right home for my music, and I'd had enough of this feeling.

I called Ryan.

"Get me out of this contract. By any means necessary."

GOD CAN'T FAIL

I WAS AT home curled up on the couch with Sy'Rai watching her favorite movie, *Alice in Wonderland*, for what had to have been the millionth time—well, I should say the movie was watching Sy'Rai and I was watching her nap peacefully, her head nestled on my shoulder. My cell phone vibrated against the cushion, and I looked down to see Ryan's face glowing on my screen. I let it go to voice mail, but he called me back immediately. This must be important, I thought. I did that careful acrobatic dance that parents learn to master when they don't want to wake their kids. I slipped out from beneath Sy'Rai and took my phone to my bedroom.

"Everything okay?" I whispered into the phone.

"Question. What do you think about Broadway?" he said.

"Huh?" I asked, confused.

"Well, a call came in. There's interest in you doing a stint as Roxie Hart in *Chicago* and—"

"Whoa, whoa, whoa. Wait, *me*, doing *Chicago*?"

I laughed out loud. Gracing the stage on the Great White Way was something I never allowed myself to fantasize about. I loved theater and *really* loved musical theater. Anytime Sy'Rai and I were in the city, we tried to catch a show. She was maybe ten or so when I took her to see *Wicked*, and her eyes had lit up as bright as the Luxor Sky Beam, the same way they did whenever she sang around the house. Stepping on a Broadway stage—let alone doing it in the sequined shoes of such an iconic, revered character as Roxie Hart—felt so far out of reach even in my wildest dreams that the idea never crossed my mind.

I'd watched performers tackle that role with precision and ferocity that seemed beyond my grasp, women who commanded every inch of the stage with the confidence of generals leading armies into battle. The thought of joining their ranks made my stomach twist into elaborate knots.

I'd forgotten that feeling. That familiar mixture of exhilaration, adrenaline, and fear that reverberates from head to toe. I felt it when I signed my first deal. And when I stepped onto the set of *Moesha* for the first time. And when I walked into the studio to meet Whitney and record for *Cinderella*.

"What do you think?" Ryan asked.

My heart was racing so fast I pressed my palm against my chest, as if to contain it. I knew what that meant.

"Yes," I said, loudly, before the voices of fear and inadequacy got a chance to try to convince me otherwise. "Yes, I'll do it."

Years of career setbacks, comments questioning my relevance, and now being stuck in a legal battle with my label had left me numb. I had nothing else to give, and no fight left, when it came to music. On paper, I was a caged bird, unable to officially release anything until we found resolve with the label.

But I'd been enjoying my television work. Back in 2011, I joined the cast of BET's *The Game*. I played Chardonnay, a sassy bartender who spoke her mind without fear—or filter. The character was a recurring role for the show's fifth season and eventually became part of the main cast. It was a chance to work with Wendy Raquel Robinson, who I knew from my days on *Thea*, and Hosea Chanchez, who I'd been friends with for years.

Beyond the opportunity to work with friends, *The Game* gave me the chance to rediscover my love for comedic acting. I loved not carrying the pressure of a lead role—which sometimes meant being in every single scene. Joining an ensemble cast was less pressure than *Moesha.* I had the freedom to enjoy the work more than I had in the past. Working in television offered me the satisfaction of structured days and clear expectations, but I missed the disciplined rigor of rehearsals, the camaraderie that comes with creative collaboration, and the exhilaration of performing live onstage.

When I stepped off the plane at JFK a week later, the crisp spring air slapped my cheeks. I felt transformed into that wide-eyed little girl showing up to Atlantic Records for her first audition, stomach fluttering with nerves and anticipation that bordered on nausea.

My heels clicked against the pavement as I made my way down Fifth Avenue toward the Ambassador Theatre, each step a tiny declaration of intent. *I am here. I am trying. I am terrified. I am alive.* The rhythm of my steps blended with the symphony of the city—car horns blaring with impatient urgency, vendors hawking their wares in musical cadences, snippets of a hundred different conversations floating past me like scraps of melody seeking harmony. The skyscrapers towered overhead, glass-and-steel monoliths reflecting the afternoon sun, and I felt suddenly, overwhelmingly small. But not in the way that diminishes—in the way that reminds you you're part of something greater than yourself.

Standing before the Ambassador Theatre, I gazed up at its marquee—golden bulbs illuminating a place where legends had been born and reborn. *Chicago*—one of the longest-running American musicals in Broadway history. I let the weight of that history wash over me, imagining all the women who had inhabited Roxie Hart before me. Ann Reinking. Bebe Neuwirth. Liza Minnelli. Christie Brinkley. Melanie Griffith. And now me.

This felt like the universe offering me a new beginning. I wasn't going to let anything get in the way of that. Not my past. Not my fears. Not the whispers of inadequacy that had become my constant companions.

Taking on Roxie required dedication beyond anything I'd experienced before. Broadway musicals, I quickly discovered, demanded a holistic transformation. Your body must become a finely tuned instrument, your voice a precision tool that cannot falter. And I had a month to master the book and the choreography.

Those first few weeks felt like beautiful torture. Hours melted into one another as I rehearsed dance moves that made muscles I didn't know existed scream in protest. The rehearsal studio became my confessional booth, my therapist's couch, my battlefield. Under incandescent lights that missed no flaw, surrounded by mirrors that reflected every hesitation, I confronted the gap between who I was and who I needed to become. The hardwood floor, polished to a honeyed glow by countless performers before me, caught my tears, my sweat, and occasionally my blood, when blisters broke open midcombination.

"Again!" the choreographer would call out, his eyes never missing the slightest misstep, his voice betraying no fatigue despite hours of repetition. "Five, six, seven, eight!"

I would dig deeper, push harder, determined to master every flick of the wrist, every subtle hip roll, every precise head turn. This wasn't some music video where clever editing could mask imperfections or where my star power could compensate for technical shortcomings. This wasn't a concert where spectacle could distract from any slight vocal weakness. This was raw, exposed, live theater where every night demanded perfection and authenticity in equal measure.

There was a time when this kind of pressure would have felt like being buried alive. Now each demanding day felt like an excavation of the parts of myself that had been buried under years of industry expectations and personal disappointments.

And when I'd get back to my apartment overlooking Central Park, I'd throw on the cast recording from the 1996 revival and sing along as I showered and had dinner. Every now and then, I'd even throw on my character's shoes and run through sequences in front of the floor-length mirror that was in the corner of my bedroom.

To build my stamina up, I took up running and boxing. Every morning, I jogged to Central Park. Sometimes I would run without any music, just the sound of my own breath and the rhythm of my feet pounding the pavement. The crisp morning air would fill my lungs, burning slightly before giving way to that runner's euphoria. Sometimes I'd stop by the reservoir, watching the sun spill gold across the water's surface, and feel something akin to peace wash over me. In the flicker of a passing second, with the city still stretching and yawning before another chaotic day began, I'd find snippets of clarity—remembering why I'd fallen in love with performing in the first place.

"You look different," Sy'Rai said during one of our FaceTime calls, her eyes studying me with the unnerving perception children sometimes possess.

"Yeah? How so?" I asked, touching my face self-consciously, wondering if she could see the new definition in my cheekbones from the weight I'd lost amid all the rehearsing.

"Your eyes," she said simply, her gaze unwavering even through pixels and distance. "There's a lightness in your eyes . . . one I haven't seen in a while."

At thirteen (going on thirty), my daughter had the ability to see me more clearly than anyone, and she was my biggest motivator—and my greatest cheerleader.

Her observation startled me. I felt *alive*—gloriously alive. Inspired. Excited about each day. I locked in, like I was getting ready for war.

My dietary regimen became strict—not in the punishing way of my younger years, but with the reverence of an artist caring for body and mind just as much as she cared for her instrument. I avoided anything that might cause dehydration or inflammation: caffeine became a distant memory; alcohol, a temptation mostly resisted; spicy foods, dairy, acidic fruits—all sacrificed at the altar of vocal perfection.

Water became my constant companion, along with the elixir I've sworn by since discovering it while working on *Cinderella*—Ginger Honey Crystals brewed with plenty of manuka honey. My voice coach—a stern woman with hands gentle enough to coax tension from the tightest muscles—became as essential to my routine as breathing. She taught me the art of vocal conditioning, showing me how to sustain notes with such control that even whispers could reach the back row. And how to sustain myself, and my voice, for eight shows a week.

I became profoundly conscious of every word that left my lips. Phone conversations dwindled to essential communications only. Even casual chatter felt like squandering a precious resource. I wrapped myself in silence when not in rehearsal, creating a cocoon where only the words of the script and the notes of the score existed.

The world outside the theater faded until the book and choreography lived in my muscle memory, until I could run the show backward and forward in the dark of night when sleep evaded me. I surrendered to the discipline, letting it remake me from the inside out.

Watching my body transform—muscles lengthening and strengthening, voice gaining more power and endurance—gave me something beyond mere confidence. It restored my faith in my own resilience. Even with my body screaming for rest, with blisters blooming on my feet like perverse flowers, and with my throat raw from hours of rehearsal, I felt a freedom I hadn't experienced in years.

Being that on point, that polished, that deeply connected to my instrument was liberating in ways I couldn't have anticipated. Embodying Roxie healed wounds so deep I'd stopped acknowledging their existence. I began to remember why I had fallen in love with performing in the first place. It wasn't the validation, though God knows I'd craved that during my most insecure times. It was purpose. I was made to tell stories with my voice, my body, my soul.

Sy'Rai got me a silicone bracelet inscribed with three simple words in hot pink lettering: "God Can't Fail." I wore it all the time, everywhere. I'd catch glimpses of it during morning workouts or afternoon rehearsals, the words becoming a mantra that carried me through held breaths of doubt when the choreography seemed insurmountable or when high notes refused to cooperate.

As we approached dress rehearsals, I'd slip the bracelet into my mic pack.

"What's that?" one of the chorus members asked, catching me kissing the bracelet before tucking it away beneath my costume.

"My good luck charm," I replied with a smile that held all the faith I'd nearly lost.

The first time I stepped onto that Broadway stage—lights blazing with their particular golden warmth, orchestra swelling beneath the floorboards like a living, breathing entity—something within me shifted fundamentally. The air felt different in my lungs, richer somehow, as if infused with possibilities I'd forgotten existed. Time seemed to both slow down and speed up, creating a pocket universe where only this stolen second existed.

I felt the power of my voice again. I understood, with sudden clarity that brought tears to my eyes midperformance, the depth of music's hold on me, the sacred joy of sharing that gift with others. For the first time in years, I released myself from expectations, from fear, from the constant internal criticism that had become my closest companion.

That night felt divinely orchestrated, as if God had reached down and temporarily removed the barriers between intention and execution. When curtain call came, it was a standing ovation. Through the blinding spotlight, I caught a glimpse of my parents, Ray, and Sy'Rai—cheering wildly, their eyes wet with tears. I imagined they weren't just cheering for the performance they had witnessed. It was for the woman who had fought her way back from the precipice.

In the end, it wasn't the role that transformed me. It was the simple, profound reminder that I could still move people with my voice.

The true measure of this transformation was reflected in my daughter's eyes when she ran into my arms backstage, the pride lighting her face. She'd seen me struggle mentally and professionally—for so long.

"You were *phenomenal*, Mommy," she whispered, her voice carrying above the congratulatory din that filled the room.

Standing under the spotlight, I realized I had finally found my way back.

Back to myself.

Back to my voice.

Back to my purpose.

UNCONDITIONAL OCEANS

SPRING 2018

IN THE GOOD BOOK, the number seven symbolizes completion and perfection, exoneration and healing, and often accompanies the fulfillment of promises and oaths. While doing *Chicago*, I promised myself that once I reclaimed my voice—not just my literal voice, but my artistic voice, and my authentic self—I would make the album that had been living inside me for years.

I wanted to sing my truth and create without compromise. I'd gotten my freedom and was ready to step out on my own—a brand-new feeling.

Recording my seventh album, after so many years away from the studio, felt like learning to walk again after injury. My muscles remembered, but they were afraid of the pain that might come with movement.

"Do you think people really want to hear from me?" I asked Sy'Rai over dinner at our favorite restaurant overlooking the Pacific Ocean. "What if I'm not . . . relevant anymore?"

She leaned forward, pushing aside her untouched black beans and rice. Her eyes—the same eyes that had seen me rise and fall and rise again over her sixteen years—held steady on mine.

"Mom, do I need to remind you who *you* are?" Sy'Rai said simply. "You're one of the greatest singers. Ever. There's a reason the world calls you 'The Vocal Bible.' Make the music you want to make. People just want to hear you."

At times, I couldn't believe the young woman who sat before me. Sy'Rai looked more and more like me. Even scarier? She'd been taking the time to slowly develop her artistry, and the voice that came out of her blew me away. She was graceful, self-assured, and aware of her power. And she stood in it.

The simplicity of it struck me. *Make the music you want to make.*

I'd spent so many years trying to sound like what I thought people wanted. But what did I want to say? Who was I as an artist now? What did my voice—my true voice—even sound like anymore?

So, I approached this album as if it were my last. What would I want my final artistic offering to sound like? To represent? To say about me?

I was ready to face the things I'd been running from—the demons I'd tucked away in the corners of my mind, the pain I'd never fully processed. The songs didn't just come to me; they demanded to be written, clawing their way out of my soul.

I'd wake up at 3 a.m., sheets twisted around my legs from restless sleep, with lyrics pouring out of me like a spell I didn't know I was under. I'd stumble to my notebook and just write. The heartbreak, the longing, the times when I thought I was broken beyond repair—it all spilled out onto the page.

For the first time in my career, I wasn't just singing about the pain. I was confronting it under the harsh light of honesty. Every note I hit, every harmony I stacked with painstaking precision, was a step closer to reclaiming my voice—not just as an artist, but as a woman who had survived the machine of fame with her soul intact.

One of the first people I called when I started working on new music was DJ Camper, an amazing artist I'd met a few years back. His approach was different from mine, but we shared a similar sensibility. His arrangements sounded like a futuristic version of *Never Say Never.* Working with him was both a rebirth and an expansion.

The other call was to LaShawn. Just saying his name still catches in my throat sometimes. He'd helped shape the sound that defined my career, had been there from the beginning when we were both just kids with dreams bigger than ourselves. There was still so much left for us to accomplish together.

We fell back into our creative shorthand, completing each other's musical sentences. It felt like the missing puzzle piece finally snapping into place.

With LaShawn, I had the freedom to be vulnerable, to strip away all the facades and just be. He could read my moods, anticipate my needs, challenge me when I needed to be pushed.

"Let's try something different," he suggested one night in the studio. He sat down at the keyboard and started tinkering around. "Sing what's in your heart—just freestyle. Anything that comes to mind."

I'd never been the main writer on any of my projects, had never done songs based off my own melodies. The thought terrified me.

"I don't know." I hesitated, wrapping my cardigan tighter around myself, a physical manifestation of my insecurity. "That's not really how we've done things before."

"Exactly. That's the point," he said, playing a simple chord progression. The notes hung in the air between us, an invitation. "Being vulnerable has never been hard for you. What's different?"

"What are people going to think?"

LaShawn let out a heavy sigh. "You can't bring that energy in here," he said. "Don't suppress your story because you're afraid of how it'll be received. The music has to be for *you* as well. It can't just be for everyone else."

I went over to the notebook that I'd had tucked away in my purse and sang the words I'd gotten out of bed in the middle of the night to jot down:

Why I'd rather suffer 'fore I'd ever let you down?
I ain't ever scared to let the truth out
Oh, they won't ever lay me down

"Keep going," he said, never opening his eyes, giving me the privacy to fail without witness. "Stop thinking so much. Just feel it."

LaShawn helped me embrace this new role and get out of my head. He'd sit at the piano, eyes closed, waiting for me to find my voice. When I'd stumble or apologize, he'd simply wave it away.

I remember one evening in particular. The sun was setting outside the studio windows, painting the room in shades of amber and gold. We'd been working for hours on this left-of-center record called "Unconditional Oceans" that kept slipping through my fingers, vocally—almost right but not quite there.

"You have to remember your tone," he said suddenly, turning to face me fully. His eyes—dark and intense—locked with mine. "It's not about the harmonies or the range. The tone is what makes you, you. That's what no one else can replicate. That's what they fell in love with in the first place."

Just as the project was taking shape, transforming from abstract concept to an album I titled *b7*, the unthinkable happened. LaShawn was gone. A car accident. The call came on a September morning. I remember the exact flicker in time because I was in the studio, listening to playback of a track we'd worked on before he left town.

The grief overwhelmed me like a tidal wave, leaving me gasping for air in its wake. I couldn't bear to enter the studio where his presence lingered in every corner. I needed to take time—to retreat, to simply mourn the loss. I had to sit with the emptiness and let it consume me, because I knew that was the only way I could move through it.

Months later, I returned to the studio. His absence was palpable—a physical ache in the room, like phantom limb pain. I sat at the keyboard where he used to sit, ran my fingers over the keys he'd played, and let the pain sit on my heart. I owed it to LaShawn to finish the album. And I owed it to myself.

I poured everything into *b7*. I created from a place of expressing everything I'd had locked inside me. It wasn't about chasing hits. It was about giving in, trusting instinct. The album was the purest, most raw work I had ever done, and it was the hardest to release. But it was also the most healing—like lancing a wound to let the poison out, painful but necessary for true recovery.

I sit cross-legged on my bedroom floor, thirty years of photos, magazine clippings, books, and journals spread out before me like an archaeological dig of my own life. The smell of the old magazine ink mingles with the jasmine candle burning on my nightstand. Outside, rain taps against the windows of my Calabasas home, a gentle percussion track to my memories. My fingers trace the worn pages of a long-forgotten hip-hop magazine that put me on its December 1995 cover. The girl on the front is staring back at me. Her braids are impossibly perfect, and she's wearing the cutest plaid miniskirt with knee-high Doc Martens and big silver hoop earrings. That girl thought fame would feel like freedom.

I grab another magazine and study the girl on the cover. She stares back at me, twenty years old with eyes that betrayed nothing of what was happening behind them.

The weight of three decades settles on my shoulders. Not just time passed, but in expectations carried, personas worn and discarded, voices—both internal and external—that shaped every move I made.

I've spent years purging the weight of judgment, but the voices of critics and naysayers were nothing—absolutely nothing—compared to the voice in my own head.

This book all began with a question: What would it mean to reclaim a life defined by others? I wrote it on a Post-it note and stuck it to my bathroom mirror, forcing myself to face it every morning as I brushed my teeth.

I started writing. Raw, unfiltered thoughts. Memories. Buried secrets. New truths. I filled notebook after notebook, the physical pressure of pen on paper somehow more cathartic than typing. The words flowed from some untapped reservoir deep within me, sometimes so quickly my hand cramped trying to keep up with my thoughts. I've learned that the stories I once thought defined me—of meteoric success, of public failure, of private devastation—were simply chapters. They were important chapters, yes, but not the entire book. Not the complete story of who I am.

No single phase of my life defines me—not the wide-eyed teenager signing her first contract, not the broken woman in a hospital gown, not the recluse hiding from the world, not the comeback queen rising from the ashes. I am all of these women and none of them. I am the through line that connects them, the consciousness that experienced them, the soul that survived them.

When I catch my reflection now, I don't feel that familiar tightening in my chest. I don't hear that critical voice cataloging every perceived flaw.

I feel peace washing over me like a warm shower after a long day. I feel power humming through my veins like the bass line that announces my entrance at concerts.

I feel, finally, that I have become who I was always meant to be.

Just me—complicated, contradictory, still evolving.

I am fiercely proud of her. And ready for more.

ACKNOWLEDGMENTS

This book lived in me long before it lived on these pages.

Writing it asked everything of me—fearlessness, vulnerability, the courage to excavate my most tender truths. It was the hardest gift I've ever given myself.

To Gerrick Kennedy, my co-writer, who met this enormity with grace and brilliance.

To John Glynn, our editor, whose steady hand guided us through.

To my team, who held me down when the weight felt too much.

To my family, whose love runs deeper than words.

And to my Starz—you shine so bright, you make everything possible.

Thank you, always.

SONG CREDITS

"Have You Ever?" written by Diane Warren © 1998 Realsongs, ASCAP

"Angel in Disguise" written by Rodney Jerkins, LaShawn Daniels, Fred Jerkins III, Nycolia "Tye-V" Turman, and Traci Hale © 1998 EMI-Blackwood/Ensign Music Publishing/Zomba Music, BMI/ Pink Jane, SESAC

"The Boy Is Mine" written by Rodney Jerkins, Brandy, LaShawn Daniels, Fred Jerkins III, and Japhe Tejeda © 1997 EMI-Blackwood/ Ensign Music Publishing/Bran Bran Music, BMI/EMI Blackwood, SESAC/Henchi Music/EMI, ASCAP

"Full Moon" written by Mike City © 2001 Mike City Music Inc./ Warner-Tamerlane Publishing Corp., BMI

"When You Touch Me" written by Rodney Jerkins, Kenisha Pratt, Robert Smith, and Nora Payne © 2001 EMI Blackwood Music Inc./ RJ Productions Inc., BMI/Songs of Windswept Pacific/Infusion Music Group/TTARP Music Publishing, BMI

"Right Here (Departed)" written by David Quiñones, Erika Nuri, E. Kidd Bogart, Rodney Jerkins, and Victoria Horn © 2008 EMI Blackwood Music, BMI/Here's Lookin' At You Kidd Music (BMI)/ Beluga Heights Music/Sony ATV Music Publishing LLC, BMI/Quda Music, ASCAP/Golden The Super Kid Music admin. by Royalty Network, ASCAP/Lady V Music Publishing, BMI

"Unconditional Oceans" written by Brandy, Kim "Kaydence" Krysiuk, and Akil "Fresh" King © 2020 Bran Bran Music, BMI, BMG Publishing/Seven Corners Music/BMI